FANNY KEMBLE

FANNY KEMBLE

Painting by Peter Frederick Rothermel. Reproduced by courtesy of the Folger Shakespeare Library, Washington, D. C.

FANNY KEMBLE

BY

LEOTA S. DRIVER, Ph.D.

NEGRO UNIVERSITIES PRESS
NEW YORK

Originally published in 1933
by the University of North Carolina Press

Reprinted from a copy in the collections
of the Brooklyn Public Library

Reprinted 1969 by
Negro Universities Press
A DIVISION OF GREENWOOD PRESS, INC.
NEW YORK

SBN 8371-2697-5

PRINTED IN UNITED STATES OF AMERICA

TO

CARL

ACKNOWLEDGMENT

MANY people aided me in the preparation of this study of Fanny Kemble. I desire to acknowledge the assistance rendered by the officials in charge of the following libraries and collections: Vanderbilt University Library, Nashville, Tennessee; Library of Congress, Washington, D. C.; Harvard University Library, Cambridge, Massachusetts; Boston Public Library, and Massachusetts Historical Society, Boston, Massachusetts; Historical Society of Pennsylvania, Philadelphia, Pennsylvania; Germantown Historical and Genealogical Society, Germantown, Pennsylvania. Mr. H. H. Ballard of the Berkshire Athenæum at Pittsfield, Massachusetts, generously loaned me some interesting material. Miss Edith Fitch of Lenox, Massachusetts, and Mrs. Margaret Davis Cate of Brunswick, Georgia, offered suggestions concerning sources of information. Miss Jane Judge of Savannah, Georgia, contributed some interesting items found during her perusal of Savannah newspaper files. I am especially indebted to Dr. Owen Wister of Bryn Mawr, Pennsylvania, who gave me information necessary for a correct solution of several problems encountered in my research.

I wish to acknowledge, too, the aid given me by my friends at Vanderbilt University. Dr. Edwin Mims, Mr. John Crowe Ransom, and Mr. Donald Davidson read the manuscript and offered many suggestions for its improvement. Dr. Frank Owsley contributed generously of his thorough knowledge of the historical background necessary for my interpretations. Miss Linda Rhea listened to all my plans during my research and writing. Then, as a further test of her patience and friendship, she read both manuscript and proof; her criticisms were most helpful. Mr. Edd W. Parks read the proof, offered many suggestions for its improvement, and contributed much to its accuracy. My husband, Dr. Carl S. Driver, was my constant counsellor. His sound judgment prevented my doing many foolish things. Without his encouragement, this study would never have been completed.

To three former teachers I am most deeply indebted, and to them it is impossible to express adequate appreciation. The late Dr. Walter L. Fleming first interested me in Fanny Kemble; I hope that I have been able to retain and to convey some small part of his enthusiastic interest in my subject. He also placed at my disposal much material which would have been difficult to obtain otherwise. Dr. Walter C. Curry is responsible for my original interest in research. He read the manuscript of this study chapter by chapter as it was written, and then reread the completed study. His suggestions were always for its improvement. Dr. John Donald Wade directed my work. He was never too busy to discuss its progress, to read the chapters as they were written, or often, to reread the revised drafts. It would gratify me to believe that some of the suggestions he made are echoed in this book—not in its details only, but in the general trend of those portions of it which essay to be philosophic.

LEOTA S. DRIVER

Nashville, Tennessee
November 4, 1932

CONTENTS

LIST OF ILLUSTRATIONS

FANNY KEMBLE

PROLOGUE

ONE HUNDRED years ago, on September 4, 1832, Fanny Kemble came to America. For more than a century her activities have interested persons on both sides of the Atlantic. Since that October evening in 1829 when she burst upon public attention as the débutante of Covent Garden, her name has retained a perpetual charm for persons in two hemispheres.

Although her life practically spans the nineteenth century, she recalls far more than one age. She was the last of the histrionic Kembles, and they were a great family. Patrons of the English stage welcomed her as the niece of Mrs. Sarah Siddons, who had appeared at Drury Lane with that supreme master, David Garrick; as the granddaughter of Roger Kemble, a contemporary of James Quin; as the great granddaughter of John Ward, who led his strollers about the countryside in the days of Thomas Betterton and Barton Booth.

One can scarcely think of Fanny Kemble without calling to mind this remarkable lineage, but she was something more than "the last of the Kembles." She was a woman of unusual talent, intellect, and versatility: poet, dramatist, novelist, critic, musician, actress, and dramatic reader. Above all, she was a vivid and engaging personality.

Temperamentally she was impulsive, self-willed, and individualistic. Proud of spirit, conscientious perhaps to a fault, she refused compromise with anything which she conceived to be wrong. To her, integrity was a virtue beyond comparison. Her beliefs, her ideas, her personality were sacred. Something within her rebelled against any restraint imposed not only upon herself but upon others, for, histrionic artist that she was, she unconsciously projected herself into the circumstances of those about her, and their wrongs became hers. Idealistic, sometimes visionary, she found no situation which could satisfy her restiveness for long. Change always seemed to offer the contentment which she sought. Her life was a long sequence of anticipations and regrets.

Although England always remained home to her, she studied in France, lived in Italy, passed many summers in Switzerland, and resided for more than forty years in the United States. Among her friends were the great and near great of two countries: musicians, artists, writers, actors, scientists, and statesmen. Queen Victoria received her at Court; Andrew Jackson welcomed her to the White House and then crowded with his fellow politicians into the tiny Washington theater to attend her impersonation of Mrs. Haller.

Life endowed her richly, but it was also cruel to her. It created her an uncompromising individual; then it confronted her with a series of paradoxes. An autonomous spirit, she found herself restrained by a custom-bound society. Her inheritance and early surroundings both predestined her for the stage. Her name is linked inseparably with the history of the theater, but throughout her life she detested acting and resented the circumstances which drove her to that vocation. When at the age of twenty-three she left London for New York, the journey meant exile. Two years later America became her home, and the happiest years of her life were spent there. From girlhood she had condemned the institution of slavery; she became the wife of a slave owner and lived on his plantation. But throughout the perplexities that confronted her, her will, her pride, and her sense of justice and right remained inviolate. She rationalized, at least to her own satisfaction, every paradox.

Something about her escapes definition. No label places her; no characterization satisfies. An indefinable quality constitutes her supreme charm. She was forever changing and still forever constant, "like a handsome piece of changeable silk; first one color, then another, but always the clean thing."

CHAPTER I

CHILD AND SCHOOLGIRL

THE FORCES of heredity and environment drove Fanny Kemble to the stage. Among her ancestors were the members of England's most numerous, famous, and devoted theatrical family. From babyhood she heard the dramatic voices of actors and actresses. One of her earliest memories recalled a picture which hung above the living-room fireplace in the Kemble home. It depicted a stormy sea and a helmless, sailless boat in which sat a dejected man, one hand on the fair curls of a girl of three. "And that," said a tender voice which repeated the story many times, "was the good Duke of Milan, Prospero,—and that was his little child, Miranda." Grown to womanhood, the little girl who listened attentively to a simplified version of *The Tempest* despised the stage and resented the circumstances which drove her to gain a livelihood as an actress. But a predilection for the theatrical colored her whole life. With all her dislike for the histrionic profession, she could never free herself from the influences of ancestry and early environment.

Frances Anne, or Fanny as she was affectionately known, was born November 27, 1809, on Newman Street, Oxford Road, London, third of the five children of Charles and Therese Decamp Kemble.[1] Although both of her parents spent many years on the English stage, the story of the family's enthusiasm for the dramatic art began with an older generation.

About the middle of the eighteenth century an Irish actor, John Ward, led his company of players around the English countryside. His strollers presented Shakespearean dramas in the tavern yards wherever they could escape the Puritan's edict: "No monkeys, marionettes or actors." In 1752 a stalwart, courteous man of thirty, who gave the name of Roger Kemble, came to Birmingham to join Ward's company. Gossip whispered that he had forsaken the hair-dresser's trade. Although he said that he belonged to an old English Catholic family of Wiltshire, the Herald's College failed to confirm the assertion.[2] Personal characteristics lent more support to his claim of gentle breeding. He possessed the serene, stately bearing and the cold ease of a Lord Chancellor. His features were striking: eyes, extremely vivid; brows, exquisitely arched; mouth, small and admirably moulded. The line of his nose seemed faultlessly straight, but, by an unusual combination of styles, the tip of it, slightly too long and too fleshy, added something powerful and personal to the cast of his countenance.[3] It was the nose of his clan.

Although in appearance Roger resembled the traditional stage hero, he proved difficult to train. He became a permanent member of the strolling company only after surmounting bitter opposition from the manager. Several influences prompted his persistence—not the least compelling was Mr. Ward's daughter, Sally. Her commanding presence and strong but sweet voice seemed created to portray the queens of Shakespeare. Her beauty instantly won Roger's devotion.

In spite of Mr. Ward's vigorous protests, he acquired an unwelcome son-in-law at Circencester in 1753. But one consolation remained to the father and he made the most of it. He wished his daughter not to marry an actor, he taunted, and in that she had complied with his wishes.[4] Although Roger Kemble may have been guilty of other shortcomings, his memory and imagination were excellent. He treasured this caustic stricture on his theatrical ability. Twenty years later he elaborated the remark into a withering diatribe against his own unwelcome son-in-law: "I had forbidden you to marry an actor," he reminded his headstrong daughter Sarah when she eloped with Henry Siddons. "You are not disobeying me, for you are marrying a man whom the Devil himself could not turn into an actor." If Mr. Ward could have read in a clairvoyant's glass a prophecy of the success reserved for his grandchildren and great-grandchildren, perhaps he would have felt ample compensation for Roger Kemble's histrionic failings.

John Ward died on October 30, 1773; his wife, Sarah, survived until 1786. Before their decease their son-in-law assumed control of the strolling company. Additions to their family came frequently while Roger and Sally Ward Kemble traversed their circuit through Hereford, Worcester, and adjacent towns. Sarah was born in Wales on July 5, 1755; John Phillip, at Prescott in Lancashire on February 1, 1757. Eight others preceded Charles, the youngest son, born in 1775. The wandering parents perhaps welcomed with a sigh each new and burdensome charge upon their resources. They could not foresee that little Sarah was to become the peerless Lady Macbeth, little John, the incomparable Coriolanus, or little Charles, the ideal Mercutio of the nineteenth-century stage.[5]

Although Roger Kemble succumbed to the lure of the stage, he determined that none of his children should make it a profession. He meant to educate them for some more dignified pursuit. Roger was a Catholic; Sally Ward, a Protestant. According to an agreement between them, the sons were to be reared in the religion of their father, and the daughters, in that of their mother. Mr. Kemble dedicated his eldest son, John Phillip, to the Church and sent him to the Catholic school at Douai. All went well until the masters reawakened his hereditary inclinations by making him read aloud during the meals Butler's *Lives of the Saints* in his splendid Kemble voice. When he observed that even in worship he could not listen to the priest without unconsciously saying to himself, "What a part!" he realized that he was not intended for the priesthood.[6]

One and all, the Kemble children drifted to the stage. Even Charles refused to heed the counsel of his father and older

brothers. After a short service in the post-office, he gave up
his position to join Mrs. Siddons and John Phillip at Drury
Lane.[7] Although they might profess to scorn the histrionic
art, the descendants of Roger and Sally Kemble could not
escape its call. Fanny received from her father a full share
of this predilection for the theater.

Far from counteracting this influence, inheritances from her
mother reinforced this irresistible fascination. Maria Therese
Decamp, goddaughter of Queen Maria Theresa of Austria,
came to England in her early childhood. Her father, Captain
George Decamp, descendant of a younger branch of the De
Fleury family,[8] served as an officer in one of the armies which
France sent to invade republican Switzerland. There he
tarried long enough to marry the daughter of a farmer from
the Berne neighborhood near the foot of the great Jungfrau range of the Alps. From childhood the young girl who
became Mrs. Decamp loved those snow-capped peaks. The
longing for another glimpse of their rugged beauty remained
throughout her bitter and disappointing years in England.

Soon after their marriage the Decamps went to Vienna
where their oldest daughter, Maria Therese, was born on
January 17, 1774, the birthday of the Empress. Mr. Decamp's
talents as draughtsman and musician soon attracted the
attention of several visiting English noblemen, among them
Lord Monson, afterwards Earl of Essex. They urged the
talented young Frenchman to go to London. There, they
assured him, his abilities, which surpassed those of the amateur,
would enable him more easily to maintain his family. In an
evil hour he yielded to the enticement of their promised
patronage. The London fog soon affected his lungs, and flute
playing became impossible. Six years after his arrival, he
died. The support of the mother and five children fell to the
oldest, Therese, not yet in her teens.[9]

Therese had begun her stage career at the age of six when
she appeared as one of the Cupidons of Novarre's ballets.
Later she transferred to Le Texier's troupe where she won

recognition as a dancer. Soon admiring ladies and gentlemen snatched up "the little French fairy" into their society. One of the Prince Regent's favorite performances consisted in placing her under a huge glass bell intended as a covering for a Dresden china group. There "her tiny figure and flashing face" produced a more beautiful effect than that of the costly work of art.

Captain Decamp intended to return to the continent as soon as he made his fortune. For that reason he neglected the teaching of English to his children. At his death Therese's knowledge of the language was meager. Even with this handicap she refused to consider any occupation except that of the stage. At first she learned the dialogue of the childish rôles by mere dint of repetition. But success came rapidly, and in 1786 she appeared as Julie in *Richard Coeur de Lion* at Drury Lane.

The following years disclosed the extent of her talents. She excelled especially in the portrayal of sprightly parts or in those which demanded pantomimic action. The celebrity of the Kembles, with whom she became allied by her marriage in 1806, overshadowed her attainments, but she possessed in a higher degree than any member of that famous family the peculiar organization of genius. She was versatile and dramatic; they were circumscribed and sometimes theatrical. Genius and talents marked all the descendants of Captain Decamp and his romantic wife.[10] Maria Therese Kemble transmitted something of their capabilities to each of her children.

This emotional Gallic strain blended with the English and Irish in the temperament of Fanny Kemble. She was the descendant of the gruff, gentleman-comedian, John Ward; of the Bohemian but regal stroller, Roger Kemble; of the reserved, cultured Mercutio, Charles Kemble. Equally potent were the inheritances from Captain Decamp, the French soldier-musician; from the liberty-loving Swiss mountaineer grandmother; from the dramatic, versatile Therese Decamp. To the splendid Kemble voice and hereditary theatrical tastes, she added a dramatic versatility, a musical ear, and the worship of beauty. In her nature, English respect for law and tradition encountered its antithesis in the emotional, romantic temperament of the Swiss-French.

According to Sir Thomas Lawrence's portrait of Mrs. Roger Kemble, Fanny bore a personal resemblance to her grandmother. She always tried to believe that the likeness to this brave, energetic woman was more than skin deep. Although the common records of the family did not reach much beyond the days of Roger, somehow the Kembles always seemed a race apart. More dominant natures and more expressive ways and looks separated them from their associates. They suggested those deities who, as muses and hunters, once visited the earth in the guise of shepherds.[11] Their daily life was heroic, and their standards of attainment, high. Handsome, passionate, objective, and confident, they had a way of making more sensitive people appear dim and devitalized.[12] Although these qualities of mind and temperament came to Fanny from her father's family, those from her mother stamped her more strongly. She added "to the fine senses of a savage rather than a civilized nature" an "instinct of correct criticism in all matters of art," a quickness and accuracy of perception, and a vividness of expression.[13]

Charles Kemble's family removed from Newman Street to Westbourne Green during Fanny's babyhood. The first impression which remained in her memory came at this second home. A gift was responsible, a pasteboard figure of a little girl with a book full of painted cardboard dresses, cloaks and bonnets. She cared nothing at all for ordinary dolls. Instead, they were rather hateful to her. She always wanted to tear them in pieces to see what was inside the sawdust. But the cardboard and the wardrobe were different. The child spent many hours in noting the effects produced on the countenance of the doll by changes in its clothing. Even before she was three years old, this predilection for theatrical matters manifested itself.

Other traits which characterized her whole life also began to express themselves—most prominent among them was "a general audacious contempt for all authority . . . coupled with a sweet-tempered, cheerful indifference to all punishment."[14] She never cried, never sulked, and never lamented or repented her transgressions. No matter what the consequences, she accepted them with buoyancy of spirits. Upon one occasion a fool's cap of vast dimensions covered her tiny head. In response to the advice from an adult member of the family to hide her horrible disgrace, the culprit seized the first opportunity and danced down the driveway. From an elevated bank she called loudly upon all passers-by to admire the penal costume. A diet of bread and water atoned for the next malefaction: "Now I am like those poor, dear French prisoners that everybody pities so," she joyfully philosophized.

Mrs. Siddons came one day just after her small niece committed an offense against either manners or morals. One of the grave elders of the household led the truant into the awful presence of the Tragic Muse. The culprit heard reprimands in those tones which "curdled the blood of the poor shopman" when the tragedienne demanded if his printed calico would wash. The passionate, dramatic tones paused; a childish voice tinkled, "What beautiful eyes you have!" Truly it was a difficult matter to obtain the "minimum quantity of obedience indispensable in the relations of a tailless monkey of four years and its elders."[15] Punishment was inevitable. The transgressor accepted it as a matter of course, for consequences failed to deter Fanny.

Her first experiences as an actress came at about this time. The famous actor, Charles Young, called frequently at the Kemble home. If the elders were absent, he made his way to the nursery. As one of his favorite diversions, he made Fanny fold her little, fat arms and, "with a portentous frown," received from him unintelligible passages from *Macbeth*. To these she replied with a lisp, "My handth are of oo toler." Years later when Charles Young acted Macbeth for the last time in London, Fanny Kemble, the youthful sensation of Covent Garden, was the wicked wife. Memories of other days came to him as he stood behind the scenes watching her paint her hands and arms. The elderly man tip-toed to her side, "Ah ha! my handth are of oo toler," he reminded her with a wistful smile.[16]

When Fanny reached the age of five, her parents began to consider the question of her education. Soon she left Westbourne Green for Camden Place, Bath, where Charles Kemble's sister, Mrs. Frances Twiss, kept a girls' school, established after she forsook the stage to marry that "grim-visaged, gaunt-figured, kind-hearted gentleman" who compiled a concordance of Shakespeare. Here the child remained during a little more than a year. Just what profit she gained, she never knew. She became neither versed in learned lore nor accomplished in the lighter tasks of leisure hours prescribed for girls of that establishment.

Again those elements of theatrical life which filtered into this rather remote center stamped themselves upon her memory. John Twiss, then a young giant studying to become an engineer officer, visited homefolks occasionally. He, too, felt the Kemble dramatic urge. The enacting of his Uncle John Phillip Kemble's famous rescue of Cora's child in *Pizarro* was his amusement. With Fanny clutched in one hand and exalted into perilous proximity to the chandelier, he rushed across the drawing-room to her terror and triumph. During her stay at Bath the future actress also witnessed her first play. Near by lay a family residence called Claverton Park, where in the middle of a spacious hall stood a portable theatre or puppet show with tragic instead of grotesque figures. There, on summer afternoons after a walk through the green meadows, *Macbeth* and similar solemnities occasionally appeared before the child's enchanted eyes.

After a year's absence from London, Fanny returned to the Kemble's new home in Covent Garden Chambers. The months with Mrs. Twiss had made few changes in her conduct.

She came back to her parents much as she had gone, mischievous, petted, spoiled, philosophical, self-willed and equal to any occasion. A happening during her brief sojourn in London illustrated the latter trait. Talma, the French actor, called upon Mr. Kemble when the elders were absent. A servant holding Fanny by the hand opened the door. The artist took some notice of the little miss. He requested her to remember his name and to tell her father that Monsieur Talma, the great French tragedian, had called. Fanny assured him that she would not forget. Then she added "with noble emulation" that her father and her uncle were great tragedians and that there was a baby in the nursery who must be a great tragedian, too. She did nothing but cry, "and what was that if not tragedy?"[17]

During this interim in Fanny's schooling, Mrs. Siddons returned to the stage for one night as Lady Randolph. Her six-year-old niece was in the audience when the performance began. Although the child remembered little about it except the appearance of a solemn female figure in black and the tremendous roar of public greeting which welcomed her, this was the only occasion upon which the future actress witnessed a performance by this supreme genius.[18] Here again the concerns of the theater impressed themselves on the child mind of the "last of the great Kembles."

After several months in London, her school life began in earnest. Mr. and Mrs. Kemble chose Madame Faudier's school at Boulogne as a suitable place for a mite of a girl to learn French. Learn French she did. There was no helping it, for French was the only language spoken there. In addition she studied music, dancing, and Italian. She mastered the beginnings of such humanities with tolerable success. But if frequency of penitences was any indication, Madame Faudier instilled the characteristics of humanity in general only after considerable effort.

Fanny still felt a grievous contempt for authority and a disdain for punishment. She was a sore torment to poor

Madame Faudier, who knew not how to manage this bit
of Irish. One day an alarmed passer-by informed Madame
that one of her "demoiselles was perambulating the house
roof." A paroxysm of rage and terror gripped her, "*Ah ce
ne peut être que cette diable de Kemble!*" she cried. Thrust for
chastisement into a lonely garret with nothing to do but look
about her, Fanny quickly discovered a ladder leading to a
trap-door. A few moments later the extensive panorama land-
ward and seaward received such homage as her Swiss grandmother would have bestowed on the Jungfrau.

Snatched from this eminence, the admirer of natural loveliness expiated her adventure in a pitch black cellar. In spite
of an attitude of nonchalance, she "suffered a martyrdom of
fear," for nature had endowed her with a highly susceptible
and excitable nervous temperament and an ill-regulated
imagination. On many occasions she "suffered from every
conceivable form of terror" when those about her thought her
indifferent. The only agreeable impression retained of these
school days, she said, was that of the long half-holiday walks.
In unrestrained freedom the girls sometimes spent the sunny
afternoon in gathering wild flowers in the secluded Liane
Valley or in telling fairy stories among the great, carved
blocks of stone, or in distant wandering along the sand dunes.

Fanny spent almost two years under Madame Faudier's
guidance. Before she left Boulogne the yearly solemnity of
the distribution of prizes took place in the presence of all
the civil and religious authorities of the town. One dignified
personage "pronounced a discourse commendatory of past
efforts and hortatory to future ones." Then Madame presented
rewards for excellence in the various subjects of the curriculum. Years later a lady present at the exercise recalled "the
frequent summons to the dais received by a small, black-eyed
damsel, the *cadette* of the establishment"—Fanny, an apt,
talented, alert child as well as a most provoking one.[19]

The Kembles lived at Craven Hill, Bayswater, when at the
age of nine she returned to England. Mrs. Kemble had a mania

for moving. She relieved her feelings by changing residences. If that were impossible, she shuffled the furniture. She detested the dense, heavy atmosphere of London with its smoke and fog. Perhaps the memory of Captain Decamp's tragic career there added to the depression which she always felt amid the deafening clamor and ceaseless uproar of its busy streets.

In consequence of this mania, as a finale to a hard evening's work at the theater, Charles Kemble often trudged five miles from Covent Garden to Craven Hill. When that became too strenuous, in addition to the rural residence, he took a lodging in Soho. Fanny sometimes remained in town with her father. One life-long recollection of these days in Gerard Street remained with her. There her father read passages from *Paradise Lost*, and she found the sonorous melody enchanting. During some years Milton remained her favorite English poet. Previously Scott held precedence over all others. Unreasonable as it may seem, at this age the future actress did not know a single line of Shakespeare.

Children's amusements, as Fanny points out, are always more or less dramatic and in the playroom of a household like that of the Kembles, dedicated to the stage, it was only natural that a miniature theater should hold an honored place. Small figures modeled from cardboard, with their feet inserted into pieces of wood, were the characters. These presented many such plays as *The Miller and His Men* or *Bluebeard*. Fanny's older brother, John, acted as manager and spokesman in these performances.

The children's attendance at a real play incited new ideas. *Meg Murdock or the Mountain Hag* and a mythological after-piece, *Hyppolita, Queen of the Amazons*, impressed the future disciple of Thespis. Fanny especially approved of the martial heroism displayed by the fair warriors who went so far as to die. With this stimulus the youthful Kembles decided to stage a performance of their own. John acted as manager, selector, and director. He considered the advisability of *Chrononhotonthologos*.

None of the actors except the manager could pronounce the name of this burlesque, and, instead, he chose *Amoroso, King of Little Britain*. No one could accuse the youthful performers of lacking ambition in their selection of an audience. Mr. and Mrs. Liston, the Amoroso and Coquetinda of the real stage, Mr. and Mrs. Charles Matthews, Charles Young, and Charles and Therese Kemble were of the number invited to witness this triumph of amateur genius.[20]

But play days ended abruptly. From the time of Fanny's return to England, Mr. and Mrs. Kemble had discussed the continuance of her education. Now she hastened her own departure again for France. She was troublesome, unmanageable, and still disdainful of all authority. Madame Faudier had failed. Even a trip to the guillotine, arranged by that lady so that the offender might see the ultimate fate of a career of wickedness, had caused no change in her conduct.

After a series of misdemeanors, affairs finally came to a crisis during a walk with Aunt Dall, Mrs. Kemble's sister. An impertinent reply followed a reproof. The aunt declined Fanny's company. Instead of returning home, the youthful tragedienne determined to end it all in one magnificent gesture. At least Aunt Dall, father, mother, all who had provoked her, should be sorry. She selected a pond in the nearby meadow as an appropriate setting for this ultimate satisfaction. But the water was thickly covered with "green slime studded with frogs' heads." A moment's contemplation revealed the inexpediency of her getting beneath its surface. With the decision that a living actress was preferable to a dead one, the child turned resolutely in the direction of London.

Between Craven Hill and London lived a seamstress who often did needlework for the Kembles. She was surprised upon replying to a knock at her door to find Fanny there all alone. Her amazement increased with the information that her visitor was on the way to London to apply for a theatrical engagement. This woman understood child nature. She suggested that a brief rest and a wee piece of bread with butter would cheer a weary traveller on her way. Several hours later Aunt Dall's entry awakened the little truant. Ignominious capture followed. The offender expiated the misdemeanor by a week on bread and water and daily confinement in a sort of tool-house in the garden. This was not cheerful, but the prisoner endeavored to make it appear so. She sang at the top of her voice whenever she heard any footsteps on the garden walk. Fanny might be sorely hurt, but those who inflicted the wound never enjoyed the satisfaction of hearing complaint. She repaid injury with contempt.[21]

At the end of the summer Fanny departed for Paris. She entered a school on Rue d'Angoulême, Champs Élysées, kept by Madame Rowden, who could refer to Miss Mitford and Lady Caroline Lamb as products of her establishment which formerly had operated at Hans Place, London. Here both secular and religious education received attention. Madame's Low Church tendencies made her a persistent church-goer, and Sunday was a day of unrest for the girls. In addition to occasional week day services, on Sunday they attended two or three devotionals either in the chapel of the embassy or at the Église de l'Oratoire. Further discipline required that they write from memory a recapitulation of the sermons heard in the course of the day. These they read aloud at evening prayers. A comparison of these with the originals doubtless occasioned many suppressed titters. Sometimes upon an appeal for mercy and a solemn protest that although they had listened attentively they could not recall a single line, Madame permitted the girls to choose texts and compose original homilies. The Kemble volume must have been an interesting comment on current transgressions and punishments.

The portion of secular knowledge which received attention varied. Although almost all the girls were English, they studied geography, history, arithmetic, and mythology in French. Latin, music, and dancing also found a place in the curriculum. Later came a course in Italian. Dante was the Italian master's "spiritual consolation, his intellectual delight and indeed his daily bread." He employed one textbook. From that "sublime, grotesque and altogether wonderful poem," *Divina Commedia*, he taught his pupils to "stammer" the Italian language and to illustrate every rule of syntax.

Madame Rowden also had a practical turn of mind. Every student attended a Saturday sewing class. When girls left her school, they could make their own dresses and do respectable darning. Among all these various studies, the one for which Fanny never felt a lack of zeal was dancing. She had "a perfect passion" for this art, a preference which long survived her schooldays. She believed even late in life that her natural vocation should have been that of an opera dancer, perhaps an echo from the "little fairy" of Le Texier's troupe.

In addition to regular pupils, Madame Rowden received a small number of parlor boarders, girls who joined only one or two classes. Occasionally when Fanny's report for good conduct was acceptable, she received invitations to tea with these special students. One evening she sat on the sofa opposite the portrait of her Uncle John as Coriolanus, the only ornament of Madame's drawing-room. While his stature grew alternately large and small before her sleepy eyes, the girl sitting by her side held a book before Fanny's face, her finger at the lines:

> It is the hour when from the boughs
> The nightingale's high note is heard.

Instantly the sleepy girl was wide awake. Quivering with emotion, she fastened a steel-like grip on the book, which she succeeded in carrying to her bedroom. At bedtime, after the supervising teacher and the light departed together, she told her companions that she had a volume of Byron's poetry under her pillow. Emphatic whispers of terror and dismay followed this disclosure. At last, conquered by their horror and tears, she hid the book in a vacant bed, and then lay awake most of the night intoxicated by those magic words That "small, sweet draught" remained indelibly impressed on her memory. During her last year in Paris, when she received news of her Uncle John's death at Lausanne and of Lord Byron's at Missolonghi, she felt passionate regret only for the man of whose poetry she had read less than twenty lines.[22]

Trips in the Champs Élysées, Jardin de Luxembourg, and Parc Monceaux interrupted the routine of her lessons. On days when the picture-gallery was opened gratuitously, the girls wandered through the old palace. There they formed their taste for art among the samples of the modern French school of painting which it displayed. Fanny's real holidays were the rare and short visits of her father. Charles Kemble enjoyed the gaiety of Paris and the brightly lighted cafés; its operas and theaters were wonderlands to his daughter. Together they strolled along the Boulevard or in the Tuileries, dined in the Cadran Bleu, and then rounded out the evening at a theater where some celebrated French actor, often Philippe, appeared.

Madame Rowden's establishment was famous for occasional dramatic representations. These formed a diversion for the girls who were, as Fanny said, as near to Patagonia as to Paris in so far as its amusements were concerned. The instructress chose Racine's *Andromaque* as a starring vehicle after Madame had summarily confiscated all copies of *Roxelane* just before the staging of that performance. She would not allow the presentation of a seraglio in her school, the horror of which the girls could scarcely understand. The heroine of *Roxelane*, a pretty French woman revolutionized the Ottoman Empire by inducing her Mohammedan lover to dismiss his harem and confine his affection to her whom he married in orthodox fashion.

Andromaque was above reproach. Fanny played Hermione, and in this rôle she gave proof of her dramatic inheritance. An imposing audience gathered to witness the play. The girls became hoarse with nervousness. They swallowed raw eggs to clear their throats, only to make themselves sick with these as well as with fright. At last the tragedy ended. Fanny had electrified the audience, her companions, and still more, herself.

Madame usually read some book of devotion before the prayers which concluded each day's labors. On this occasion she chose the story of a fashionable lady extremely fond of the theater. One day, so the story went, she expatiated with great vivacity to the Reverend Doctor Somebody upon the delights which she derived from the stage. "First you know, Doctor, there is the pleasure of anticipation, then the delight of the performance, and then the enjoyment of the recollection!" "Add to which, Madame," interposed the amiable divine, "the pleasure you will derive from all these pleasures on your death-bed." Fanny could not suppress a smile at this implied condemnation of her whole family's vocation. It seemed a rather powerful piece of sensational religionism for a lady who ornamented her room with John Kemble's Coriolanus.[23]

As Madame bade Hermione good-night, she concluded, "Ah, my dear, I don't think your parents need ever anticipate your going on the stage; you would make but a poor actress." Just what prompted this remark Fanny never knew, but she said that the mistress must have accepted her performance as either "a threat or a promise" of dramatic power. But after all, Madame Rowden perhaps was not far wrong. Fanny always remained a poor actress in so far as devotion, zeal, and love of a profession were necessary to success.

Three busy years passed at Madame Rowden's school. Fanny was fifteen when Charles Kemble came to take her home, to a different home, of course. Mrs. Kemble had moved several times during her daughter's absence but anywhere in England was home to *la plus anglaise des anglaises*. The student prided herself on a knowledge of Latin, Italian, and French, a taste for the tragedies of Racine and Corneille, a love of the *Divina Commedia*, a passion for dancing, and the reputation of a

FANNY KEMBLE

*From the engraved frontispiece of Records of a Girlhood,
published by Henry Holt & Co., in 1879.*

talented amateur actress. Her will, determination, and self-assertiveness remained, but age slightly curbed their manifestations. Among her more tangible possessions was a book of her own verse, for Fanny had felt the poetic urge. She wrote rimes without stint or stopping—a perfect deluge of doggerel.

On the journey across the Channel a stiff breeze snatched away the young voyager's bonnet. In London she so far imposed upon her father's masculine ignorance in such matters as to induce him to replace it with a full-sized leghorn flat. Under the circumference of this immense sombrero, Fanny seated herself beside her father in the afternoon coach for Weybridge. A nervous fear gripped her heart, fear that she should not recognize her mother after an absence of three years.[24]

The sun disappeared beneath the clouds in the west. The blue aromatic pine woods and the fields of golden gorse and purple heather became more and more indistinct in the waning light. Darkness fell before the stage arrived at the straggling, picturesque village. "Is anyone here for Mrs. Kemble?" inquired a womanly voice, when at last the coach stopped in front of the inn. Fanny could not see the questioner, but she knew those tones. In a moment the little traveller, leghorn hat and all, tumbled from the carriage into her mother's arms.

CHAPTER II

DRIFTING TOWARDS A VOCATION

BY THE time of the girl's return from Paris, Mrs. Kemble's rural yearnings had carried her to a tiny cottage on the outskirts of Weybridge. But for her admirable contrivance, she could never have found room in that bird-cage for her family. Such was her skill that all except Mr. Kemble delighted in it. But, as Fanny has said, one could scarcely expect a man to relish a residence where he was too long and too large for every room. Mrs. Kemble preferred even a small cottage away from London to a roomy house in the noise and fog. While her husband spent the weeks in his comfortable house at Number 5 Soho Square, she packed herself and the children into their crowded rural quarters.[1]

Fanny was delighted with this new home. She felt carefree, a blessed release after the sewing classes and devotionals of Madame Rowden's school. She now passed the days in the open air on the heath, in the wood above the meadows of Brooklands, or in the picturesque inclosure of Portmore Park. There the tenantless, half-ruined mansion surrounded by its noble cedars above the winding river Wey made a picture worthy of any artist's brush. A purpose other than the admiration of its beauty frequently drew the Kembles to that vicinity. Mrs. Kemble was passionately fond of fishing, and the family spent whole days by the river pursuing this sport. Although all the children took part, only Fanny inherited her mother's enthusiasm; but at this period of her life even she preferred a book and a shady, grassy spot by the riverside while Mrs. Kemble waited patiently for a nibble.

The girl followed no systematic studies. The year of her return from Paris marked the beginning of a period of indiscriminate reading. She read every book which fell into her hands no matter what its subject. She found her chief delight in such German literature as translations enabled her to become acquainted with. She studied La Motte Fouqué, Tieck, Wieland's *Oberon*, and Goethe's *Wilhelm Meister*. In addition to her reading she continued to scribble verses, some "in very bad Italian" and others in "indifferent English." She felt compelled to write. Perhaps "an eruption of such rubbish" was safer than "keeping it in the mental system."

John and Henry occasionally interrupted their sister's mental labors. They needed a short-stop or some other sort of stop for their "insufficiently manned . . . games of cricket." A severe blow on her instep from a ball which she failed to hold seemed a severe price to pay for the honor of sharing her brothers' pastimes. Another sport in which Fanny joined with more satisfaction was shooting at a mark, an exercise of skill which she much preferred to "that dreadful watching and catching of cannon-balls at cricket." John owned two guns, with the use of which he tried to familiarize her. The rifle felt unsupportably heavy; the fowling piece kicked unmercifully. After the first shot she declined all further experiments with either. Instead, she reverted to the "little, ladylike pocket pistols" as preliminary training for the honor which came to her years later of firing an American cannon on the practice grounds at West Point.[2]

The happy Weybridge summers which succeeded each other for three years brought to Fanny one incident of special importance—her catching of the smallpox. Her sister Adelaide had had a light attack, at first diagnosed by the village doctor as chickenpox, but later proving to be varioloid. Mrs. Kemble had lost all faith in vaccination, and she decided that a natural attack, like Adelaide's was the best preventive of the more serious disease. Without considering the difference in the ages and constitutions of the two girls, she summoned Fanny home from London to contract the disease. Although Adelaide's illness had been mild, Fanny very nearly died. She had returned from France a pretty girl with sparkling black eyes, black hair, a clear, vivid complexion and smooth features. Besides marking her face perceptibly, smallpox left her complexion thick and muddy and her features heavy and coarse. In the years which followed, she sometimes keenly felt the disadvantages which this loss of her good looks imposed upon her. "Well, my dear, they can't say we brought you out to exhibit your beauty," Mrs. Kemble remarked when they were considering the probability of Fanny's début on the stage. Throughout her life, friends commented on the variations in her appearance. Sometimes her features looked clear and smooth; on other occasions, the markings were noticeable and her complexion, muddy. "Fanny Kemble, you are the ugliest and the handsomest woman in London," her old friend Mrs. Fitzhugh once exclaimed.[3]

The Parisian education did not achieve at least one anticipated result. Fanny's French dancing lessons failed to give her a graceful carriage or to teach her to hold herself upright. She stooped and slouched, stood with one hip up and the opposite shoulder down. Such deportment could not be tolerated among the Kembles, who prided themselves on their patrician bearing. Her parents resorted to strenuous correctives. Among other engines of torture they tried one of the "backboard species," a flat piece of morocco-covered steel, strapped to the waist with a belt and to the shoulders by two epaulets. A steel collar encircling the throat and fastening in the back completed this "portable pillory." The expected reformation failed to materialize even after the wearer's endurance of considerable torture.

Finally the girl threw off the "iron shell" and became the pupil of a sergeant of the Royal Foot Guards. His methods were more successful. After a number of exercises such as he practised on awkward squads at the parade grounds, he pronounced his pupil fit to march before the Duke of York, then commander of the forces. Throughout her life Fanny thanked her drill-master for her "well-placed shoulders, an erect head, upright carriage, and resolute step."[4]

During the winters the family returned to a house at Bayswater or at Soho. Fanny still practised her music and pursued her unsystematic reading. Dr. Malkin, master of the grammar school at Bury St. Edmund's, where John prepared for admission to Cambridge, frequently visited in the Kemble home and occasionally suggested books for her reading. As a useful exercise he set her to translating Sismondi's *Les Républiques Italiennes* which he wished her to abridge for publication. Evenings often found her at Covent Garden, where in 1826 Weber's opera *Der Freyschütz* held a long popularity.

By the spring of 1827 the migration to a slightly larger abode at Bayswater permitted Fanny the dignity of an unshared bedroom. This she made into a small study, the privacy of which she enjoyed immensely. A window opened above the suburban garden. Many hours passed while she watched the changing light on the distant sloping meadows and dreamed of castles in Spain. She had decided to make a name for herself as a writer. John was still only a student at Cambridge, but he meant to become a lawyer, perhaps Lord Chancellor of England. Henry studied at Bury St. Edmund's. His vocation was still undecided, but it would be a worthy one, of course. Adelaide's girlish voice already displayed unusual operatic promise. A Lord Chancellor, a prima donna, and an authoress! Charles and Therese Kemble should never regret the sacrifices and skimpings necessary to educate their children. Poems accumulated by the dozen. An authoress! Yes, in that direction fame seemed to lie.

Fanny was not yet seventeen when she first went to Hertfordshire to visit her aunt, Mrs. John Phillip Kemble. After Mr. Kemble's death at Lausanne, his widow accepted a home offered by her husband's friend, Lord Essex, on the Cashionbury estates. Fanny enjoyed the days there. Mrs. Kemble allowed her to follow her own inclinations. When she chose, she wandered from Heath Farm around the environs of Cashionbury Park or visited with the neighbors. Her "production of doggerel suffered no diminution" when she began a historical novel inspired by Wraxall's *Memoirs of the House of Valois*, found in her aunt's library. Mrs. Kemble's book shelves held many attractive volumes. Fanny's choices included Byron and Jeremy Taylor. "I read them on alternate days," she said, "sitting on a mossy-cushioned lawn, under a beautiful oak tree, with a cabbage-leaf full of fresh-gathered strawberries and a handful of fresh-blown roses beside me, which Epicurean accompaniments to my studies appeared to me equally adapted to the wicked poet and the wise divine."[5] At last she could read to her satisfaction those poems of which a mere glimpse had intoxicated her imagination at Madame Rowden's school.

At Heath Farm, Fanny first met the dearest friend of her life, Harriet Saint Leger. Miss Saint Leger was almost thirty, more than twelve years older than Fanny, when the two exchanged confidences while rambling over the countryside in Hertfordshire. In spite of the difference in their ages, enduring friendship followed their meeting. Harriet was an intellectual woman. She delighted in metaphysical subjects, and her habits of thought and reading were profoundly speculative. Her manner and countenance expressed her nobility, intelligence, and tenderness. *Haut et Bon* was the device of her family; it was also a description of her. Her tall, thin figure wanted roundness and grace, but it was straight as a dart. Her vigorous, elastic movements and springing step gave to her bearing a character like that of the fabled Atalanta. Although she was not beautiful, her clear grey eyes and sensitive mouth were impressive. Her dress was eccentric: she ignored all shades except black or grey. Her clothing lacked ornamentation, but she always experienced difficulty in procuring cashmere fine enough for her skirts, cloth perfect enough for her short spencers, or lawn exquisite enough for her collars and cuffs.

Fanny's meeting with Harriet Saint Leger was one of the

momentous incidents of her girlhood. For more than fifty years these two remained the most devoted friends. Harriet's philosophical, speculative intellect presented many thoughtful questions to her young associate. They served as a kind of balance to Fanny's inherently emotional and romantic trend of mind. Fanny felt a perfect confidence in Harriet's judgment and integrity. Not that the two always agreed, but each was willing to give her friend's ideas a hearing. Their friendship counted for much in the lives of both.[6]

The autumn of 1827 found the Kemble family living on St. James Street, Buckingham Gate, Westminster. In October, Mr. Kemble returned from Paris, where he had won acclaim while presenting "Shakespeare the Barbarian" to the classically minded French audiences. Fanny's projected historical novel had given place to a dramatic version of the Valois story entitled *Francis I*. Against the background of French struggles to maintain supremacy in Italian tributaries and to escape the grasping hand of Charles of Spain, the drama told the story of the unscrupulous and petty selfishnesses of Francis and his mother, Louisa of Savoy, which resulted in the downfall of both. Undisciplined passions made them ready tools in the hands of a supposed monk, Gonzales, in reality a Spanish nobleman, Garcia, an agent of Charles, who came to France to revenge the betrayal of his sister by a French nobleman, Laval.

As one might expect, the play followed the pattern of the Shakespearean drama. Influences of the early histories were especially potent in its structure and material. In spirit and plan it belonged with Elizabethan drama. It moulded together and connected by agents incidents which seemed unrelated. An almost imperceptible moral link also united remote but tragic events with the immediate, domestic interest. In reality the historical setting was subordinated to the fatal love story of Laval, Francis, and Françoise. The motive force, revenge, exhausted itself at the end of the fourth act, and the scenes of act five existed primarily for the proper administra-

tion of poetic justice. Many characters, all important in the
events of the story, crowded the drama. Their vigorous delineation was the most striking quality of the tragedy. Each person
stood out, strongly and vividly, motivated by an outstanding
trait.

Francis I seems an unusual play for a girl of seventeen to
have written. Naturally the reader never loses sight of the
fact that the author is young and immature. A kind of naïveté
is one of its principal charms. But it forecast dramatic success
for its author. It marked her as a person with possibilities.
She recognized tragic material and dramatic situations; she
realized that vivid characterization was essential to drama;
she understood that every event must have a plausible motiva-
tion. Several scenes displayed more than usual dramatic power
in their execution. The production revealed, too, how thoroughly even at this age the future actress had imbibed Shakespearean
traditions. She drew upon Shakespeare's dramas for situations.
His idiom colored almost every line of her dramatic expression.

Fanny felt pride and satisfaction in the finished product.
Considering the age and sex of the author, she thought it a
tolerably fair play. Her father wanted it acted; her mother
preferred to have it published first. While they discussed,
praised, and criticized it, the girl wished that she might see her
father in the costume of Francis and hear the alarums of
the fifth act. In the meantime her thoughts turned to the idea
of a comedy. It was to be Italian and mediæval so that one
character might be "one of those bewitching creatures, a
jester."[7]

When five years later, in 1832, John Murray published
Francis I in London, it was an immediate success. One edition
followed another until it reached the tenth. In 1833 Peabody
and Company of New York brought out a sixth American
edition. With the publication of this tragedy, its author took
rank not only as one of the greatest living actresses but as
one of the foremost dramatists of that day.[8]

Several times weekly throughout the season of 1827 the

young playwright attended Covent Garden, where Edmund Kean, Charles Young, and Charles Kemble made one of Shakespeare's plays something worth seeing. When she saw Mr. Kean as Shylock, she returned home "a violent *Keanite*." Mr. Kemble frequently lamented the sad want of a capable actress at either London theater. Fanny felt half inclined to give Covent Garden one, but the thought remained unexpressed to her father.

John occasionally came from Cambridge accompanied by one or another of his student friends—Arthur Hallam, the Tennysons, the Malkins, the Romillys, Frederick Maurice, John Sterling, Richard Trench, William Donne, Edward Fitzgerald, James Spedding, William Thackeray, and Richard Monckton Milnes, who were to become important figures in nineteenth-century history. John brought, too, his fervor concerning political questions. The homefolks heard continuous discussions and explanations. He was neither whig nor tory, he said, but a radical, a utilitarian, an adorer of Bentham, a worshipper of Mill, and an advocate of the vote by ballot. He opposed hereditary aristocracy, the church establishment, and the army and navy. As Fanny listened, she wondered who would care for peoples' bodies and souls in his reformed society, but a sister's questions failed to shake his conceptions of an Arcadia. He labored for hours daily writing arguments against these condemned institutions.[9]

In the midst of this excitement, Fanny felt restless. Her mind and temperament were "in a chaotic state of fermentation." She was vehement, excitable, and violently impulsive. Her wild imagination was ill-regulated. From a state of feverish agitation on one day, she lapsed to low-spirited despondency on the next. The reading of Mrs. Jameson's *Diary of an Ennuyée* added to her desire for isolation and independence. She considered chimerical projects of settling in the south of Europe, perhaps in Italy, "and there leading a solitary life of literary labor."

She believed that she possessed talent. The hope of developing it was her "meat, drink, and sleep," but that thought dragged another consideration after it. Could she live by her wits, by the product of her brain? Her father's property was almost gone. She must depend upon her own resources for a livelihood. She dismissed the thought of marriage, for her temperament militated against her becoming an obedient wife or an affectionate mother. Her imagination was paramount. She would be unhappy as the mistress of a household and the cause of unhappiness to others. She might fall in love some time, but, if so, she determined "to fall out of it again" hastily. She would never so far lose sight of her best interests and happiness as to enter into a relation for which she felt unfit. She must depend on her own resources, she decided, although she knew that the remuneration of a young author was likely to be pretty meager.[10]

In a fit of despondency she threw into the fire between seven and eight hundred pages of her verses, but the paper no sooner crumbled into ashes than she regretted her rashness. Although they were ridiculous verses, they represented time and pains. Why had she foolishly destroyed something which she treasured? She must curb that impulsiveness, she knew. One dare not spend one's life destroying treasured possessions in fits of despondency.[11]

One evening she overheard her father say, "There is a fine fortune to be made by any young woman of even decent talent on the stage now." A fine fortune seemed a fine thing. As for the decent talent, Fanny knew that she had "a passion for all beautiful poetry." From her babyhood she had heard discussions of stage technique. A career behind the footlights need be no barrier to the continuance of her creative work. It might be of assistance. The theatrical lust which tore Roger Kemble from his hair-dressing and Charles Kemble from the post-office stirred in her blood. She spoke to her father and mother about the matter, and with some reluctance they replied that she might succeed. Charles Kemble hesitated to encourage her aspirations, for he also inherited his father's

and grandfather's prejudice against their children's respond-
ing to the call of the stage.[12]

In February, 1828, Fanny fell ill with the measles. Remembering the severity of the smallpox, she made her will and
sent it to Harriet Saint Leger for safe keeping.[13] Sickness and
graveyard reflections were scarcely calculated to improve her
emotional state. Fortunately just at this time her cousin, Mrs.
Henry Siddons, came from Edinburgh to visit the family. In
her own young womanhood, the gentle, self-controlled Mrs.
Siddons had curbed an impetuous temper and passionate
emotions of her own, and therefore she understood Fanny's
nervous, irritable, stormy character. She saw, too, that the
young girl possessed the same traits which Fanny Kemble's
mother had never disciplined in herself, and that the mother's
temperamental emotions excited and irritated her daughter.
When Mrs. Siddons's visit came to an end, she obtained permission for Fanny to accompany her to Edinburgh.

The stay prolonged itself for a year, the happiest year of
Fanny's life, she said. The calm, equable and all but imperceptible control of Mrs. Siddons succeeded the anxious, de-
spondent, irritating tenor of the girl's London life. The fascination which the older woman exercised over her deepened into
profound respect and confidence. Fanny was at the worshipping
age; Mrs. Siddons became her idol.[14]

Edinburgh was then the small but important capital of
Scotland, and still preserved its regular winter season of
fashionable gaiety when the nobility and gentry came from
their country residences to their town houses. It was also a
brilliant and intellectual center of a society strongly marked
with a national character. Scott, Wilson, Hogg, Jeffrey,
Brougham, Sydney Smith, and lesser giants "held mental
dominion over the English-speaking world," under the standard of the *Edinburgh Review*. Mrs. Siddons's position in the
city, Fanny noted, was peculiar, "her widowed condition
and personal attractions combining to win the sympathy and
admiration of its best society, while her high character and

blameless conduct secured the respect and esteem of her theatrical subjects and the general public.''[15] Fanny participated in many of the privileges extended to her cousin.

The glamor of historic and romantic interest quickly seized upon the girl's imagination. The picturesque beauty of Edinburgh contrasted favorably with the dinginess and ugliness of London. She renewed her devotion to Scott and added an allegiance to the ballads. She read every available collection from the *Border Minstrelsy* to Smith's six volumes of *National Scottish Songs*. Nowhere, she thought, could one find "a truer expression of passion, anguish, tenderness and supernatural terror." "The older ballads . . . the clarion-hearted Jacobite songs, . . . and the bewitchingly humorous songs of Burns, with their enchanting melodies," were her study and delight.[16]

Although Fanny could point to no event which made a distinctively serious or religious impression on her thoughts, her mind became more interested than ever before in religious considerations. Mrs. Siddons never made religion a subject for inculcation or discussion, but her family regularly fulfilled the observances of the Church of England, and the spirit of unselfishness and affection governed her life. Perhaps the influence of the religious teachings of Fanny's Parisian school days returned to the surface of her mind. Perhaps, as a young clergyman once told her, she had a natural turn for religion.

As an immediate result of these graver thoughts, she determined to lay Byron on the shelf. The effort was a painful sacrifice. *Cain* and *Manfred* especially stirred her with "a tempest of excitement," which left her "in a state of mental perturbation." The poems of Byron, she said, touched in her the spirit of the time which was common to both, for "the spirit of an age creates the spirit that utters it, and though Byron's genius stamped its impress . . . upon the thought and feeling of his contemporaries, he was himself, after all, but a sort of quintessence of them, . . ." Thus the mere fact that temperamentally she was *un enfant du siècle* rendered her "liable to the infection of the potent, proud, desponding bitter-

ness of his writings."[17] Two years later, when she again turned
to his poems, all their noble beauty remained, but she no
longer felt their power of wild excitement.[18]

All too soon the happy year in Edinburgh came to an end.
Fanny returned to the home on St. James Street in the spring
of 1829. She found her parents overwhelmed with care and
anxiety. After having himself entered at the Inner Temple,
John renounced his preference for the bar. His passion to
uplift his fellow creatures according to the theories of Bentham
and Mill gave place to a decision to prepare for the Church.
He left Cambridge without taking his degree after the committee had deferred a favorable report upon his examination
until he could satisfy its members that he had studied Locke
and Paley. He had confined his answers to arguments against
their doctrines. When a Kemble rejected the stage, he found
it difficult to settle upon a career. Mr. Kemble was bitterly
disappointed, for he had anticipated his older son's becoming
Lord Chancellor. That John was later to renounce his clerical
aspirations and become one of the first Anglo-Saxon scholars
in Europe would have seemed hardly an equivalent honor
even had the father foreseen this distinction.[19]

The tangled affairs of Covent Garden were still burdensome
and depressing, a Damoclean dagger which threatened every
moment.[20] In 1803 John Phillip Kemble had purchased one-
sixth interest in Covent Garden for £23,000. On September
30, 1808, the theater burned, entailing an estimated loss of
£150,000, of which insurance covered only £50,000. Eight
months later a more splendid Covent Garden rose from the
ashes of the old. An enormous debt encumbered the new
theater, a debt which its owners never liquidated. After John
Phillip's retirement from the stage, he gave his share in this
building to his brother, Charles. The gift received as a bene-
diction proved to be a curse. Charles became manager in 1822,
but he was neither fortunate nor judicious. The rental of
£12,500 per annum was in itself a staggering amount to be
paid from the earnings. By the autumn of 1829 affairs were

at their worst. Distraint warrants for rates and taxes to the amount of several thousand pounds placed the theater in the possession of the bailiffs.²¹ Inevitable ruin seemed to stare the hapless lessee in the face.

Mr. Kemble was absent on a professional tour in Ireland when his wife returned home one day from a walk, much depressed: "Oh, it has come at last," she said, bursting into tears. "Our property is to be sold. I have seen that fine building all covered with placards and bills of sale; the theater must be closed, and I know not how many hundred poor people will be turned adrift without employment!" A kind of terror seized Fanny. Like the Lady of Shalott she felt that the curse had come upon her, but she spoke affectionate and consoling words to her mother. Then she wrote an urgent entreaty to her father begging that she be allowed to seek employment as a governess, so that he would be relieved at least of the burden of her maintenance.²²

Although Mrs. Kemble consented to the posting of the letter, she sent another by the same mail requesting Mr. Kemble to withhold his answer until his return. On the following day Mrs. Kemble asked her daughter whether she believed that she possessed any real talent for the stage. During almost two years Fanny had given no thought whatever to a stage career. Indeed, the "former fancy about going on the stage, and passionate desire for a lonely, independent life in which it had originated, had died away with the sort of moral and mental effervescence which had subsided during my year's residence in Edinburgh."²³

Every thought connected with the theater gradually became more and more distasteful to her. It seemed the cause of much of the anxiety and humiliation to which her father was sacrificing his life. The emotional energy exacted by the stage left its devotees passionless and artificial in their everyday life, and the false stimulation of the emotions burned up one's nervous energy. That supreme tragedienne, Mrs. Siddons, remained an uninteresting, unemotional husk of a woman, and Fanny valued too much the integrity of her own sensitiveness to accept willingly such a future.[24] Then, too, the presumption of impersonating one of Shakespeare's creations seemed a sacrilege. "Pasteboard and paint, for the thick breathing orange groves of the south; . . . rouge, for the startled life-blood" of Juliet! Actors were mimickers, sham creatures; the stage, "a disgusting travesty."[25]

In response to Mrs. Kemble's request to learn some part, Fanny chose that of Portia, her ideal of perfect womanhood. When she recited it, her mother merely commented, "There is hardly passion enough in this part to test any tragic power. I wish you would study Juliet for me." Study to Fanny meant memorize, just what it meant, she realized, "unfortunately long afterwards." When she had learned the part of Juliet, Mrs. Kemble listened to the recitation without making any comment, and when Mr. Kemble returned, Mrs. Kemble told Fanny that they both wished to hear her recite. So one evening she stood before them and repeated her first lesson in tragedy.

"Very well—very nice, my dear," each commended at the conclusion of her effort. Fanny escaped from their praise, sat down on the stairs, and found relief from her repressed nervous fear in a flood of tears. A few days later Mr. Kemble took her to Covent Garden. He wanted to know whether her voice possessed strength enough to fill that large auditorium.

The stage, with its racks of pasteboard and canvas forests, banqueting-halls, streets, and dungeons, was empty and silent. Not a person stirred in its depths, which seemed to stretch back into infinite space behind her. In front, the great amphitheater, equally empty and silent, was dark except for a long, sharp thread of light, which focused in a vivid spot of brightness on the stage. Set down in this strange place with no sound except her father's voice coming from the darkness, Fanny "was seized with the spirit of the thing; . . . and completely carried away by the inspiration of the wonderful play, I acted Juliet as I do not believe I ever acted it again, for I had no visible Romeo, and no audience to thwart my imagination."[26]

Fanny thought that the auditorium was deserted. But in the back of one of the private boxes sat an old friend of her father's, an amateur actor and a capable critic. At the end of the performance he joined Mr. Kemble. "Bring her out at once," he advised. "It will be a great success."[27]

The theater had claimed another Kemble!

CHAPTER III

A DEBUTANTE OF COVENT GARDEN

CURIOSITY drew the throng toward the ponderous structure, patterned after Minerva's Temple, in the old gardens of Saint Peter's Abbey. The statues of Tragedy and Comedy niched under the Doric portico on Bow Street looked with surprise at the milling crowd which sought entrance into Covent Garden. When the doors opened, pit, galleries, and boxes of the dove-and-gold theater soon overflowed with persons eager to witness another début.

First appearances were nothing unusual to London theatergoers, but this one was exceptional. Miss O'Neill had come to the metropolis after many successes in Dublin; Edmund Kean was the sensation of the provinces for years before a London audience gave him a hearing; Talma came heralded as the premier tragedian of France. Their fame had preceded them, but the talents of this débutante were untried. Nothing vouched for her ability except her family name, a name which every patron of the drama recognized as synonymous with theatrical prowess. While they waited, one problem troubled many anxious minds. This débutante possessed the Kemble name. Had she also inherited the family genius?

Although an incessant chatter resounded from pit to gallery, all did not join in the confusing uproar. Memories of other nights at Covent Garden filled the thoughts of many who had followed that theater through both gloomy and fortunate days. In their imagination, Grimaldi convulsed his audience with an impersonation of Scaramouche; John Phillip Kemble inspired awe and admiration as the proud, unyielding Coriolanus;

or Mrs. Siddons held her auditors spellbound through the tragic grandeur of Lady Macbeth's sleep-walking scene. But Grimaldi had answered his last curtain call. After life's fitful fever John Kemble slept at Lausanne. Only Mrs. Siddons remained. Eyes of the spectators wandered from the footlights to an unobtrusive box.

There sat that septuagenarian matriarch of the English stage now waiting with fear and anxiety for the first appearance of her niece. Recollections of her own first attempt to win the favor of a metropolitan audience and its miserable failure at Drury Lane more than fifty years before increased her apprehension. By her side fidgeted young Henry Kemble, intensely, deliciously happy. When Mr. Kemble cast about in search of a suitable hero for Fanny's début performance, this younger brother barely escaped the rôle of the lovelorn Romeo. Henry was young and handsome, but he had an insuperable dislike for acting. Although he obeyed his father and memorized the part, he utilized his slight inheritance of the family talent to stage a ludicrous burlesque of the balcony scene, which dispelled all idea of his being the lover for his sister's first public appearance.[1]

Near by in another box sat Mr. Talfourd, the dramatic critic, with pencil and paper ready to note every expression, every word, every gesture. In yet another sat Sir Thomas Lawrence, who had painted portraits of the Kembles until he unconsciously made them the models for his every artistic conception. He was to paint this débutante as Juliet. He, too, must observe every expression and every pose. Occasionally his eyes wandered to the white-haired, silent woman in that unobtrusive box. If he had dared he would have hastened to greet her. But that could never be. They had been strangers for years now, strangers since the dying Maria Siddons exacted from her sister the promise never to become Lawrence's wife. Memories and shadows peopled the stage and the boxes of historic Covent Garden.[2]

At seven o'clock the confusion suddenly ceased. The curtain

rose. Noises of the enemy servants' clashing swords penetrated to the dressing room. Mrs. Kemble, returned to the stage for this one night after an absence of twenty years, hovered near the door of her daughter's room. Within, Aunt Dall and a maid garbed Fanny in the traditional white gown of Juliet and placed her in a chair with the long satin train carefully laid over its back. There she sat ready for execution, palms of her hands pressed convulsively together and tears trickling down her rouged cheeks.

At last came a quick rap on the door: "Miss Kemble called for the stage, Ma'am!" On the opposite side from that by which her mother advanced upon the stage, Mrs. Davenport, the Nurse, and Mr. Keely, her servant Peter, tried to reassure Fanny. " 'Never mind 'em, Miss Kemble!' urged Keely in that irresistibly comical, nervous, lachrymose voice of his, . . . 'Never mind 'em! don't think of 'em any more than if they were so many rows of cabbages!' " "Nurse!" called Mrs. Kemble, and Mrs. Davenport waddled into view on the stage. Turning, she called back in her turn, "Juliet!" Aunt Dall gave Fanny a push. She ran across the stage, her eyes blinded by a mist. The green baise floor seemed to rise against her feet. She seized hold of her mother and stood confronting the huge theater full of staring, curious human beings, "like a terrified creature at bay." Applause sincere but more restrained than that which had welcomed her father, the Mercutio of the cast, resounded through the immense theater a second time. Fears of overwhelming a débutante slightly subdued Fanny's reception.[3]

Could that frightened girl clinging to her mother as though life depended on her grip redeem the fortunes of Covent Garden? Where were the Kemble poise, suavity, and air of superiority? But the terrified girl's features were striking. A nobly formed head, dark eyes full of a gifted soul, and an expansive brow shaded by black hair signified an extraordinary intellect. Although in stature she was scarcely above middle height, her finely proportioned form and erect carriage minimized this handicap. Seeing her was almost like looking at Mrs. Siddons through the diminishing end of an opera glass.[4] With that striking resemblance, she could not be entirely lacking in theatrical talent.

After moments which seemed ages to the frightened girl, the applause subsided. A new and untried Juliet uttered her first lines. The trembling voice gradually gained confidence. "I do not think a word I uttered during this scene could have been audible," reflected the actress. "In the next, the ball-room, I began to forget myself; in the following one, the balcony scene, I had done so, and for aught I knew, I was Juliet; the passion I was uttering sending hot waves of blushes all over my neck and shoulders, while the poetry sounded like music to me as I spoke it, with no consciousness of anything before me, utterly transported into the imaginary existence of the play."[5]

Before the end of the first act, spectators felt assured of her success.[6] Each succeeding scene verified this confidence. There was the anxiety and hurry of the innocent girl awaiting the return of the embassy to Romeo; the awakening of sterner energies after Tybalt's death; grief in every word and look when she bandied meanings with her mother; composure while she listened to the Friar's proposals. She seemed too petulant upon entering the Friar's cell and delivered the soliloquy before taking the potion with too much violence. But these were minor blemishes especially for a first attempt. When the last curtain fell on the tragedy of the enemy lovers, the applause was tumultuous and rapturous. The large audience hailed this girl of nineteen as the worthy successor to her incomparable aunt.[7] Excepting Pasta, she more nearly than any other actress of the time approached the boldness and dignity of Mrs. Siddons.[8] She moved with ease and decision. Her conception and interpretation of the Italian girl presented a true Juliet, tender, graceful, dignified, energetic, and occasionally sublime.[9]

Congratulations, tears, embraces, and a general joyous

explosion of relief occupied the friends and the family behind the scenes. With difficulty, Fanny's parents tore her away from this unrestrained, hysterical rejoicing. When at last she returned home and sat down to a long belated supper, she found a little gold Geneva watch by her plate. She immediately christened it Romeo. The meal remained almost untasted while she admired the first watch which she ever possessed. Soon she was fast asleep with this new treasure hidden under the pillow.[10]

This success of October 5, 1829, determined Fanny's future. She was to devote herself to a vocation which she never had liked or honored.[11] During her theatrical career in London, the young actress played Juliet one hundred and twenty times to the delight of the patrons of Covent Garden[12] These early performances revealed all the unevenness, irregularity, and immature inequality which characterized her entire theatrical career. Mrs. Kemble, who attended each appearance and who always remained her daughter's most exacting critic, sometimes commended with an air of satisfaction, "Beautiful, my dear!" Quite as often, if not oftener, the verdict was, "My dear, your performance was not fit to be seen! I don't know how you ever contrived to do the part decently; it must have been by some knack or trick which you appear to have entirely lost the secret of; you had better give the whole thing up at once than go on doing it so disgracefully ill." That was awful, the actress confessed, and made her heart sink down into her shoes, regardless of the applause with which the audience greeted the performance.[13]

Fanny soon became accustomed to this new existence. As compensation for her three weekly performances, she received a salary of thirty guineas.[14] This seemed quite a handsome sum, especially when she compared it with Mrs. Siddons's miserly reward of five pounds during her first successful weeks at Drury Lane.[15] At noon on the days preceding evening appearances, the actress dined on a mutton chop—she "might have been a Harrow boy for diet." Then Aunt Dall took her to the theater late in the afternoon, and there in her dressing room Fanny worked with some piece of needlework or tapestry until her tragic sorrows began. When the call for the stage sounded, Aunt Dall carried the long white train to the entrance, spread it out and adjusted the folds carefully as Fanny went on. Then she waited until her niece's stage tribulations were ended, when she gathered up the aggravating train and escorted its wearer back to her tapestry.

By the end of three weeks the conditions of Fanny's life, so she said, had altered as by the touch of a fairy's wand. Instead of an insignificant schoolgirl she was a little lion of society. Formerly she existed on an allowance of twenty pounds per year squeezed from her father's hard-earned salary. Now as long as her health and faculties remained unimpaired, she had an assured income of at least a thousand pounds a year. No more trudging long distances afoot through the muddy London streets to save coach hire! She now owned a comfortable carriage. She soon bought a horse (and one for her father, as well), and took riding lessons from Captain Fozzard, who claimed as pupils all the best horsewomen in London. Fashionably made dresses of fresh colors and fine textures replaced faded, threadbare, turned and dyed frocks. Visitors besieged her door; social civilities and courtesies poured in from every side. If her parents had thought it prudent, she might have passed every free evening in the gaiety of the London season. Dancing was her passion, and it required all of Mrs. Kemble's watchfulness to prevent an over-indulgence.[16]

Lest the public tire of the uninterrupted performances of *Romeo and Juliet*, the manager decided to offer a different drama on December 9. Belvidera in Otway's *Venice Preserved*, "a bundle of two or three emotions dressed in black satin and nicknamed a woman,"[17] was this second rôle. Fanny heartily disliked the portrayal. She was "no longer sustained by the genius of Shakespeare, no longer stimulated by the sublime passion and exquisite poetry." The miserable situations were

Sketches of MISS FANNY KEMBLE *in the character of* Belvidera, *in* Venice Preserved. *Robert Fridenberg, Inc.*

revolting and disgusting. Nothing inspired sympathy for the creature whom she impersonated.

Here, too, she encountered a difficulty which remained a constant handicap during her theatrical life in England, a comparison with Mrs. Siddons. Her aunt's effects in the various rôles were the only acceptable or possible ones to a London audience. Fanny could not imitate the great tragedienne even if she had desired to attempt it. Nature had settled that in making her of small stature. This limitation compelled her to devise gestures and effects different from those to which her audiences were accustomed. Too many frequenters of Covent Garden still recalled the overpowering poses of the Tragic Muse. Comparisons with her must have resulted unfavorably for any actress, and especially for one who had just celebrated her twentieth birthday.

As often happens, critics praise a creation which the artist condemns. Fanny's characterization of Belvidera decided, they thought, the question of her capacity and energy of mind. She possessed more than a mechanical talent and facility which, accompanied by youth, made many other actresses successful in the rôle of Juliet. Belvidera proved that this impersonator was gifted with strong feeling, fine imagination, and a cultured intellect. Were she not something more than an actress, her acting could not have been what it was.[18]

Then followed Murphy's *Grecian Daughter*. To the actress's disgust, opinion pronounced Euphrasia her *chef d'oeuvre*. No one could play Juliet ill, observers said, but very few could portray Euphrasia well. In this rôle she excited that most expressive kind of applause, dead silence and low murmurs, the involuntary expressions of inward emotion.[19] Fanny's genius was never of the tearful variety. One admired it or was dazzled by it without being harrowed by the grief which some theater goers rejoiced in.[20] Thomas Moore steadfastly refused to be touched by her acting. He was unmoved enough during the pathetic moments of a performance to look around the house for symptoms of weeping. One lady was using a handkerchief, he said, but only for a cold in the head.[21]

During a performance of the *Grecian Daughter*, an accident, anticipated from the night of Fanny's début, materialized. Mr. Abbot, old enough to have been her father, was not a bad actor put a perfectly uninteresting one in tragedy. Wanting passion and expression, he resorted to vehemence as a substitute. In moments of powerful emotion he became unsteady on his limbs. The actress felt a premonition that disaster would follow one of his headlong lurches about the stage. It came when Phocian, after a painful and eventful separation, rushed to meet his wife. Just as he seized her, his underpinnings gave way. He and the disgusted Euphrasia landed in a confused heap upon the floor. Fanny remained in mortal terror of his embraces. Ever afterwards she steadied herself on her feet and braced her whole figure, determined to stand fast, whenever he made the slightest affectionate motion in her direction.[22]

The part of Mrs. Beverley in Moore's *The Gamester* introduced the actress in a new rôle on February 25, 1830. This character elicited her sympathies, and it became one of her most finished impersonations, exalted in its conception of character and powerful in its delineation.[23] In her portrayal of this part, Fanny realized as never before a curious phenomenon of acting, a "sort of double process which the mind carries on at once, . . . in diametrically opposite directions." The player enters heart and soul into the character without ever forgetting his own identity. A "watchful faculty, perfectly prosaic and commonplace in its nature," never deserts him. "The whole person appears to be merely following the mind in producing the desired effect and illusion upon the spectator." In reality "both the intellect and the senses are constantly engrossed in guarding against the smallest accidents that might militate against" the spectator's illusion. Even in the last scene as Mrs. Beverley, when tears almost blinded her, the actress calculated the space necessary for her father's fall and accordingly moved her train. This double action of the mind, she thought, was the most singular experience of the stage profession.[24]

The actress's development and improvement in the five months following that memorable October evening when she first played the part of Juliet surprised even her most hopeful observers and partisans. In this interval and apparently with little effort she had won a firm place in the admiration of the London theater goers. Even the delectable Garrick first achieved that distinction after years of diligent study and trials. Mrs. Siddons won their acclaim only after one miserable failure followed by seven years of drudgery in the provincial theaters. But in a few months Fanny was the idol of the play-going public. Shop windows featured reprints of Lawrence's sketch of the actress. Gentlemen proudly displayed buff neck-handkerchiefs decorated with minute copies of the drawing.[25] This vogue led to plates and saucers ornamented by miniature figures of her as Juliet and as Belvidera. "We were all of us in love with you and had your portrait by Lawrence in our rooms," Thackeray confided to her twenty years afterwards.[26]

Fanny worked more diligently during those first months than at any other period of her theatrical career. If she had failed on the first night, that would have ended the matter. Her pride might have suffered, but she would not have felt deeply sorry. She then could have pursued some more congenial profession. But after that first success, she dared not fail. Neither Mr. nor Mrs. Kemble let any opportunity pass to make helpful suggestions. When in town, Lawrence never failed to attend her performances. On the next morning she always received a letter containing detailed criticisms of her voice, gestures, and poses. One morning while she was reading his observations on her portrayal of Belvidera, Mr. Kemble entered the room and said in a low voice, "Lawrence is dead." The shock stunned her. Only a few days before, she sat for a pencil sketch—his last completed work. Had he lived, Fanny might have worked more faithfully. No one else called to her attention every fault in the inflection of her voice and every undramatic pose or gesture. Even with this irreparable loss, the girl sometimes wondered whether his death was not a fortunate happening for her. His kindness and warm interest in her success inspired a grateful sense of appreciation. During their few months of friendly relationship she already felt something of that fatal fascination and charm which had blighted the lives of her two cousins. If she had sat for the projected Juliet portrait, she feared that she, too, would have loved this handsome, melancholy man,[27] although he was sixty, and she, twenty.

After the success of *The Gamester* Fanny at last appeared as her "favoritest of all Shakespeare's women," Portia. "Juliet, with the exception of the balcony scene, I act," she explained; "but I feel as if I *were* Portia—and how I wish I were!"[28] This rôle, her first attempt in comedy, demanded a sort of skill different from that required for the tragic heroines.

But her inheritance from the Decamps endowed her with a versatility which no other Kemble possessed. Portia was as intellectually conceived and presented as any other of the actress's characters. If any fault were found, it concerned her interpretation of the trial scene. Contrary to the traditional idea, this impersonator recognized Portia's secret fear that Shylock might read the passage from her law-book. She was the Portia who duped the old Jew out of his lawful pound of Antonio's flesh. Although the London audience found it difficult to sanction any variation from traditional dramatic interpretations, it accepted her Portia as a modest, sincere, and intelligent presentation.[29]

Many weeks passed with no new rôles to learn. Then rehearsals for two new characters, Isabella in Southerne's *The Fatal Marriage* and Mrs. Haller in *The Stranger* interrupted Fanny's readings in an expurgated edition of the old English dramatists. Finally, on May 28, as Lady Townley in *The Provoked Husband*, she bade Covent Garden and her London audiences farewell.[30]

The season had proved a financial success. She had given

one hundred and two performances.[31] The receipts on those
nights averaged from three hundred to three hundred and
fifty pounds.[32] After he deducted all expenses from the proceeds, Mr. Kemble paid thirteen thousand pounds of the debt
on the theater.[33] The débutante's course through this first year
was one of unclouded brightness. She revived the national
attachment to the stage and duplicated for the failing fortunes
of Covent Garden Kean's achievement at Drury Lane.[34]

A summer tour led first to Bath, the town to which Fanny
had gone at the age of six in the hope of being "bettered" by
her aunt, Mrs. Twiss. Since Mr. Abbot remained in London,
she at last had a Romeo whose agility did not threaten disaster.
John Mason, her cousin, made the tour with the company.
Crowded and sometimes overflowing houses greeted the performers. Usually actors practised their art upon the provincial
audiences before London saw them, and all felt a desire to
judge an actress who had walked directly on to a metropolitan
stage without this preliminary novitiate. Some auditors expressed warm admiration for her talents. Others, in true
provincial style, considered her a mere novice who could not
even pronounce her words correctly.[35]

From Bath the troupe journeyed to Edinburgh. Here Fanny
experienced the frigidity of the Scotch audiences which in
former years often provoked Mrs. Siddons to pant out in
despair, "Stupid people, stupid people!" The theaters were
crowded, but the spectators evinced no emotion. To the
actress's surprise, most of the critical strictures concerned her
diminutive stature and irregular features. Jeffrey, like many
of his fellow-townsmen, complained because she was not
prettier. She was sorry for it, she confessed, and heartily wished
she were more beautiful; Mr. Jeffrey was not handsome, either,
and he did nothing about it.[36] A breakfast with Sir Walter
Scott compensated for all the less inspiring experiences. His
acquaintance was one of the pleasant results of her theatrical
vocation.[37] His words of commendation removed the sting from
Jeffrey's strictures: "Went last night to Theatre, and saw Miss

Fanny Kemble's Isabella, which was a most creditable performance. It has much of the genius of Mrs. Siddons, her aunt. She wants her beautiful countenance, her fine form and her matchless dignity of step and manner. On the other hand Miss Fanny Kemble has very expressive, though not regular features, and what is worth it all, great energy mingled with and chastened by correct taste."[38]

The company journeyed from Edinburgh to Glasgow, where the audiences were less apathetic. When a three days' vacation came as a result of King George's death, Fanny visited Loch Lomond and Loch Long. She forgot that theaters existed. Her appreciation of natural beauty suddenly crowded out all other interests. How could people attempt to describe such places, she wondered. "A volume might be written on the mere color of the water, and give no idea of it." When she returned, she carried "an appropriate nosegay . . . a white rose from Dumbarton, in memory of Mary Stuart, an oak branch from Loch Lomond, and a handful of heather, for which I fought with the bees on the rocky shore of Loch Long."[39]

The Glasgow engagement concluded the Kembles' schedule in Scotland. From there the company crossed to Ireland. Dublin audiences were far from cold. After the first play, a bodyguard of several hundred men shouting and hurrahing like mad escorted Fanny's carriage to the hotel. On the second night a similar group surrounded the carriage at the private entrance. As soon as the father appeared: "Three cheers for Misther Char-*les!*" rang out. Aunt Dall followed, and "Three cheers for Misthriss Char-*les!*" Then came Fanny: "Three cheers for Miss Fanny!" "Bedad, she looks well by gaslight!" exclaimed one admirer. "Och, and bedad, she looks well by daylight too!" retorted another.

On the Dublin stage occurred one of those ludicrous incidents which relieved for the actress the tedium of her despised vocation. The play was *The Provoked Husband*, performed miserably enough to provoke any one. During the performance

FANNY KEMBLE AS ISABELLA

Robert Fridenberg, Inc.

of the play, when Lord Townley complained of his wife's late hours, she insolently retorted: "I won't come home till four, tomorrow morning." "Then, madam, you shall never come home again," thundered the irate husband as he made an impressive exit. The actress stood motionless for a moment as though aghast at the threat. During this breathless pause, one of her gallery auditors, thinking she lacked proper spirit in not making some rejoinder, blurted forth, "Now thin, Fanny!" Needless to say, the gravity of the situation dissolved into irrepressible mirth.[40]

During August and September, threatrical activities divided attention with other matters. While in Liverpool, the actress received a letter from her brother John, mailed from Algeciras, Spain. He supposedly was spending the summer in study preparatory to taking orders in the Church. In reality, he, with several college companions, Sterling, Barton, and Trench, decided to lend their aid to the cause of Spanish liberty then represented by the rising of General Torrijos. Fanny understood the gravity and danger of her brother's position. To increase her distress, he forbade her writing to him or speaking of his plans to any one. Months passed before another message relieved her anxiety.[41]

At Birmingham and Manchester visits to numerous factories especially interested her. Power-looms and spinning jennies were astonishing machines, but the process of casting iron pleased her most. It seemed incredible that solid masses of iron-work were cast in molds of restless, shifting sand. Finally as a climax to her sight-seeing came a ride on the line of railroad then under construction between Liverpool and Manchester. The "curious little she-dragon" of an engine consisting of a boiler, a stove, a small platform, a bench, and a barrel, drew its passengers along the rails at the "astonishing speed of thirty-five miles an hour." No one could imagine the sensation of cutting the air at that rate, Fanny told her friends. It was delightful, and, though strange beyond description, it aroused no feeling of fear. Several weeks later she enjoyed another ride as one of the passengers at the official opening of the road. Finally, October found her back in London, preparing for another year at Covent Garden.[42]

On October 4, the season opened with a performance of *Romeo and Juliet*—the beginning of a none too successful year. Several causes combined to hurry on the impending disaster of the old theater. Among other forces, injudicious management and the changing taste of the public were prominent. Those in authority depended almost entirely upon the unaided attraction of their star, Miss Kemble, and on the dramas which had brought success during the preceding year.[43] Of the new plays attempted, several were ill-chosen. *The Jew of Aragon*, written by an ambitious young actor, Mr. Wade, was hissed from the stage.[44] *The Fair Penitent*, a feeble adaptation of Massinger's *The Fatal Dowry*, was also a failure, an illustration of what generally happened in the attempt to fit old dramas to modern theatrical requirements. The removal of objectionable matter left an undramatic lump of lead.[45]

Leigh Hunt, never under the spell of Fanny's acting, thought the interest in the novelty of a girl actress was waning and that she no longer held the attention of theater goers. After witnessing the opening performance of Juliet, he classed her as an entirely artificial performer. Although she might be apt in catching all that could be learned about acting, she was not essentially superior to many others who held but a brief day of repute.[46] Portia received his more favorable comment. She exhibited no more genius in the performance, but she smiled like an ordinary woman.[47]

Critics ascribed the declining interest in the stage to the culmination of a trend in progress throughout the early nineteenth century. Public taste, as well as public habits, was changing. The hour of dining, the establishment of clubs, the desertion of the theater by fashionable persons, now more eager to dance the new dances—all helped to bring about the decay.[48] An utter indifference to theatrical amusements similar to that which marked the closing years of the seven-

teenth century seized the public. Dr. Wilson graphically sum-
marized the situation in his *Noctes Ambrosianæ:* "I meet young
gentlemen now who formerly used to think it almost a crime
not to go to the theater," he said, "but now they ask, 'Where-
abouts is Covent Garden Theater?' although the same people
would faint away if it were thought they had not been to the
Italian Opera."

Several new rôles added during the year brought flattering
recognition to the actress. Bianca in *Fazio* by Milman became
a favorite character. To this, Fanny added Beatrice with much
pleasure but Lady Macbeth and Constance with fear and
misgiving: "And so I am to act Lady Macbeth! I feel as if
I were standing up by the great pyramid of Egypt to see how
tall I am!"[49] Even Leigh Hunt pronounced her Beatrice clever.
With a few less peacock-like movements of the head and gait,
and a little more abandonment to Beatrice's animal spirits,
he said, the character would merit comparison with her
father's Benedick.[50]

The repetition of well known impersonations allowed Fanny
time for other interests. Dancing was still for her an incomparable pleasure. Many nights found her in the ballroom until
the early morning hours. Formal affairs where one looked
dignified, spoke incoherently to several people, and received
introductions to several others were boring. She could not
afford to waste her time on those. A quiet evening with Shakespeare, Milton, or Shelley was preferable. Often, too, she
attended the opera where Pasta starred in *Medea.*

When the theatrical season finally closed in June, Fanny
was heartily tired of London. Even the prospect of another
provincial tour offered some relief, for any place became tiresome to her when she stayed too long. She hoped for another
journey to Ireland and a visit to Ardgillan with Harriet Saint
Leger. Instead, engagements took her to Bristol, Bath, Exeter,
Plymouth, Southampton, Manchester, and Birmingham.[51]

Early in July, Charles Kemble's thoughts began turning
towards America. He knew that nothing short of a miracle

could prolong his hold on Covent Garden. Empty houses on the remaining nights neutralized the advantages gained from Fanny's performances.[52] His depleted fortune recalled to his mind the successes of other English actors beyond the Atlantic. Already in the eighteenth century, Bernard had imparted the news of his discovery that Americans frequented theaters and compensated actors liberally, and others followed in his wake. In 1798 Thomas Cooper arrived in New York, and, although Stephen Kemble had detected no talent in this young aspirant, he immediately attained recognition.[53] In 1810 George Frederick Cooke's brilliant successes marked an epoch in American stage history.[54] Edmund Kean, initiated by John Kemble into the mysteries of tragedy as one of the infant imps about the witches' cauldron in *Macbeth*, appeared in the principal American cities in 1820.[55] Six years later William Macready followed Kean to America.[56] Each received a genial welcome from his audiences, and, what interested Mr. Kemble more, in each instance this cordiality heralded thousands of dollars. From similar returns he expected to replenish his fortune swept away by the losses at Covent Garden. He could offer an additional attraction to his audiences. None of his predecessors possessed a daughter who had won the acclaim of London and provincial assemblages.

Spurred on to her supreme efforts in order to escape going to America, "that dreadful place," Fanny acted with renewed vim when the season again opened at Covent Garden. The house, the carriage, and the horses might go, and yet she could be comfortable and very happy if she need not leave England. But go to America! That would be terrible![57] The old theater made a last struggle to cope with its more fortunate rival, Drury Lane, which catered to the corrupt taste of the London audience and presented mutilated operas, promenade concerts, tight-rope dancers, and finally, Van Amburg, the lion tamer.[58]

Although supported by her father and the veteran Charles Young, Fanny lamented bitterly the short-sighted management which required her to appear in impersonations demanding physical as well as mental maturity for their portrayal.[59] Dressed in imitation of Harlow's famous portrait, her girlish figure scarcely able to sustain the weight of the velvet and ermine, she appeared as that "quintessence of religious, conscientious bigotry and royal Spanish pride," Queen Katherine.[60] Critics cried shame upon a public taste which allowed *Henry the Eighth* to be performed to empty seats. Truly the public was a wayward and ungrateful child.[61]

Then followed the long and severe illness of Mr. Kemble, and further staging of tragedies awaited his recovery.[62] Weeks passed before he could return to his work. Those who had hoped against hope for the salvaging of Covent Garden gave up in despair. The final performance remained but a matter of time.

For months scenes of a play based on the Lope de Vega theme of the *Star of Seville* had tortured Fanny's thoughts. This period of partial inactivity seemed the proper time to unburden her mind of its persistence. Night after night, whenever the mood possessed her, she sketched out scenes. At last on January 14, 1832, she completed her drama.[63] Was it as good as a second piece ought to be, she wondered. At times it seemed dead as ditch-water; at others, animated in parts. The completion of even a poor drama meant something, and she felt a sense of pride in hers. Although the story came from a Spanish source, nothing except the setting, the names of the characters, and the title of the play—*Star of Seville*—bore witness to its origin. In her hands its spirit and characters became English. It savored of the early English dramatists, Massinger and Ford. Other scenes disclosed the devotee of the early Shakespeare. Although the Spanish dramatist separated his lovers, her Don Carlos and Estrella died together. Like her earlier play, *Francis I*, its idiom was thoroughly Shakespearean.

Perhaps the play was as effective as a second work should be, but a practically unrelated sub-plot destroyed its unity.

4

Although it presented excellent opportunities for startling theatrical effects, it was not dramatic. Things happened too suddenly; characters were not convincing. They seemed puppets rather than people. Friends and critics objected to certain low comedy set in a tavern and to a bedchamber scene as unladylike. Strangely enough the tavern scenes were the most convincing presentations in the play. A dramatic writer depicted coarse and common men and women as well as courtly and refined ones, she replied to her critics. Each character must speak the language of his nature and circumstances. The conventional regards of age and sex had nothing to do with works of art. The dramatist pictured life as he saw it. Fanny really cared little what anyone thought of her writings. She wrote for her own pleasure and because something within drove her to write.

The interruption in the dramatic performances had somewhat whetted the public appetite, and enthusiastic audiences again greeted Fanny's return. Before her final leave-taking, two triumphs fell to her lot. On March 15, her own tragedy, *Francis I*, was performed. The author opposed the production and declared she gladly would forfeit a hundred pounds rather than act in it. She objected to its mutilation, although the length and the numerous cast were not suited to the stage. On the theory that a work of art might be shortened just as though it were a log of wood, the director chopped off the fifth act entirely. When he had completed the shortening process, even the author scarcely recognized her work. It filled the house for several weeks—the actress said curiosity alone accounted for that—and then gave place to Sheridan Knowles's *The Hunchback*.[64]

The rôle of Julia in this drama, written especially for Fanny, suited her style of acting. It abounded in effective stage situations, and the production received unstinted praise. Rumor whispered that Julia was to be one of the actress's last creations. She intended soon to marry and leave the stage, it said. If she continued to act as in that play, such a happening must never be, critics replied. Certainly someone with the interest of the drama at heart would forbid the banns.[65]

Fanny appeared at Covent Garden in 1829 the favorite of the public; she left it three years later, amidst the shouts of Bravo! as Julia. On the night of June 22, 1832, she bade a last farewell to the old stage which John Kemble built, where he and his famous sister took leave of their vocation, and where she had made her first entrance into that make-believe world. Handfuls of kisses were a farewell token of affection to the cheering audience; copious, bitter tears saddened the goodbyes to the pretty little maid who had attended her for three years and to old Rye, the property man. A month passed quickly in a final tour of Edinburgh, Manchester, and Liverpool, where the performances were marked by all the absurdities usually encountered on a summer tour. Then the last extremity of misfortune overtook her—banishment to "that dreadful America."[66]

CHAPTER IV

FIRST YEARS IN AMERICA

AMERICA! The word spelled exile to the English girl who on August 1, 1832, sailed from Liverpool for New York. Home and all the world remained in Britain. The single encouraging reflection, the thought that two years must end some day, afforded scant consolation. A foreboding that she should never return home deepened her melancholy. When the shore line slowly receded from view, she turned from the deck of the *Pacific* an expatriate.

The modern tourist can scarcely understand the inconveniences encountered by travellers of that time. Before the third decade of the nineteenth century, few men and fewer women undertook the passage for pleasure or curiosity. Business affairs alone prompted such a venture. Steam had not yet narrowed appreciably the barrier between world and world. The most favorable voyage a passenger need anticipate required a month.[1] The hardships of the Atlantic deterred many; reports of the few who braved this hazard and observed conditions in the United States discouraged their even more adventurous fellow-countrymen.

Prior to 1820 the majority of English visitors to America concerned themselves with practical investigations. Henry Wansey canvassed the prospects for woolen manufacturers.[2] In 1806 John Melish planned to open a market for cotton goods through Savannah.[3] John Bernard, the English actor, discovered that a continent called America existed beyond the sea where some of the people were white, spoke English, and went to see plays.[4] Such men represented the middle class.

They found in the crudity and hardships of American life nothing to surprise or repel them. Utilitarian inquiry prompted their observations. Although the more learned sensed a lack of cultural advantages, the political situation compensated for this deficiency.[5] Most of these travellers tended toward political radicalism. Many shared the sentiments of Melish, who characterized the United States as a republic—the only republic on the face of the earth that deserved the name—where all people lived under the equal protection of laws made by themselves. Even though political theory remained at least two centuries in advance of its practice, America was a freer and more prosperous country than Britain.[6]

But the tone of British estimates changed just before the third decade of the century. Instead of men who came to trade or to farm, representatives of the upper and professional classes began to make the voyage. They came as seekers after new and strange sights. These people brought with them a supercilious preconception in regard to American crudities. and their reports verified their previously formed opinions, These accounts, together with the activities of the Tory reviewers, exerted a pronounced influence on popular opinion. In 1817 Wilson and Lockhart of *Blackwood's* joined Gifford of the *Quarterly* in denunciations of America. Naturally these reactionaries could not neglect the country which furnished the world's great object lesson in democracy and liberalism. As early as 1814 the *Quarterly* indulged in an angry insult to America.[7] *Blackwood's* began the year of 1819 with articles which rejected American claims to any real education. It asserted that all books produced there might be burned without loss. Nothing existed to awaken the fancy in that land of dull realities.[8] In 1820 the *Edinburgh Review* made room for Sydney Smith's famous condemnation.[9] This censure, taken up and exploited by the lesser periodicals, insensibly affected the judgment of travellers, even those who thought themselves fair and liberal.

The conditions which later gave birth to the Reform Bill

of 1832 spurred on conservatives and reactionaries to the defense of old English institutions. They chose an attack on American democracy as one method of protection. Although some of their party admitted that democracy constituted the best form of government for the America of that time, all bitterly opposed any imitation of it in Great Britain. Captain Marryat branded republicanism as mob rule. He insisted that Americans selected second-rate men as their officials—agents of the majority who were as often wrong as right.[10] Thomas Hamilton and Godfrey T. Vigne commended the material progress of the United States, and approved of the system of government. It seemed well adapted to conditions west of the Atlantic.[11] But any change in English government would overthrow time honored systems. Reform measures were a live issue. To the reactionaries, anarchy seemed near at hand. They saw in the political and social life of this new country a consummation of the demands now arrayed against their principles. When a Chartist leader enumerated the rights of the working man, he referred to a state similar to that said to exist under American republicanism. Conservatives hastened to refute the claims of these more favorable observers.

In defense of these English animadversions it must be recalled that travellers of the late twenties came to a country in which manners had changed for the worse since the time of Wansey and Bernard. Jacksonian democracy dominated politics. The frontier permitted a relaxed tone in habits and speech. Observers before 1820 confined their peregrinations among the gentility of the seaboard where social refinement was most widely diffused, but by 1825 the newcomers penetrated as far west as St. Louis. Beyond the older communities they saw a society afflicted by many unmannerly traits: tobacco-chewing steamboat passengers, quick-feeding hotel guests, and illiterate, drawling, impertinent loafers.

Americans soon writhed under the descriptive vividness with which English pens traced these characters. The censorious harridan, Mrs. Trollope, defined the chief distinction between

England and the United States as the latter country's total want of refinement. In Cincinnati, she conversed with a strait-laced ignoramus, who knew Byron only for his immorality. This puritanical moralist had never heard of Massinger or Ford. He declared Shakespeare was obscene and thanked God. that Americans were sufficiently enlightened to have found it out. This, she said, was her best literary conversation in America. Rarely had she heard a sentence elegantly turned or correctly pronounced during her stay in the new world.[12] Although her scathing generalizations surpassed most travel records in acridity, her representations embodied the extreme English conception of American life. By 1830 readers began to reject the records of humanitarian inquiry and in their stead accepted such documents of Tory condescension.[13]

The prospect of a two years' sojourn amid such surroundings was not inviting to any devotee of Dante and Shakespeare. To the English actress the journey meant the severance of all intellectual ties. Her interests in music, painting, sculpture, and literature must be forgotten, for these arts did not exist beyond the Atlantic. She left friends and country. Messages could reach her only after a month's delay. She was to work very hard at a distasteful vocation among strangers from whom she could not expect the invariable kindness and indulgence of her own people. Only one friend, the ever faithful Aunt Dall, would share her successes and disappointments, for even in America the white satin train must not gather up the dust along the path from the dressing-room to the stage entrance. Although her companionship lessened a little the bitterness of leaving, to Fanny the voyage meant banishment into an occidental desert.[14]

After she waved a last goodbye to the fading outline of Liverpool, she retreated to her stateroom. Nothing mattered very much now; England lay behind; America, ahead. The tears came again and again whenever the voyager thought of her miserable plight. During the weeks while the little ship tossed on the stormy Atlantic, she tried to forget her unhappiness, but her efforts brought only partial success. Mock trials, games of dumb crambo, and disputes between an ardent Bostonian Clayite and an equally enthusiastic Jacksonite provided an uncongenial amusement. Throughout many days and nights the traveller craved nothing except solitude and rest, for a stormy sea convinced Fanny that even nature itself opposed her leaving her native country. Thirty-five days passed, before the little sailing vessel drew up to the dock in the New York harbor. All hurried ashore, and for the first time the actress "soiled her pretty English shoes with Yankee dirt."[15]

Then came the American Hotel. The stateroom on shipboard had been stuffy and uncomfortable, but accommodations at the hotel were even more nearly unbearable. The rooms displayed a mixture of French finery, Irish disorder, and dirt. Sitting-rooms suddenly became sleeping quarters if more than the customary number of guests arrived. Servants slept anywhere they fancied in the public rooms rented to families. Fanny soon decided that no such thing as privacy existed in America. Visitor or servant opened a door and entered nonchalantly as though every room were his own.

In the early autumn, to make matters worse, guests spent most of the hours between darkness and daylight in battle with "multitudinous beasts of prey." Every evening at sunset, clouds of mosquitoes began their war dance. In addition to these "winged devils," lodgers found swarms of flies, an army of fleas, a closet of bugs, and two or three ants' nests in each bedroom. Horrible! the plagues of Egypt were a joke to them.[16]

Those first days in New York severely tried Fanny's self-control. Rehearsals added one more nuisance. When the actress arrived at Park Theater and glimpsed her leading man, she believed her eyes must be deceiving her. But they were all too accurate. Mr. Keppel, a "washed out actor" who once on the London stage had failed as her Romeo, had heard of the inducements offered by the American theater. Here he was, ready to vex Fanny's patience again. While devotees of the New York stage anxiously waited to judge her ability,[17] she rehearsed *Fazio* and tried to decide in what position she might expect to find Mr. Keppel each time he participated in the action of the drama.

The manager decided upon September 18 as the date for her début. The intervening days allowed her some opportunity for cursory observations of this strange, new city. Mr. Kemble carried letters of introduction from Mr. Vaughan, the British Minister, to Mr. Philip Hone, a prominent New York politician. An exchange of calls preceded a dinner at his residence on September 15.[18] This marked Fanny's introduction to American society. She of course missed the formality of English social functions. The women came in a sort of French demi-toilette with bare necks and long sleeves. The dinner was plenteous and tolerably well prepared, but poorly served. Servants were scarce; water-glasses and finger-glasses, lacking. After the meal, she tried to sing for the company, but the piano was pitched too high. Besides, the wall, which the musician was obliged to face, absorbed all her voice.[19]

Her host seemed more enthusiastic about Fanny than she about her introduction to New York society. While listening to her, he almost forgot to eat dinner. Although he was delighted with her wit, her air of indifference and nonchalance seemed not at all calculated to make her a favorite with the beaux, he said. She appeared especially ungracious in receiving the advances of those who desired to pay her attention, but she could be charming when she chose.[20]

With all the actress's repeated protests against the theatrical profession, she could not long resist it. Lester Wallack's performances at the Park Theater during those first weeks in New York soon attracted her. She attended his presentation of *The Rent Day* and cried bitterly throughout the performance, because, she said, in the very first scene the hero asked his wife whether she would go with him to America. That was too much for Fanny to bear quietly.[21]

Then came September 18 and her own début at Park Theater. Never before, critics said, had expectation reached such a pitch. Every available space in the gold-carved, red-curtained auditorium was packed with delighted spectators. They were not disappointed in her interpretation of *Fazio*, and she could have hoped for no higher compliment.[22] The final curtain fell amid the deafening shouts and plaudits of an astonished audience.[23] None present had seen her equal on the American stage. Auditors hailed her as the preëminent female genius of the day.[24]

According to that ridiculously comical, facetious journal, *My Conscience*, Fanny felt amply repaid for the effort of showing an American audience what real acting was.[25] Seriously, she wondered how she had accomplished it, for Mr. Keppel almost swamped her. He studied his rôle in haste and, in consequence, possessed no knowledge of it. He did recall that sometime during the performance he must fall on his knees, and, fearful lest he overlook the proper occasion, he sank down every few minutes. Apparently no other circumstances of the drama disturbed his memory. Rid of her encumbrance after the second act, the actress began to move more freely—she gathered up her strength and set to work comfortably by herself. Her success was greater than she could have anticipated.

Those who followed her performances systematically during the following weeks noted certain features common to all her portrayals. Mind was the distinctive characteristic of her acting; intellectual excellence distinguished each conception. Her faults were those of the Kemble school: a monotonous delivery of elaborate passages, a failure at times to give force to striking lines, and the assumption of a stately manner for an ordinary remark. In her impersonations distinct enunciation and fitting by-play compensated for these failings.[26] Although the Kembles' performances seemed tame to many spectators accustomed to the "stamp-and-stare-and-start-and-scream school of acting," their quieter and more intellectual characterizations won many plaudits. Before two weeks passed they attracted audiences of the most refined and thoughtful persons.[27]

Oliver Wendell Holmes, who at the first opportunity at-

FANNY KEMBLE
Painting by Thomas Sully.

tended a portrayal, described the actress as a very fine affair.[28] After a lapse of thirty years Halleck could not speak without enthusiasm of her first appearances in New York. He especially admired her Bianca, Julia, and Portia.[29] A lifelong friendship followed their meeting at a dinner party. The poet's sister wondered what the actress could find in him to admire and charitably attributed this interest to Fanny's fears of his reputation as a satirist. Halleck confessed—he said in justice to the English girl—that no one else ever accused her of fearing anything.[30]

Contemporary estimates dated the beginning of a new era in American stage history from this first engagement of the Kembles in New York. They attracted to the theater people who for years were strangers to its walls—the serious and the gay, the aged and the young, again sat side by side to pay homage to the masters of dramatic art.[31]

Four performances each week together with daily rehearsals left few leisure hours. When Fanny reflected on her meager opportunities for observing these strange people about her, she often wondered whether her opinions of them were always just. But the inconsistency and narrow-mindedness existing in a free and supposedly enlightened country appalled her. Dr. Wainwright, rector of the most fashionable church in New York, met her and Mr. Kemble at the hotel and greeted them enthusiastically. This was his first opportunity to pay his respects, he explained. His congregation would not tolerate a pastor who called on actors or invited them to his home, and his presence in a theater could not be contemplated. Should he be guilty of any such enormity, deserted pews and "forced resignation of his cure of souls" would follow.[32] Another inconceivable prejudice came to her attention when an intelligent and obliging servant sought a pass for admittance to a performance. He explained that it must be for the gallery, for people of color were not allowed in any other part of the theater.[33] A few days later the English girl heard an account of slave flogging in the South. As she listened, her face flushed, tears came into her eyes, and indignation strained every muscle of her body.[33a] This was a new version of American freedom and equality. These brothers in black won her sympathy immediately; years before she saw slaves she became their advocate.

The conditions of the laboring class offered more agreeable reflections. If in the city the faces of workers bore the impress of toil and care, outward signs of a debasing pursuit of wealth, on rest days these same people were happy and cheerful. Their frequent picnics to Hoboken indicated the prosperity and contentment of these unskilled laborers. Artisans and common workers with their well dressed families flocked there from their confined vocations for pleasure and exercise. What a contrast with the mill people of Manchester or Birmingham! No other spectacle gave a foreigner, especially an Englishman, "a better illustration of that peculiar excellence of the American government" which guaranteed freedom and happiness to the lower classes. These people were well fed, well clothed, and well housed. Their capacities for physical enjoyment seemed fully satisfied.

But another consideration troubled her. What of those who, like herself, possessed a higher degree of mental cultivation and whose estimate of happiness included something more? Where were the art galleries, the works of science, the cultivated and refined society, and the associations with men of genius? "The heart of a philanthropist," she said, "may indeed be satisfied, but the intellectual man feels a dearth that is inexpressibly painful; and in spite of the real and great pleasure which I derived from the sight of so much enjoyment, I could not help desiring that enjoyment of another order were combined with it. Perhaps the two are incompatible; if so, I would not alter the present state of things if I could. The losers here are decidedly in the minority."[34]

No Americanisms provoked from her more bitter censure than insatiable curiosity and lack of politeness. A casual acquaintance sat at his hostess's table, examined the cards of the various callers, and asked a dozen questions about each. Shopkeepers were either condescendingly familiar or insolently indifferent. A washerwoman sat down before her employer. When a shop boy brought articles for inspection, he not only appropriated the nearest chair but kept on his hat. Such impertinences were not tolerated in London. These breaches of good manners doubtless had their origin in a misapprehension which confused ill-breeding with independence. Workers fancied they elevated themselves when they discharged their duties and obligations discourteously.[35]

But even these Americans were not entirely bad. In addition to other commendable qualities, honesty compensated in part for such rudeness. If a maid wore her mistress's slippers, she admitted the appropriation. When the landlady asked a peddling farmer whether the eggs were fresh, he confessed, "No, we eat the fresh ones ourselves." Fanny could not imagine similar frankness from English laborers. In two years she did not notice a single instance of brutality to animals such as one saw hourly in the streets of any English town.[36]

At six o'clock on the morning of October 8, the actress bade goodbye to the bugs and mosquitoes of the American Hotel and departed for Mansion House, Philadelphia. This journey by steamboat, coach, and train awakened in Fanny's heart a deep sympathy for any traveller in America. A fourteen-mile trip in a coach-and-four traversed "the wickedest road, . . . the cruellest, hard-heartedest road, that ever wheel rumbled upon." Visitors always remarked that in America the face of nature was gigantic, "and," said Fanny, "truly we found the wrinkles such for so young a country. The ruts were absolute abysses."[37]

Once in Philadelphia, she preferred that city to New York. An air of stability and occasionally of age reminded her of England. The smaller city was also quieter, cleaner, and more comfortable. Although people of the United States lived and died with a haste and bustle unknown in other countries, this nervous rush seemed more subdued here.[38]

Most agreeable as individuals, the inhabitants made intolerable audiences. Nothing except the traditional Scotch assemblage could compare with their frigidity. Here as in New York, Mr. Kemble made his first appearance unassisted by his daughter. His impersonation of Hamlet at Chestnut Street Theater on October 10 disappointed his hearers. They prophesied that he would not be popular; his manner was correct and elegant but stiff and lifeless, the critics said.[39] This estimate immediately recalled to Fanny a New York auditor's disapproval of *Venice Preserved:* "Lord bless you, it's nothing to Cooper's acting—nothing! Why I've seen the perspiration roll down his face like water when he played Pierre." The school of acting condemned by Hamlet apparently had established a new stronghold in America.

Fanny's first rôle, Bianca, received a cordial welcome, and her success was immediate.[40] By the fifteenth of October lithographic portraits from Sir Thomas Lawrence's drawing of the actress found eager purchasers. Soon after her arrival a fragrant nosegay came to her room. A laconic note signed "A Philadelphia Friend"—the word friend underlined as though it signified Quaker—accompanied it. When two days later another followed, Fanny would have given half the flowers to have known the name of their sender.[41] Few evenings during her stay in Philadelphia failed to bring similar bouquets. She welcomed them enthusiastically, too rapturously for their sender to have remained a stranger.

Four performances and six rehearsals weekly engaged most of the actress's waking hours, but she did enjoy a few leisure afternoons at her favorite recreation, riding. The conventional demands of society, receiving and returning visits, necessitated the sacrifice of other evenings. The Chestnut Street exclusives accepted her. Her reported standing in English society and the pride, reserve, and hauteur with which she received advances of the rank and fashion of Philadelphia aided her theatrical success in that city.[42]

The excitement attending the pre-election weeks greatly interested her. No one could ignore the shouting and window

breaking which attended political rallies. Politics, it seemed
to her, resolved itself into two motives: the aristocratic desire
for elevation and the democratic desire for demolishing and
levelling. Every citizen was a politician, and political events
occurred incessantly. A citizen never for a day forgot his party.
His politics were "as inseparable from him as his clothes" and
as mixed up with the discharge of his ordinary avocations.
In New York the actress noticed an "Anti-Bank Hat Store,"
so that a loyal Democrat need not purchase his beaver from
a Whig. Elections for various offices all the year long turned
the country into a "perpetual contest for votes." During an
election of mayor or alderman, shopkeepers lived "in as fierce
a state of excitement, as if the choice of a perpetual dictator
were the question in point." Discussion became so spirited
during the general election period that a violent Whig blamed
the President with everything, including the cholera scourge.
Had not Clay predicted battle, pestilence, and famine if
Jackson came into power? This prophecy was fully realized.
The nation had a war with the Indians; cholera raged; people
fleeing from the infested cities to the country ate half the
farmers out of house and home. Like many an older head the
English girl confessed that the subject of American politics
was far beyond her limited powers of comprehension.[43]

Two weeks after the dramatic critics prophesied Charles
Kemble's failure on the Philadelphia stage, they eloquently
acknowledged his daughter's success. Before her arrival the
fashion and intelligence of the city, they said, were strangers
to the theater. Managers found it necessary to cater almost
exclusively to the pit and gallery. Tasteless and lifeless productions by worn-out actors, a miserable compound of senseless rant and dumb show, had driven Shakespeare from the
stage. Now the classic drama had regained the favor and
patronage of the intelligent,[44] and well dressed ladies again
crowded the boxes. The actress's connection with the master
spirits of the English stage, her real or fancied resemblance
to Mrs. Siddons, and her own literary reputation all prepared

the public to expect a wonder. Although curiosity brought
many to a first performance, admiration of her acting prompted
their attendance on later occasions.

The Kembles closed their initial engagement on November
4 with *Romeo and Juliet*. An incident of this performance
illustrated the strength of the illusion created by Fanny's
acting. During Juliet's soliloquy before she drank the draught
prepared by the priest, the house became quiet as a grave.
At length she knelt, "Romeo, I come! This do I drink to thee."
At this critical moment a poor fellow in the pit who watched
the whole affair with ill repressed emotion cried out with a
ludicrous accent of despair, "Down it goes!" Even poor Juliet
looked as if this honest display of sympathy lightened her
sorrow and disposed the lips trembling with grief to express
quite a different emotion.[45]

From Philadelphia the Kembles returned for a second
engagement at Park Theater, where receipts from the first
performance of *Taming of the Shrew* netted $5,000.[46] After a
month in New York, a second engagement at Chestnut Street
concluded their schedule for 1832. One report estimated their
earnings since their first appearance on September 17 at
$30,000.[47] Fanny admitted that their success was gratifying.[48]

New Year's Day, 1833, found them in Baltimore for a week's
stay at Holliday Street Theater. This city reminded the
travellers of the outskirts of Manchester or Birmingham. It
looked newer than either of the others which they had visited.
Bright red brick houses in rows of three or five with gravel
pits and patches of meadow between gave it an untidy,
straggling appearance. Daily rehearsals and nightly performances again made detailed observations impossible. All afternoon the actress pinned up ribbons, feathers, and flowers and
sorted out theatrical adornments. All evening she enchanted
audiences, prompted her "fellow-mimes," and wished "it had
pleased Heaven to make me a cabbage in the corner of a
Christian kitchen-garden" in Hertfordshire or any other shire
of England—the precise spot would not have mattered.[49]

On the evening of January 13, the Kembles arrived at Gadsby's Inn, generally regarded as the most popular and comfortable hostelry in Washington. Fanny thought differently. The place was overrun by members of Congress and their wives, who by their airs seemed to imagine themselves members of Parliament, she facetiously remarked. The inhabitants of the place were half savage and half civilized. From the West the voters had sent a "learned baboon" christened Davy Crockett to a seat in the House of Representatives.[50] This learned aborigine thought far better of her than she of him. When he attended one of her performances, he was captivated. Any theater was good enough, he said, if it offered such a pretty play-actor as Miss Kemble. She reminded him of "a handsome piece of changeable silk, first one color and then another, but always the clean thing."[51]

Washington was the city in America which the English girl most desired to visit. Here she expected to meet again Washington Irving, who had often visited the Kemble home in London. She carried letters of introduction to President Jackson, Henry Clay, and Daniel Webster. Then, too, Washington was the capital, and, although she knew there could be no similarity, the word suggested London and Paris. The contrast could scarcely have been more appalling, for it seemed the ugliest place in the world. In 1833 Washington was not a capital city but merely a capital. Pennsylvania Avenue was just being paved. All other thoroughfares lay hub-deep with mire or dust, depending on the weather. A quagmire reeking with miasma occupied the present Smithsonian grounds. Cows pastured along many of the streets and challenged the right of way with Henry Clay or Chief Justice Marshall. Street lights did not exist. If a pedestrian failed to provide his own lantern, he frequently sounded the depths of various mud-holes. Aside from the Capitol and the White House no public buildings of architectural distinction attracted visitors.[52]

Fanny made the customary round of the tourist. She visited the Senate, where Webster was speaking, the House of Rep-

resentatives, and the library. On the following day she went
to the War Office to see the Indian collections. Finally she
journeyed to the White House, "a comfortless, handsome-
looking building, with a withered grass-plot enclosed in wooden
palings in front." Here the "fine old well-battered soldier,"
President Jackson, paused long enough in his battle with the
Nullifiers to receive the actress. The old general could think
of nothing except the South Carolina rebels. He spoke of that
state's waywardness and entered his protest against scribbling
women. The whole of the southern disturbance, he assured
his guest, had its origin in no larger source than the nib of
a lady's pen. Truly, thought Fanny, the lady must have
scribbled to some purpose.[53] Then the President hurried
away and left her to talk to a squat, bald-headed Dutchman
who hoped to be president after Jackson.

Washington Theater reminded her of a doll's playhouse.[54]
The proprietors were poor, the actors poorer, and the equip-
ment inadequate. But eager spectators contested for seats at
each performance, where the Kembles turned the heads of
old and young alike.[55] Amusements at that time were few and
crude, and celebrated artists came seldom. John Marshall and
Justice Story were regular attendants. When Fanny portrayed
Mrs. Haller in *The Stranger* and the audience felt moved to
tears, the Chief Justice shed his in common with the younger
eyes. His associate on the bench expressed in poetry his tribute
to her art. Those were inspiring audiences with Marshall,
Webster, Clay, and Irving in the boxes, inspiring not only in
genius but in capacity to enjoy.[56]

In April the Kembles journeyed to Boston,[57] where Mr.
Kemble appeared first on April 15 at the Tremont Theater,
again in the rôle of Hamlet.[58] Fanny, who made her début
on the following evening as Bianca, thought this audience
received her more kindly than any other in the United States
had done.[59] To followers of the theater, the English girl seemed
the superior of any other actress who had ever appeared on
the Boston stage. In the impersonations of others there had

been too much ranting, too much riving a passion to tatters for the sake of immediate effect. Her portrayals were free from this defect.[60] The most talented company she found outside of London contributed materially to this effect. The actors possessed a devotion to their profession. Their faith in it invested their work with dignity.[61]

Week after week eager listeners crowded into the Tremont. The élite came from Brookline.[62] As long as funds held out, a procession of Harvard students hastened over the road to Boston every evening. Once at the theater they massed in the narrow entrance alley until the doors opened. Then with danger to flesh and raiment, they finally scrambled into the pit where they sat on unbacked benches, too absorbed to know where they were.[63] Among them came a pale, slender youth who seldom allowed anything to interrupt his study. Now, an attraction stronger than books drew him to Boston, and night after night Charles Sumner walked through the snow from the campus to the theater. Although he worshipped his idol from a distance, anyone who met the actress could expect special attention and favors from this scholarly senior. Not until years later and during a less happy period of her life was he to count her among his acquaintances. Perhaps he never entirely escaped from this first fascination. Throughout his life he evinced an unusually keen interest in her affairs. Whenever possible, he was at her service.[64]

Boston enchanted Fanny, for it resembled an English city. Many houses constructed of granite radiated an air of wealth and solidarity. The Commons was like Constitution Hill; Beacon Street, like a bit of Park Lane. The recently opened Tremont Hotel offered more comforts than any other establishment of its kind in the country.[65] Single rooms with locks for every door insured privacy just when she had come to the conclusion that Americans had an aversion for solitude under any circumstances. Every room had its own bowl and pitcher and free soap, innovations truly luxurious. The most modern plumbing procurable in 1830 provided eight "bathing rooms" in the basement of the hotel. These were an incomparable satisfaction to the actress, who hoped that if she ever went to heaven, she would find plenty of bath tubs and soft rain water. Although whale-oil lamps lighted the guest rooms, another novelty, gaslight, illuminated the public rooms. The Tremont prided itself on being the world's largest and grandest hotel.[66] The visitor wished that she might remain its guest during all her sojourn in America.

One window of Fanny's room overlooked the box office of the theater. An unusual procedure attracted her attention during the first days of her engagement there. A group of purchasers, inspired, she thought, by the characteristic New England desire for gain and abetted by a singular resourcefulness, smeared their clothes with sugar, molasses, and other abominations in order to force decently clad competitors from the ticket office.[67] After the box office supply of tickets was exhausted, these scalpers sold theirs at a substantial profit. To prevent this malpractice, the proprietors finally auctioned the boxes and tickets.[68]

In Boston the English girl found also a society which delighted her. The claims to preëminence in the cities of North America, it seemed to her, rested on varying requirements. In New York wealth determined status; in Philadelphia, birth; in Boston, mental cultivation. Democracy might govern the land, but throughout society a contrary tendency showed itself wherever it could find the smallest opportunity. In other cities, persons of distinction called upon her. But when she attended some function in so-called best society, she rarely met individuals noted for their intellectual attainments. American best society, to her, included Halleck, Irving, Bryant, Paulding, Catherine Sedgwick, and persons of lesser fame interested in similar matters. Only Boston among the cities which she visited accorded social recognition for literary achievements. Here she could accept invitations assured of interesting companions.[69]

After five weeks in Boston the Kembles returned to the Park

Theater for the final New York engagement. To the last performance they remained an undiminished attraction.[70] Then came a short stay in Philadelphia before they departed for Canada on a well-earned vacation.

On the morning of June 30, the actress hurried from the American Hotel to board the steamship which was to carry her up the Hudson. In company with her father and Aunt Dall she stopped first for a brief visit at Cold Spring, the home of Gouverneur Kemble. Here she inspected the iron works which cast the first successful cannon in America. Then the group continued to Albany, where Fanny and her father played a three nights' engagement.

Exactly twenty years had passed since the first Kemble appeared on the Albany stage. In 1813 Mrs. Whitelock, Charles Kemble's older sister, reigned as the first star in its theatrical history.[71] It always seemed to Fanny that no matter where she went she could never get away from these relatives of hers. When she walked down the street of Philadelphia, pictures of Mrs. Siddons and John Phillip Kemble confronted her. She made her London début not as Fanny Kemble, but as another Kemble. She stepped upon the American stage acclaimed the reigning star, but another Kemble was there before her. Ancestral figures always overshadowed her. She could never escape from their mannerisms, their fame, and their triumphs.[72]

With the conclusion of the Albany theatrical engagement, the travellers proceeded to Niagara. From the day of her arrival in New York the phenomena of nature fascinated Fanny. English sunsets could not equal in splendor those of America; storms were more awe-inspiring here. Neither could anything in England compare with the Hudson or the Catskills. More mountains, rivers, and frontier towns, and then she saw Niagara. No words could describe it. One might imagine "the sea pouring down from the moon," she said, but even that gave no idea of "this glorious heap of tumbling waters." As she stood on the brink of the abyss for the first time, she felt an almost irresistible impulse to jump into the foaming water. But for the strong arm of Edward Trelawney, who had joined the party in Albany, she "might very well have taken the same direction as the huge green glassy mountain of water. It literally seemed as if everything was going down there, and one must go along with everything."[73] After three days by the falls, the travellers crossed Lake Ontario. In an open boat they ran the rapids of the Saint Lawrence, sang Canadian boat songs, and soon found themselves "safe and sound, only half roasted, in His Majesty's dominions."[74]

When Fanny returned to New York in September, she knew that with the coming season she would bid farewell to the stage. A rumor had already reached London that as soon as she fulfilled contracts already agreed upon she would marry an American gentleman of large fortune[75]—Mr. Pierce Mease Butler, a lawyer-musician, the son of Dr. James and Sarah Butler Mease. His maternal grandfather Pierce Butler, third son of Sir William Butler, came to America in 1766, a major in the British army. Four years later he resigned his command to ally himself through his marriage to Miss Polly Middleton on January 10, 1771,[76] with one of South Carolina's first families. When Major Butler's only son and one daughter contracted marriages of which he did not approve, he left his fortune to a second daughter, Frances. At her death either of his grandsons, Pierce or John Mease, who assumed the Butler name might receive her estate. Pierce complied with the terms of his grandfather's will.[77] Thus an imposing ancestry and an exalted social position were the heritage of this wealthy young lawyer-musician who proposed to share his fortune with the young English actress. Although exclusive Philadelphia society may have gasped in astonishment, few blamed him for winning if he could the charming young descendant of English strollers. One none too enthusiastic editor said there was more noise about Miss Kemble and her marriage than ninety-nine stage actresses could create about sane people: "He who weds her for an angel will discover, we opine, ere a fortnight *that she is nothing more or less than a woman*, and perhaps one of the most troublesome kind in the bargain."[78]

The year's success interested Fanny on account of her father's future rather than because of her own. Contracts took her back to Philadelphia, Baltimore, Washington, Boston, and New York.[79] Hearty receptions awaited her upon each return to these cities. In Philadelphia the young American actor, James Murdock, appeared as a member of the company and achieved a triumph even greater than his friends had anticipated.[80]

As the season again neared its close and those interested in the theater reviewed the successes of the year, each acknowledged the Kembles' theatrical supremacy and their contributions to the American stage. Other renowned English actors had performed before audiences in the larger cities of the United States, but no other actress to win like recognition had appeared. The Kembles' quiet and refined characterizations brought about a change in the prevalent ideas of acting. The only parallel in American stage history attended the successes of George Frederick Cooke in 1812.[81]

Spring did not bring all acclaim, gladness, and dreams to the actress. On the nights of the final engagement in Boston, she rushed from the cheers of the audience to the sick-room where Aunt Dall lay critically ill. Months of suffering, the result of an injury sustained when a carriage overturned, came to an end on April 20.[82] Patient, unselfish Dall's devotion to her favorite niece had ceased.

Although Aunt Dall had always seemed happy, her satisfaction, Fanny realized, was one of sacrifice to others. Years before she ever won her affectionate nickname from the stumbling syllables of little Henry Kemble, Adelaide Decamp's own happiness had ended. Obliged like all her family to earn a livelihood, she turned to the stage and found employment with Mr. Stephen Kemble. During her theatrical apprenticeship, a young officer of a militia regiment, son of a wealthy Yorkshire squire, became her admirer. His father demanded that he forget the young actress. He refused. The angry parent instantly summoned his servants and tenants. In their presence he disinherited and disowned his son, whom he branded as illegitimate. Crushed and humiliated, the young officer immediately enlisted for India. With a bankruptcy of love and hope which would have embittered and hardened many hearts, Aunt Dall came to live in Charles Kemble's home. Apparently without any memory of the past, she gave her whole life in patient, unselfish devotion to her sister's children. She died as she lived in their service, forgetful of her own happiness.[88] Fanny left her on a green slope under the trees in Mount Auburn cemetery. Then, disconsolate, she departed for New York. A sense of irreparable loss, of unbearable loneliness, crept into the actress's life. Aunt Dall had been confidante, counsellor, and comrade. The world seemed empty and futile without her companionship.[84] For the first time Fanny knew the meaning of grief.

On June 6, 1834, the Kembles appeared for the last time at the Chestnut Street Theater, Philadelphia.[85] On the following morning at Christ Church Fanny married Mr. Pierce Butler.[86] Some months previously, in reading Smith's *History of Virginia*, she had criticized Pocahontas for marrying an enemy. If she had been a wild she-American, she said, one of her hunters should never have tamed her. Did no voice warn her that persons animated by opposing ideals might become enemies? Mr. Butler, a young cavalier of the Old South, the descendant of English dukes, would demand exact and unquestioning obedience to his every command. In his view, he possessed his wife as he possessed his slaves—body, mind, and soul. She owed an unmitigated acquiescence to his will in return for his protection, his confidence, his wealth, and the privilege of being his wife. Fanny had experienced freedom. She was self-reliant and independent, with radical opinions of woman's sphere. Implicit obedience to any man was not in her code. She believed that all persons possessed the right of personal liberty. Of course, she remarked in her criticism of the Indian Princess, love might bring harmony from the discords of dissimilar natures.

If she considered the matter at all, she trusted it to bring happiness to her, too. Her ears were not yet attuned to the dissonant rumblings from the clash of the pro-slavery advocate and his attacker. She should have known that the discords in the natures of the Englishman and his Indian bride were easily resolved when compared with those of the traditionalist and the radical, or of the planter and the abolitionist. But no such thoughts troubled her mind. She was happy. Temperateness was not one of her virtues. She felt intensely and acted impulsively or not at all. Now she loved blindly, passionately. She knew that a woman's chances for happiness always ran an immense risk when she entrusted them to another. But she believed hers were safe.

One brief engagement in New York; then farewell to the paper and paint profession! No more incessant rushing from city to city to amuse strange herds! Never again need she look into the future years and picture herself doomed to a vocation which she disliked. She was escaping from the stage before habit rendered its excitements necessary to her contentment. She need not anticipate an old age of vacuity, deadness, and indifference such as she observed in persons who devoted their lives to the theater. Her energies should no longer be subjected to the withering influence of the emotion and agitation inseparable from a stage career.

Instead of this unnatural existence she dreamed of a home of her own where she could find leisure to study, to think, and to work. There were to be hours for the poems she intended to write, hours for the books she wanted to read, hours for her music, and days of companionship and sympathy. She planned for the future years, oblivious to the discordant natures which must be harmonized, oblivious, too, to hundreds of black beings who wallowed in the soil of rice and cotton fields by day and in wretched, filthy hovels by night—black spectres which were to haunt her; dark shadows which were to blot out the last shimmer of her dreams.

CHAPTER V

MISTRESS OF THE FARM

ON JANUARY 1, 1835, the Butlers took possession of Butler Place, six miles from Philadelphia on the old York road.[1] During the summer months they had travelled and visited at well-known watering places. From autumn they had resided at the home of Mr. Butler's brother in Philadelphia.[2] While they waited for workers to renovate the old farmhouse, Fanny busied herself in copying the journal of her observations during her first years in America. Mr. Butler objected strenuously to its publication, but he soon found that he opposed a will as unyielding as his own. He then began a vigorous criticism and expurgation of the manuscript. When he became too persistent, Mrs. Butler informed him that rather than submit to further curtailment of material already sold she would leave him and manage her own affairs.[3] Rumor had it that he offered the publisher $10,000 to suppress the diary, but the firm anticipated a far greater profit from its sales.[4] In less than six months the temperaments and ideals of the conservative husband and his self-willed wife had come into conflict.

The accommodations at the Farm—Fanny chose that homely appellation instead of the more pretentious title of Butler Place—seemed not in the least superior to those in a second-rate farmhouse in England. Still both husband and wife preferred this three-hundred-acre estate to a town home in Philadelphia. With an Englishwoman's notions of country life, duties, and occupations, Fanny anticipated interests in the near-by village and its poor. A garden and a dairy were to be her special hobbies. Her point of view, that of the rural sections of her native country, failed to make allowance for the distinctive qualities of the American rustic inhabitant or the realities of life on a small farm.

In after years, Fanny realized how ludicrous her expectations must have appeared to those familiar with the conditions surrounding the Branchtown estate. Instead of a well-kept garden she found three acres set apart for the cultivation of vegetables and a quarter of an acre divided into three straight strips where a few flowers struggled for their lives. Although three men called gardeners worked constantly, the boxwood hedge around the plat looked "mangy." Adam and Eve landscape-gardened in Paradise, Fanny reflected. How she wished their descendants had inherited some little knowledge of the craft.[5] But at this time the property did not belong unreservedly to Mr. Butler, and his wife's busy visions of gardening and greenhouse improvement were indefinitely postponed.[6]

Her first attempt at the cultivation of her neighbors' good will also resulted in disheartening failure. She offered to teach the small children of the gardener and the farmer as well as any village children who cared to join them. Contemptuous amazement met this benevolent proposal. Branchtown supported a village school where children received instruction for which they paid willingly. There these "small students made their exits and their entrances without bob or bow, pulling of forelock, or any other superstitious observance of civilized courtesy." Parents and progeny alike sniffed at her gratuitous education and misunderstood the spirit which proffered it.

On the first Fourth of July spent at Butler Place, the mistress planned a feast and rejoicing such as she thought should mark the birthday of American Independence and the expulsion of the "tyrannical English" from the land of freedom. She set a table under the trees and spread a dinner for thirty-two persons, the number of workers and children on the farm. She provided beer and wine for the due honoring of the even-

ing. No one touched either. They were objects of moral reprobation rather than sources of bodily comfort to her Quaker
farmer and his family. The farmer, indeed, remonstrated
repeatedly that it seemed a "shame and a pity to waste such
a fine day for work in doing nothing." With a doleful conviction
that her hospitality was as little acceptable to her neighbors
as her teaching had been, she bade her guests farewell. These
people and their children wanted nothing which she could
give them. The women liked the make of her gowns, she said,
and would have borrowed them with pleasure, but they desired nothing else from her.[7]

Of all her blunders that which in after years appeared the
most ludicrous concerned the dairy. After eating stale butter
for several weeks, she decided to obtain daily a newly churned
supply for home consumption. Ignorant of the entirely independent position of her workers, she went down to the farmhouse and interviewed the dairy maid. Words failed to express
that woman's amazement. She always churned twice each
week. Fresh butter every morning? Twice-a-week butter not
good enough for anybody? Who ever dreamed of such vagaries?
After the petitioner had exhausted her prettiest vocabulary
of requests and persuasions, the quiet, sober Quaker dairy-
maid followed her to the door: "Well—anyhow—don't thee
fill theeself up with the notion that I'm going to churn butter
for thee more than twice a week." Fanny failed to realize that
nobody could bring a small lump of butter in the enormous
churn used in the dairy, and the maid did not even dream
that machines of lesser dimensions existed.[8]

The plan for any humane occupation among the poor of
her village neighbors soon came to naught. No poor people
lived in Branchtown, at least none in the English acceptation
of that word. The abject class of ignorant, helpless, hopeless
paupers who depended upon charity and substituted alms-
taking for labor formed no part of the population here. Visits
among employees as practised by English women could not
be attempted because of their failure to understand her inten-

tions. Many changes had come about in this new land once claimed by England as its own.[9]

Although these misunderstandings of her motives wounded her, the English girl found happiness at Butler Place. The meadows and woodlands which she explored on horseback were beautiful, and, gradually she improved the appearance of the yard and garden. She read, studied, and wrote reviews for a magazine. She was undisturbed even when her *Journal* came from the press, and many reviewers flayed her unmercifully. "One of the most deplorable exhibitions of vulgar thinking and vulgar expression ever encountered," said one.[10] "The authoress has unsexed herself," cried another.[11] As usual Fanny had been indiscreet. She dubbed reporters the press gang. They felt obliged to retaliate and defend their honor.

Those less biassed against unfavorable criticisms found many praiseworthy characteristics in this diary record. Composed of intermittent entries from the date of her leaving Liverpool to her first sight of Niagara in the summer of 1833, the journal narrated the young actress's doings and impressions. Although her likes and dislikes sometimes obscured her vision, an individual tone sounded the keynote of the book. Instead of getting up for the book sellers a record which a hundred other travellers could have manufactured just as well, she offered a vivid reality which mere authorship could not have created. It seemed genuine and sincere.[12]

Indeed, the account possessed all the freshness, confidence, and indiscretion of an intercepted correspondence. Although her strictures on American manners and institutions were biting, Americans were perhaps oversensitive. There was not a single deliberate attempt to misrepresent or depreciate her adopted country.[13] The candid critic found much to admire as well as many instances to censure—beautiful descriptions, just and forceful observations on the conditions of society, numerous anecdotes, and discriminating criticisms of actors and acting, which compensated for faults of language, sturdy prejudices, hasty opinions, and ungenerous sarcasms.[14] Reviewers who condemned the record because its author used colloquial expressions, found fault with hotel accommodations, and painted an uncomplimentary picture of American political and social affairs, were more prejudiced and less just than the author whose work they deprecated.

Perhaps in further defiance of the press gang, two other journals, scarcely more than pamphlets, were published in 1835. *My Conscience! Fanny Thimble Cutler's Journal of a Residence in America whilst Performing a Profitable Theatrical Engagement: Beating the nonsensical Fanny Kemble Journal All Hollow! ! !* parodied the earlier journal and caricatured the incidents and characteristics which critics had assailed most bitterly. This diary, "Published to purchase for the authoress a Wedding Gown, being about to honor Fierce Cutler, Esq., with her hand in Wedlock," began with an account of her arrival in New York. Then followed descriptions of her experiences at the hotel: abominable meals of peaches, grapes, plums, cantaloupes, and watermelons, maggoty cheese, and sour bread; rooms with the floors covered by thousands of bugs which cracked like torpedoes under her feet. It narrated the impudence of American servants—on the third day after she employed a maid, the independent hired girl boxed her mistress's ears until they rang with pain. American social usage came in for its share of exaggerations. At the dinner which introduced her to American society, a Negro went around the table and wiped the diners' faces and hands with a sponge dipped in whiskey—the American substitute for finger bowls. Then followed humorous accounts of her experiences in the different cities visited and stories of her meeting with Mr. Fierce Cutler and their courtship. No one could accept seriously a line of these facetious accounts. They ridiculed powerfully the inconsequential strictures which reviewers made on her original journal.

The second publication, *Fanny Kemble in America, or Journal of an Actress Revised with Remarks on the State of Society in America and England by an English Lady Four Years Resident in the United*

States, especially aped the tone of authority with which the authoress discussed affairs in her *Journal.* It purported to be extracts from the earlier record exhibiting the "singular mind of the intellectual Fanny" which qualified her to become the censor of the morals and manners of the people among whom she travelled. The "English Lady Four Years Resident" of course was enamored of America and saw only its admirable features. Few of the reviewers' jibes escaped ridicule. It ended with Fanny's death at the printing office of Carey, Lea, and Blanchard on May 2, which halted the revision, for even this hardened critic felt respect for the dead. The authoress, so the story ran, had survived her favorite child, the *Journal,* only a few days. An epitaph by an unknown hand appropriately concluded the review:

> Here lies one who—*never lied*
> Save "prostrate on the floor";
> So *lying* lived—she *lying* died;
> And lies—to rise no more.[15]

Fanny's revenge on the press gang was complete. She turned their strictures against themselves by rewriting the kinds of scenes and criticisms which they tried to find in her *Journal.* She enjoyed shocking excessive primness wherever she found it, and she doubtless indulged in numerous laughs at the reviewers' expense. What the public thought about her writings worried her not at all.

On May 28, 1835, the arrival of little Sarah increased the family to three. Fanny loved children. Possessing one of her own meant the realization of a long cherished hope. Her life followed in a tranquil, serene, and even course which after the excitement of the past few years was both agreeable and wholesome. From the time of her début at Covent Garden, she had lived, she said, "at the rate of three years in every one . . . in point of physical exertion and exhaustion." Those years spent in a turmoil of action and emotions were ended. The remainder of her life seemed to stretch before her like a level, peaceful landscape. Human foresight could see no change likely to disrupt this contentment except, she recalled, one source from which this peaceful existence might receive a shock—the South.

Her husband possessed an interest in extensive plantations in Georgia. Her daily experience and her faith in the justice of God forbade the continuation of that abuse by which one race held another in bondage. Opinion was at work silently and strongly in the hearts of men. Although people of the North opposed the theory of slavery, they still tolerated its practice in another part of their country. This situation could not continue. The selfishness with which men clung to their interests increased the vigilance of the planters at this time; but wealth in slaves remained a property crumbling beneath their feet. A few years more and the black population would be free. Fanny heartily disliked the toil which gave her sustenance in the past, but she readily would have resumed that profession in order to have freed her family from support by that grievous sin against humanity.[16] Slavery and her relations with that institution continually troubled her although all feelings of self-condemnation seemed gratuitous on her part. When she married Mr. Butler she had not known of the hundreds of slaves on his Georgian plantations.[17] Unwillingly and ignorantly she became a participant in that unjust system of labor. In 1835 she paused in her heterogeneous reading of Alfieri's *Life*, Irving's *Tour on the Prairies*, and *Dr. Faustus* to write a long and vehement treatise against slavery, but she refrained from publishing it lest fellow-citizens tear down the Butler residence and make a bonfire of the furniture, a favorite mode of remonstrance, she had learned, against those who advocated the rights of the unhappy blacks.[18]

One day her husband explained that the cotton lands in Georgia would soon be exhausted. In Alabama, he said, large tracts of wild soil lay idle. Anyone who possessed the Negroes necessary to cultivate these lands might realize an enormous fortune in a few years. He questioned jestingly whether she would be willing to go there. Gladly, she replied, if her doing so would place their slaves "upon more humane and Christian footing." How much might be done if two persons possessed the energy and courage, the humanity and justice, to attempt it! Although they might not educate the blacks even to read, no law prevented the owners from living among their servants and teaching them all that example and personal influence could impart.

She formulated a plan for such a project. The owner would explain to his slaves that in a certain number of years he intended to free all whose conduct proved them worthy of freedom. In the meantime each was to receive a profit from his labor. In a savings bank established by the master the slave would deposit his earnings. At the end of his probation each would possess small funds with which to begin an independent life. Throughout the intervening time the owner and his family were to live continuously on the plantation. Each person, Fanny believed, had some appointed task in life; this experiment seemed her and Mr. Butler's peculiar duty.[19] To her the Negro was a downtrodden, intelligent Englishman with a black skin. If she should explain her project, he could not fail to comprehend or to respond.

Associations with individuals of abolitionist tendencies at this time exerted a strong influence upon her ideas. After her marriage she had forsaken her Episcopalian training to accept the Unitarian preference of the Butlers, and Dr. Channing had become an admired acquaintance. His eloquent sermons and fervid depth of devotion inspired her.[20] She also read his articles on slavery. She had never seen a slave before her marriage, but she had opposed slavery on theory, for she had spent her early life in the atmosphere of reform which pervaded England during the first decades of the nineteenth century. Before she left London sentiment had freed the last slaves held in British dominions, and abolitionists had already initiated a campaign against that unjust system in America. Her interest in the institution naturally became more personal after her alliance

6

with a slave owner, for she now unwillingly possessed black servants, and her child must own them after her. She trembled for the future of those dear to her, for an all merciful Father's patience could not endure an unjust affliction of His children forever. In America her ideas in regard to slavery developed; her championship of abolition became more ardent; but a firm conviction of its injustice and inhumanity had come with her from England.[21]

Fanny was disappointed when in the fall of 1836 Mr. Butler and his brother departed for the South without her. The overseer inhabited the only cottage there, and he could not provide accommodations for his employer's wife and child. Although she was glad on Sarah's account, she would have endured many discomforts in order to have seen the plantations on the Altamaha River. She realized, however, that if she had gone, her hands would have been tied. She could not have freed any servants, paid them for their labor, or taught them to read. But a mere personal influence, she believed, often accomplishes much, and through the influence of example she hoped to do something.[22]

Rather than spend the winter alone at Butler Place, Fanny sailed from New York on November 1, 1836. Twenty-seven days later, accompanied by Sarah and the nurse, she arrived in London. Mr. and Mrs. Kemble now lived at Park Place, Saint James's. There she spent most of the weeks during her ten months' stay in England. Her return at that time brought renewed acquaintances with many remarkable persons. Sydney Smith's keen wit and genial humor especially pleased her. Through the kindness of Lord Lansdowne she attended the first meeting of Queen Victoria and the Houses of Parliament. On several occasions she met Samuel Rogers and William Wordsworth. Once she met them walking in a park, and enjoyed their conversation, "the gentle rill of the one speech broken into and interrupted by sudden loud splashes of the other." Later Rogers told her that in the magnificent library at Althorpe Wordsworth always kept a volume of his own poetry in his hand,[23] a circumstance which exceedingly amused his admirers.

Fanny found London "more beautiful, more rich, and more royal, than ever." Liberalism, she said, had gained a much stronger and wider influence than it had exerted four years earlier. Liberal opinions had spread, while Toryism had remained steadfast in its old stronghold. Tories held firmly to their political faith and feared everything which differed from it. As a result of this fear they mixed less with their opponents than formerly and expressed less tolerance for differences of opinions.[24]

But the turmoils and dissipation of London life, as much as it amused her for a time, soon began to pall. Her visit there tended to reconcile her to a life comparatively remote from the best refinements of civilization and all enjoyments of society. She felt no desire to desert America and the duties that belonged to her there.[25] She hastened to Liverpool early in August to meet Mr. Butler. After a fortnight, each day spent in "heart-eating suspense," the long delayed vessel finally arrived, and the reunited family hastened to London. After a brief sojourn they sailed for New York on September 10. The re-assembly of the Pennsylvania Constitutional Convention on October 17 cut short Mr. Butler's first visit to England.[26]

On August 7, 1837, a few weeks before Fanny's return to America, the management of Walnut Street Theater, Philadelphia, produced her tragedy, *The Star of Seville*.[27] Its publication during the same year brought to light a work which she had completed before her arrival in America. Perhaps these events again turned her thoughts to creative writing. During the year after her return she completed her third play.

She based an *English Tragedy* upon an event which had recently stirred fashionable London to its foundation. Lord de Ros, premier Baron of England, cheated his fellow-gamblers at the Club. Although all acquaintances knew him to be one of the most profligate men of the day, exclusive circles disregarded all other remissness. To the author, his laxity at dice constituted his mildest shortcoming. In her drama she attempted to present his philandering activities for which society should have condemned him. Under the name of Lord Alford he wormed his way into the affections of Anne, the wife of his aged friend, Judge Winthrop. Although he ruined their lives, he escaped all censure. But when a companion noticed that he shot loaded dice, Alford immediately became an outcast. Only violations of honor in gambling counted against reputation.

This dramatization the author thought the only worth while thing she ever wrote. She was not entirely wrong. It represented her best effort in drama, and although some scenes were over-sentimentalized, the play presented dramatic possibilities and impressive theatrical effects. The writer's stage experience aided in adjusting material to stage conditions. This tragedy showed a decided improvement over its predecessors. The dramatic promise of *Francis I* was renewed and augmented. An *English Tragedy* presented a more unified structure and the most impressive poetry which its author ever wrote. Shakespearean scenes, imagery, philosophy, and idiom again dominated her dramatic conception.

> The waters of my life have run to bitterness
> And the failing fountain trickles cold and slow,

Judge Winthrop mourned after Anne's death. This work marked Fanny's last serious attempt at the dramatic form.

William Macready, lessee of Covent Garden, to whom she submitted the completed manuscript recognized its merit: "Finished the reading of Mrs. Butler's play which is one of the most powerful of the modern plays I have seen—most painful, almost shocking, but full of power, poetry and pathos."[28] Although he expressed his high opinion of the genius which sustained the drama throughout and thought that its merit challenged representation, the management decided not to stage it because of the startling character of the plot. It was too tragic, Fanny said, too shocking to be accepted as truth. Only in real life were such events enacted. Mr. Butler objected to the publication of the work from the time of its composition.[29] Not until twenty-five years later did it appear in print.

Fanny thought of following this drama with another kind of composition, a treatise in defense of Providence. She sickened of the prevalent notion among her neighbors that Providence foreordained every ill although no one mentioned fortunate occurrences as coming from the same source. They laid all misery, all suffering, every premature death, and all disease to the charge of the Father in Heaven. No matter what calamity visited them, they failed to reflect upon their own instrumentality in the business. With a resignation more provoking than praiseworthy, they turned their eyes upward, folded their hands, and miscalled it a dispensation of the All-Powerful. To Fanny it seemed that a profound sense of the Creator's justice rendered all things endurable; but the idea of an arbitrary infliction of misery put her whole soul in revolt. She always recalled a devout old Scotch lady's interpretation: "Hech, sirs, I'm never weary of reflecting on the gracious dispensation of Providence towards myself, and its righteous judgments on my neighbors!"[30]

Fanny felt no interest in creeds, theologies, dogmas, or systems. She read accounts of the history and authenticity of the Gospel narratives in order to give some reason for the faith which she felt. She believed that "Christ received the last and perfect revelation of moral truth, brought it into the world, preached it by his practice, and bore witness to it by his death." Since his coming, his teaching and example have moulded every holy life and death wherever people knew his name. Even those individuals least inclined to acknowledge it have imbibed unconsciously the influence of the inspiration which he breathed into the soul of humanity.

In her opinion, civilized societies and nations which called themselves Christian had scarcely begun to comprehend, to believe, or adopt his teaching. When people understood his meanings, his influence would bring about the regeneration of the race. It would extend above and beyond all discoveries of science and developments of knowledge; more and more it would prove itself the only moral and spiritual theory able to carry forward or even to keep pace with the progress of humanity.[31] With this philosophy she wished to contradict the prevalent ideas about Providence.

On May 28, 1838, little Frances Anne, soon nicknamed Fan, came to join in the celebration of her sister Sarah's third birthday.[32] Fanny was disappointed at first that her children were not boys. The lot of women usually appeared unhappy, principally because of the many serious mistakes which were prevalent in the education of women. Surely the Creator could not have intended any of his creatures to lead the sort of life that many women do.[33]

The problem of educating a girl was even greater in America than in England. Even the accomplishments were not well taught, and seemed flimsy, frivolous, and superficial in both quality and quantity. More solid acquirements were almost unknown among Fanny's lady acquaintances. The species of ignorance occasionally displayed was so absolute and profound as to be amusing and curious. While quite enough native shrewdness, worldly acuteness, and smatterings of shallow reading existed, they combined in a result worthless and vulgar to a pitiable degree. Exceptions to this narrowness and aridity could be found, but, unless Fanny had been unfortunate in her associations, this happened rarely.[34]

The family went to Rockaway on the shore of Long Island for the warmer months of 1838. From there in the latter part of August Fanny and the children journeyed to Lenox, Massachusetts. No other place in America possessed for her a charm equal to that of the Berkshire country. Green hills, small valleys, thick woods, jewel-like lakes, and distant jagged crests where troops of clouds, wandering showers of rain, and sunbeams chased each other, completed a grander pageant than that which Prospero raised on his desert island. Here, too, her most esteemed American friends, the Sedgwicks, resided.

In associations with them she found a community of intellectual interests lacking in her other acquaintances.

At the little Red Inn where she stayed, she found two other friends, Mary and Fanny Appleton, who came for a week's rest.[35] Here these guests pursued an unceremonious existence with an absence of all form or inconvenient conventionality. This short vacation was an incomparable relief after the months of isolation at Butler Place. But a brief dispatch interrupted the joy of her last few days in Lenox. A message told Fanny of her mother's death in far away England.[36]

In December, Mr. Butler, his family, and the children's nurse departed for the rice and cotton plantations. He anticipated a total change of his wife's opinion of slavery as a result of her residence there.[37] She prepared for the journey torn by conflicting thoughts. That she was not permitted to accompany her husband in the past had disappointed her, for, ever since she had first learned of his possessions in the South, she had desired to see conditions as they actually existed on his plantations. Mr. Butler was just recovering from a severe illness, and she believed that the warmer climate would be beneficial to him. On the other hand, the journey and residence meant hardships, and the whole circumstances of existence would be repugnant to her. Life in a half-furnished house located in a rice swamp with slaves as habitual company and alligators from the Altamaha as the only visitors was not alluring. The ordinary comforts of life were almost unknown, and the care of two small children would be a problem.[38] A thousand-mile journey with one child of six months and another of three and one-half years through regions where accommodations remained far from ideal meant in itself considerable hardship for the mother.

In 1838 any traveller in the United States encountered many privations and annoyances. American impetuosity and hurry led to numerous risks. Within a mile of Philadelphia the Butlers crossed the Schuylkill on a bridge of which the principal pier was incomplete. The railroad carriages reminded Fanny of green-houses on wheels. In the center of the car built to accommodate sixty-four persons stood a sheet-iron stove. Passengers froze and suffocated by turns. The seats arranged along either side of the vehicle left a kind of aisle in the middle, where the restless part of the travelling population fidgeted up and down continuously, and tobacco chewers expectorated at will.

At Baltimore the party transferred from the train and proceeded to Portsmouth, Virginia, by steamer. Ornamentation rather than comfort concerned the furnishers of the boat, as was shown by the fact that it displayed seven expensive looking mirrors, but only one towel for each wash room. Upon their arrival at Portsmouth, Fanny saw slaves for the first time in her life. Her first glimpse did not tend toward an alteration of her previously formed opinions on the subject of their state. These creatures were poorly clothed and horribly dirty. In their manner was the lazy recklessness always exhibited by persons without responsibilities.

After a day in a railway carriage the travellers arrived at Weldon, North Carolina. The Dismal Swamp which they had crossed "looked like some blasted region lying under an enchanter's ban." The Pine Barrens seemed more cheerful but still gloomy enough. People had told Fanny that North Carolina was the poorest state in the Union, and her observations indicated the accuracy of this statement.

Weldon pretended to be a town, but it seemed, Fanny said, rather the place where a town intended to be. At the dilapidated hotel the landlady showed the women into a filthy room where tattered articles of clothing filled most of the space between three beds. In the diningroom the dirt on the table cloth, in the food, and on the clothes of the Negro waiters deprived the guests of all appetite. When the diners rose from the meal, the gentlemen guests hastened to one end of the apartment where folding doors closed after them. The rule separating men and women travellers was rigidly observed in this section by all journeying Americans. Although such a peculiar and amusing custom perhaps was necessary, Fanny felt an inclination to quarrel with the procedure. It deprived a woman of a companion's society, assistance, and protection. Twice on this southward trip colored cabin girls peremptorily ordered Mr. Butler to withdraw from the apartment when he found it necessary to converse with his wife. Men who travelled with female companions passed their time in "prowling about the precincts of the 'ladies apartment'; while their respective ladies pop their heads first out of one door and then out of another" until her man should come by.

More days passed on trains and in stage coaches, and nights, in wretched hotels. The roads ran by many beggarly houses; squalid inhabitants crowded around the travellers at each stop. These conditions seemed typical of those existing in warmer climates the world over, Fanny thought to herself. Invariably, inhabitants of southern countries, where the soil produced unurged the means of livelihood, were easy-going and inclined to shiftlessness. Sooner or later they became the prey of northern conquerors. In the past, "bleak regions of upper Europe and Asia have poured forth from time to time the hungry hordes, whose iron sinews swept the nerveless children of the gardens of the earth from the face of their idle paradises." A similar situation was developing in the United States at this time. While southern people surrounded by their slaves grew poorer, New England adventurers came among them and by stern vitality turned into wealth the ground they stood upon. Perhaps, she reflected, "this northern tide of vigorous life flows forever toward the countries of the sun, that the races may be renewed, the earth reclaimed . . . and all its various tribes, rescued from disease and decay."[39]

At Wilmington the travellers boarded a steamer for Charleston. Although they arrived at five o'clock in the morning, the boat did not leave until one in the afternoon. To the nearest inn, a mile from the railway, the sleepy guests trudged on foot in the bitter cold of the December morning. Although they had fasted most of the previous day and night, the host pleasantly informed them that the public breakfast would not be ready for several hours and that meals were not served at other times. The comforts or preferences of the individual received no consideration.

On Christmas morning the Butlers awoke in Charleston. Here they found it necessary to remain for several days, for the boat to Savannah made only one trip weekly. Communication between even the principal Southern cities was still slow, infrequent, and inefficient in 1838. But for once Fanny enjoyed waiting. Charleston seemed like one of the older country towns in England. After the "red-brick-and-white-board fever" of the North, a glimpse at a house which looked "as if it had stood long enough to be warmed through" was a privilege.

This city lacked the smug mercantile primness of northern towns. Instead it possessed an air of eccentricity and peculiarity. Every house seemed built to its owner's particular taste: on one street one could imagine himself in an old English town; on another, in some continental city of France or Italy. The foliage of evergreens screened almost every house. In the evening at nine o'clock a most ominous tolling of bells and beating of drums suggested an old fortified frontier town of the Continent. Here the curfew sounded and patrolmen watched not because of an expected foreign invasion but in fear of domestic insurrection.

The absence of anything like bustle or public celebration of the holiday season was somewhat akin to the English custom of spending Christmas at home in hospitable festivity. Charleston seemed to her more aristocratic—or was it more democratic for each person to follow his own preferences—than any other city which she had visited in America. Here at least a few people were fighting valiantly against the new-world tendency toward standardization.[40]

On Thursday the travellers departed for Savannah. The owners did not consider the boat seaworthy, and it followed the inner passage. After two nights and one day spent in tedious navigation through cuts and small muddy rivers where the boat sometimes stuck on the bottom, it drew up to the wharf of Savannah. A few hours of rest, and then the party again boarded a small steamer, this time for Darien.

When the irregular buildings of the little town appeared, it seemed to Fanny that she had touched the outer bounds of civilized creation. But as soon as the Butlers advanced on deck, things began to happen. Black men in two pretty boats alongside hailed them: "Oh massa! how you do, Massa? Oh, missis! oh! lily missis! me too glad to see you!" accompanied by certain shrieks, whoops, whistles and grunts which could be written down only in Negro language. The strangeness and wildness of the whole scene, the affectionate welcome of the people who hailed the visitors as descending deities, and the strange contrast with anything which she had experienced in the past brought tears to Fanny's eyes.[41]

The travellers transferred to the larger of the two boats, crossed an arm of the river, and passed through a narrow canal dug years before by General Oglethorpe's men. After crossing another arm of the Altamaha, they approached the low, reedy bank of Butler's Island. As they neared the wharf, the steersman took up a huge conch and in the barbaric fashion of early times in the Highlands sounded their approach. A group of Negroes appeared, "jumping, dancing, shouting, laughing, and clapping their hands."

When the visitors stepped on the landing, the enthusiastic blacks seized, pulled, pushed, carried, dragged, and all but lifted their guests into the air. They kissed the clothes and hands of massa and missis. One tall, gaunt Negress flew at the family and tried to embrace all four of its members at the same time. Fanny felt almost frightened. Not until they entered the house and shut the door upon their riotous escorts could master and his wife indulge in a fit of laughter, a merriment induced as much by nervousness as by amusement. At last Fanny was in Negroland.[42]

CHAPTER VI

THE GEORGIAN PLANTATION

MISSIS sat in the living room at her pine-wood table where evening after evening she recorded the day's events. Candles flickered in the warm breeze tinged with the scent of peach blossoms. At the opposite end of the room, light from huge blazing logs in the fireplace chased shadows along the walls.

From time to time an outer door opened noiselessly. One after another, men and women glided through, their naked feet falling all but inaudibly on the bare boards. By the hearth they squatted down on their hams, where in the dim firelight they resembled a circle of ebony idols. No one spoke; each contemplated missis, charmed by her evening gown. All felt compassion for the white hand which wrote incessantly, to them a task which seemed more strenuous than field labor. Why should missis work when she had numerous niggers to wait upon her, they wondered. Fanny looked at the dirty, ragged creatures. "I hope," she confided to her journal, "this sojourn among Mr. ......'s slaves may not lessen my respect for him, but I fear it."[1] The day's story finished, she questioned suddenly, "Well, what do you want?" Each black figure sprang up as if moved by machinery. Replies came in unison, "Me come say ha do, missis." Then they stole out silently as they had entered, "like a procession of sable dreams."[2]

Fanny Butler went to her husband's plantations prejudiced against slavery. Her marriage with a southern planter had not shaken her conviction of the injustice and cruelty of the "peculiar institution," for she was an Englishwoman, to whom the absence of such a bias would have seemed disgraceful.[3] But she went prepared to find palliations in the system; she anticipated much kindness on the part of the masters and much contentment on that of the slaves.[4] The weeks since her boisterous reception at the wharf of Butler's Island had disillusioned her. She watched these servants at their tasks, visited their filthy cabins, listened to their petitions, and attempted to lessen their suffering.

Her contact with the Negro had not shaken her confidence in his mental capacity. He remained to her the downtrodden, unlettered Englishman, conscious of the oppressor's hand. Although his skin was black, beneath that ebony, love of liberty rebelled against the tyranny which continually forced him lower. She understood better, perhaps, than any African who ever toiled beneath the driver's lash what it meant to be a slave.

Even a preliminary survey convinced Fanny that she would not be dazzled by the splendors of a southern planter's residence. She frequently had listened to some enthusiast's description of the great house containing twelve or more rooms built on a river bluff or among a grove of live oaks which distinguished the estate of the prosperous planter. Tall trees, shrubs, gravelled walks and marble statues dotted the ideal grounds. A colonnaded house with its wide hall, ample staircase, high ceilings, portraits of family celebrities and the plain but massive furniture completed a stage worthy of the beautiful ladies who commanded adoring servants.[5]

But Fanny found no colonnaded mansion here. The great house on Butler's Island consisted of three small rooms and three still smaller, more appropriately designated as closets. The largest apartment, fifteen by sixteen feet, served as sitting, dining, and living room. A dingy wooden partition ornamented with hooks, pegs, and nails to which caps, hats, and keys hung in graceful irregularity divided it from the adjoining bedroom. The nursery occupied a third room, a sort of loft above the larger apartment. The overseer, who lived as a member of the family, appropriated one of the closets as his sleeping quarters and a second for his office. The remaining one Mr. Butler used as a dressing room and business office. There he gave audiences to the Negroes, redressed grievances, and distributed red caps to meritorious slaves.

Wooden latches raised by means of small bits of packing thread fastened the doors, for locks on dwelling houses were unknown on this plantation. When one desired aid, he jerked a pack-thread bell rope suspended in the living room or raised a window and his voice until lung power summoned a servant. A wooden recess used as a pantry, and a kitchen, a mere wooden outhouse with the bare earth for a floor and a congregation of filthy Negroes for furniture, completed the master's mansion.[6] Not a single hint of spacious hallway or massive furniture rewarded Fanny's inspection. Instead, she found tables, sofas, and clothes-presses of white pine planed smooth as marble but neither veneered nor polished—not very luxurious but in harmony with the house itself.

Fanny really had not anticipated an elegant residence, for nineteen years had elapsed since the owner of the plantation had lived there. She went to Butler's Island prepared to encounter inconveniences, but she believed that in these half civilized surroundings she could find compensations for the absence of supposed necessities. Aspects of nature in the New World always requited in part the lack of conveniences and luxuries. Here on the outer edge of creation, that heritage from the Swiss strain in her temperament responded to the wild, natural loveliness about her, and she could forget the ugly residence. Dykes shut out the turbid water from the swampy land; beautiful, rattling sedges sheltered snakes and alligators; bald-headed eagles stooped from the sky to alight on straggling mossy trees; mocking birds kept up a resounding jubilee among the undergrowths of varnished evergreens. As the peculiar orange light of the southern sunset fell upon such a scene, she almost expected to see canoes of red men dart from the river banks.[7] Thirty-five years later when she called to mind

SCENES ON BUTLER'S ISLAND

where the "Georgian Plantation" was located. Above, the Fanny Kemble House; below, the slave quarters. Courtesy of Mrs. Margaret Davis Cate.

that winter in the South, she confessed that the wild, singular beauty of those sea islands and the solitary half-savage freedom of the life on their rivers and sounds fascinated her. Except for slavery she would have enjoyed her existence there.[8]

To her, the theory of slavery, the idea of holding fellow-beings in bondage, was repugnant. It violated her sense of justice and her idea of Christianity. Although Christ had not specifically denounced the practice, an omission which slave owners quickly seized on, He did so by implication when He forbade anyone's doing otherwise than as he would be done by.[9] But the practices instead of the theory of the institution made life on the Altamaha plantation unbearable.

Her first walk about the islands led by the threshing mills and then to the slave quarters. Four villages or camps consisting of from ten to twenty huts housed the slave population.[10] Near the center of each camp stood a small shed called the cook's shop. There in spacious caldrons, with the oldest wife of the village as officiating priestess, boiled the allowance of grits and rice for those who worked at the threshing floors.[11] The surrounding cabins exhibited a careless, reckless, and filthy indolence such as brutes would not tolerate in their lairs. Each building consisted of one room twelve by fifteen feet and several closets smaller and closer than staterooms of a ship. The inhabitants slept with gray moss for a mattress and a "filthy, pestilential-looking blanket" for a covering. Two families, sometimes eight or ten persons, resided in one of these huts, mere wooden frames pinned to the earth by brick chimneys. Firewood and shavings littered the floor; half-naked children cowered over smouldering cinders. The moss supposed to fill the chinks and crannies of the walls trailed into the dirt on the ground. The back doors of these huts, opening upon an unsightly ditch, stood wide open so that ducks and other fowls might travel in or out at their own pleasure. In the middle of the floor, or squatting around the hearth, would be four or five children aged from four to ten years, the latter caring for the babies of their respective households. Since the mothers were "driven afield as soon as they recover from child labor," the care of the infant devolved upon one of these little nurses who, supposedly, watched her charge, and, when it required nourishment, carried it to its mother who toiled in the field.[12]

Another short journey brought the visitor to the infirmary, where the misery of the sick aroused her resentment. Half of the casements contained no panes. Dingy shutters excluded light as well as cold. Embers of a few sticks of wood glimmering in the fireplace provided the only warmth. Around these, cowered all the sick women who were able to be there, some on wooden settles, but most of them on the ground. Those wretches too ill to rise lay prostrate on the floor without bed, mattress, or pillow, buried in tattered and dirty blankets. And this, the visitor reflected, was "the hospital of an estate where the owners are supposed to be humane, the overseer efficient and kind, and the negroes remarkably well cared for and comfortable."

As soon as she recovered from her dismay, missis told old Rose, who had charge of this room, to open the shutters of the three glazed windows. In the meantime Fanny proceeded to rekindle a fire, but when she lifted a log for that purpose, "a universal outcry of horror" arose. Old Rose attempted to snatch it from her exclaiming: "Let alone, missis—let be; what for you lift wood? You have nigger enough, missis, to do it!" After an explanation of her views concerning the purpose for which nature appended hands and arms to the human body, she lighted the fire. At her command the old Negress tidied up the floor and placed in a more comfortable position those patients unable to rise. Her supervision concluded here, missis passed on to the upper rooms appropriated to the use of men who were ill. Here all the windows were devoid of panes, and the inmates had to choose between complete darkness or the uninterrupted draughts of January air.[13]

Upon Fanny's return to the dwelling she gave vent to her indignation to Mr. Butler and his overseer. It seems probable that she counted one enemy on Butler's Island from that hour. The overseer regarded his management of the plantation as successful—the estate returned a full income under his management, a test of success not yet abandoned by business enterprises. Such men had no time to squander on sick slaves, "tools, to be mended only if they can be made available again; if not, to be flung by as useless, without farther expense of money, time, or trouble."[14]

This was the beginning of Fanny's complete alienation from her husband's interests. In a short time she became to him a meddlesome woman disseminating ideas dangerous to her own family's safety and perilous to the institution of slavery. Her zeal to ameliorate the conditions of these people led to many acts which the master could neither sanction nor condone. Her consecration and devotion to beings who called her "missis" forced open a breach which never again could be bridged between her and their owner. The residence undertaken with the hope of adding to the cheer and contentment of these charges wrecked her own happiness and peace of mind.

She had journeyed south determined to see with her own eyes the palliations as well as the injustices of this system. During the first months of 1839 she passed each day in observation of the actual workings of the slave system. No conversation upon the subject escaped her ear. She hoped to understand the planter's point of view and to comprehend his defense of the institution. Something deeper than an idle curiosity prompted her fervor; she was fighting for her future happiness. No one suspected the grim struggle in the mind of the mistress whose daily walks brought cries of satisfaction from the busy Negroes. Least of all did her husband suspect that he was on trial and that a slight shift in the balance meant the difference between his wife's respect and her loathing.

Apparently he saw nothing repugnant or unjust in the management of his plantation. To him dirty slaves, filthy cabins, and unhygienic infirmaries were ordinary matters. His Negroes considered themselves especially fortunate when

7

they compared their lot with that of the slaves on neighboring plantations. He accepted slavery as an institution decreed by God, uncondemned by Christ, and sanctioned by the Apostles. Bondage in the days of Solomon, villeinage in England, serfdom in Russia, peonage in Mexico, and domestic slavery in the North American colonies represented only different phases of the same institution. In each instance slave labor had proved effective. All enduring achievements of human art and industry remained as monuments to the everlasting benefits of slavery, said the apologist for slavery.

Providence in reality had dealt kindly with the Negro in trusting him to the tender solicitude of his white master. Contrast his situation on any southern estate, especially on Butler's Island, with that from which the merciful slaver rescued him. Of the fifty millions who existed beneath the scorching African sun, forty millions bowed under the yoke of bondage. There, in addition to his duty as a beast of burden, each sleek, healthy black might serve on any day as his pampered master's dinner. Certainly he escaped this dread on the southern plantation. Want of mental energy, a natural aversion to bodily labor, and overpowering animal propensities seemed to mark the Negro as a member of an inferior race unfit for freedom. So, argued the planter, fate had provided for his necessities by entrusting him to his white masters. Society and Christianity softened his disposition, sharpened his intellect, and aroused his sensibilities. His was not an unpaid labor, but a small return to his owner for his care while young, his clothes and food during his whole life, and his escape from African bondage into the keeping of a civilized master.[15]

Mr. Butler could not imagine how any thoughtful, intelligent person could fail to grasp its amenities once he observed the system. Such anticipations accounted for Fanny's presence in Georgia, a circumstance which suggested forcibly how completely he failed to understand this English woman even after five years of married life. Fanny believed that a wife should love her husband "better than anything on earth except her own soul,"[17] and this love and a sense of loyalty to his interests sharpened her eyes for the more favorable aspects of the institution. There were also the two little "missises" who some day must inherit the island plantations and their dusky workers. For their sakes she sought mitigating conditions in the system. But her long fostered belief in the cruelty and injustice of slavery perhaps magnified its darker phases. In the records of her observations she made no attempt to present conditions on the Butler plantations as typical of those existing elsewhere under the slave system. Indeed, she reminded herself that the Negroes on Mr. Butler's plantation were "generally considered well off."[17a] What she saw or thought she saw on Saint Simon's and Butler's Island, not the institution in general, influenced her future life.

During the weeks which followed her preliminary inspections, Fanny continued to study the management and activities of the plantation. When in residence, the owner exercised complete control over his property, and his privileges were uncircumscribed. In his absence he delegated this authority to an overseer. During nineteen years previous to Fanny's sojourn on the islands, an overseer's hand managed affairs, the owners having visited their estates only at irregular intervals.[18] An agreement curtailed his authority, but for months in succession he resided there as the only white man. Since a slave's testimony never received a hearing, no true restraint in the overseer's dealings with his charges existed. This fact influenced Fanny in her acceptance of the Negroes' stories of maltreatment.[19] The apportionment of tasks, the supplying of food and clothing, care of Negroes when ill, and the administration of punishments offered many opportunities for malpractice. During those long periods of the owner's absence, Negroes claimed that they frequently suffered indignities at the overseer's hands. Excessive punishments as well as unmerited ones, tasks apportioned without a consideration of the laborer's physical

condition, lack of proper medical attention, and the appropriation of girls and wives to his own desires provided the basis
for many complaints.[20]

Since one man could not supervise personally all the tasks
or perform all the duties which devolved upon the overseer,
he chose a head driver from among the slaves to care for
routine duties. This office, second to that of the overseer himself and in his absence equal to it, made this Negro slave
responsible for the conduct of many affairs. When his superior
was absent, he appointed the work, gave permissions to fellow
Negroes, pronounced punishments, and indeed exercised all
the functions of undisputed mastery over his fellow blacks.
A head driver on the sea island estates found frequent opportunities to use this full authority. From early spring until late
autumn all white men left the islands for the mainland before
sunset and returned only after sunrise. A damp, humid atmosphere and thousands of malarial mosquitoes made the nights
unbearable for whites. In consequence a head driver found
himself sovereign over a small principality during more than
twelve of each twenty-four hours.[21] At all times this slave kept
the keys for the stores and distributed the weekly rations. In
the execution of duties he might at his own discretion inflict
three dozen lashes upon any slave.[22] One wonders whether
he ever exceeded this limit when intoxicated with the knowledge
of absolute power.

Other Negroes in addition to this head driver commanded
their fellow slaves. On Butler's Island in accordance with the
prevailing custom where planters adopted the task system of
labor, a gang driver supervised the labor of each group. On
one of her walks Fanny noticed one of these blacks standing
over his workers with a whip, a short stick of moderate size
with a thick, square leather thong attached, in his hand.
Regardless of his protest, "Oh, missis, me use it for a measure;
me seldom strike nigger with it," she knew that he might
inflict a dozen lashes upon a refractory slave whenever he
chose.[23]

The master, or in his absence the overseer, planned the tasks and stipulated the amount of labor exacted of each worker, but the gang driver enforced his superior's orders. Although the amount of labor professed to be graduated according to the sex, age, and strength of the worker, this differentiation was not always made. When Mr. Butler first visited his estates, he found men and women who labored in the fields performing equal tasks. This, to Fanny, seemed "a noble admission of female equality." Although such a situation had existed for many years, the master immediately altered this distribution and deprived the women of a striking concession to the feminine sex.[24]

Not all slaves were employed in the fields. Each plantation needed house servants and specialized workers. These groups, to Fanny's mind, refuted the claim of Southerners that the Negro possessed little mental capacity. Association with their white masters invariably occasioned an improvement in their mental development and habits of life. They worked only as occasion demanded and then under the more immediate direction of owner or overseer. To them came many of the hours of ease as well as the condemnations for laziness which advocates of slavery flouted in the faces of abolitionist crusaders. They escaped many of the severities possible under the institution of slavery.[25]

No planter ever thought of the slave as an unpaid laborer. True, he received no monetary remuneration for his days in the rice fields, but he never lacked the necessities of life: a home, food, and clothing. Fanny saw his home, the dirty vermin-infested shack pinned to the ground by a chimney. Could his return in clothing and food compensate in even a small measure for his toil, she wondered. Here, again, she had listened to graphic accounts which described the young mulatto maid arrayed in the still fresh dresses of her young mistress or the young pickaninny who, unburdened by conventions, lolled in unmitigated happiness beneath the shade of orange trees clothed in Eden's garb.[26] The latter condition was a reality except for the absence of orange trees. But no maid appeared in crinoline or organdy. Instead, each slave received as a yearly allowance a certain number of yards of flannel, an equal amount of "plains," an extremely stout, thick woolen cloth, and two pairs of shoes.[27] These garments seemed intolerable for any person in the climate of the plantations. Why might they not be allowed more flannel and underclothing for winter and dark chintzes for summer, she wondered. Already in January requests came to her for summer clothing and soap which if "Missis only give we, we be so clean forever."[28]

Neither could she regard the food allowance as outstanding in its liberality or variety. The field hands subsisted daily on two meals of Indian corn or hominy. At daybreak they departed for the fields carrying their day's allowance. Toward noon, and not until then, they kindled a fire, cooked, and ate their food where they worked. A second meal followed at night after their tasks were completed, six hours at least after the previous meal—properly so called for it consisted of meal and nothing else—with no intermission for rest or refreshment.[29] Occasionally a piece of meat enriched their usual fare.[30] Often fish caught from the river, eggs, or perhaps vegetables from their small gardens made their meal more palatable. Fanny noticed with disappointment that most of these scraps of ground were untended and uncultivated.[31] When she enquired about this neglect, the Negroes replied that by evening fatigue prevented their further labor. By the collection and sale of moss, or from the proceeds of their eggs or poultry sold at the neighboring village of Darien, the more enterprising families occasionally added to their frugal evening meals. It was the rule of the plantation that whatever a Negro might earn during non-working hours could be appropriated as he preferred.[32]

Occasionally, with proper precautions, social privileges interrupted the monotony of plantation drudgery. Dancing dispelled the memory of cotton or rice harvest. Boat-loads of guests from the cotton plantations on Saint Simon's journeyed the fifteen miles to Butler's Island in order to participate in a ball which honored the arrival of massa and missis. The heaven-defying combinations of color in their gala attire, the contortions, springs, flings, kicks, and capers, and the antics of an enthusiastic banjo player expressed the abandon of the festive occasion.[33]

Singing relieved the tedium of other hours,[34] and religious activities also constituted a phase of the Negro's recreational life. Although the master frequently questioned the expediency of allowing the free congregation of his slaves with those from neighboring plantations—the horror of an insurrection was a never absent fear—he encouraged religious instruction. Each slave might attend church at Darien once each month where the minister neglected "Whatsoever ye would that men should do to you" for the more appropriate exhortation, "Servants, obey your masters."[35] On other Sundays some assembled under the direction of London, an old slave who in some manner had learned to read, and listened to his prayers, scripture lessons, and extemporaneous exhortations.[36] During her sojourn, missis sometimes read the service to all who chose to come to her sitting room.[37] The master controlled the spiritual life of his slaves with the same sovereignty which he exercised over their bodies. His dissent sometimes precluded the ceremony of baptism. Upon reflection Fanny sincerely hoped that rite was not essential to salvation, else some might be damned in spite of themselves.[38]

These few privileges for recreations, the interest in the slave's religious life, the small gardens, and the graduation of tasks by the master, were palliations in the drab drama of slavery. Fanny saw them, and rejoiced in them; they argued for her future happiness. But they were an infinitesimal ray of light in the blackness. The privilege of keeping poultry did not compensate for the fifty lashes of the overseer or the dozen of the gang drivers.[39] An uncompleted task, a complaint of excessive labor, absence without permission, pretended illness, or real ailments should the overseer doubt their genuineness, the unauthorized appropriation of thine as mine, or a woman's resistance to the overseer's advances—each brought its punishment.[40] One female justified actions which her mistress condemned: "Oh, yes, missis, we know—we know all about dat well enough; but we do anything to get our poor flesh some rest from de whip."[40a]

Fanny knew that these dependents frequently needed correction. Hams disappeared mysteriously, and some Negroes were lazy—they were human. She could tolerate the chastising of a strong, healthy man, but the trussing up and flogging of mothers who left three-week-old infants at their cabins was another matter.

Neither did the privilege of occasional religious instruction compensate for the insecurity of domestic relations. No slave could marry without his master's consent. Even if a choice received his sanction, dangers still lurked near. If the overseer heard of a disagreement between a man and a woman calling themselves married, he immediately separated them and bestowed each upon some other available party.[41] Doubtless this enforced felicity lessened family quarrels, but it seemed a rigid requirement and a standard to which few masters could have proved equal. Many men possessed wives on each of two different plantations, a practice known and condoned by both master and overseer.[42] The number of young mulattoes who graced the plantations testified to occasional lacks of the benefit of clergy.[43]

Sometimes, in desperation, Fanny tried to escape from the contemplation of these intolerable conditions. With Jack, the young Negro delegated as her special attendant, she learned to row her little canoe which she affectionately named Dolphin. Together they paddled to Darien where she made necessary purchases at the store.[44] Again, social custom demanded the return of calls, journeys prompted only from a sense of duty. Southern ladies were unattractive to their English neighbor. They were "extremely sickly in their appearance—delicate in

the refined term, but unfortunately sickly in the truer one
. . . languid in their deportment and speech. Sameness and
stupidity" characterized their conversation. But the monotony
of "their most vapid existence," it seemed to her, would soon
deaden any intelligence, obliterate instruction, and "render
torpid and stagnant any amount of natural energy and vivacity." Better die a thousand times than live the lives of these
Georgia planters' wives and daughters.[45]

Oftener Missis and Jack spent the afternoon fishing, for
Fanny now was an addict of her mother's favorite sport. Had
it not been for the lingering, fidgeting, gasping agonies of the
creatures after being caught, it would have been an unexcelled
recreation. Although Fanny felt not the slightest compunction
about killing, she possessed infinite revulsion against torturing.
Her experimentation with the hope of finding some speedy
mode to end their pain gave Jack an added duty. She ordered
him to knock each fish on the head the instant he took the
hook from its gills, but he banged the poor things so clumsily
that she longed to hammer him against the side of the boat.[46]
It was a horrible recreation, she admitted, but at least a
diversion.

Sometimes, too, she listened to the wild but plaintive songs
of the slaves as they rowed the long-boats to Darien or between the plantations. Some of their airs possessed in general
character a strange affinity with European and especially with
Scotch melodies.[47] She noticed that "the note for note reproduction of 'Ah! vous dirai-je, maman?' in one of the
most popular of the so-called negro melodies with which all
America and England are familiar is an example of this very
transparent plagiarism." Although the accompanying words
were "astonishingly primitive," another tune clearly traced
its ancestry to "Coming through the Rye":

> Jenny shake her toe at me
> Jenny gone away

> Jenny shake her toe at me
> Jenny gone away
> Hurrah! Miss Susy, oh!
> Jenny gone away.

"What the obnoxious Jenny meant by shaking her toe," Fanny could never ascertain, but the pause made on the last "oh" just before the final announcement of her departure indicated a general satisfaction and contained much dramatic and musical effect.

Usually the words of the Negroes' songs seemed devoid of sense. One, an extremely plaintive, and original air, consisted of but one line repeated with a sort of wailing chorus:

> Oh! my massa told me, there's no grass in Georgia.

The singers explained this wail as "the lamentation of a slave from . . . Virginia or Carolina where the labor of hoeing the weeds, or grass as they call it, is not nearly so severe as . . . in the rice and cotton lands of Georgia." Another "very pretty and pathetic tune" began with words which promised something sentimental:

> Fare you well, and goodby, oh, oh!
> I'm goin' away to leave you, oh, oh!

"but immediately went off into nonsense verses about gentlemen in the parlor drinking wine and cordial, and ladies in the drawing-room drinking tea and coffee." Fanny had heard that many masters and overseers prohibited melancholy tunes or words and encouraged nothing but cheerful music and senseless words, since the peculiar musical sensibility of the Negroes made them "especially excitable by any songs of a plaintive character, and having any reference to their particular hardships."[48]

Soon after February 14, the oppressive heat on the swamp island necessitated the family's departure from the rice plantation for the cotton lands. Could those mitigations for which she had searched in vain on Butler's Island be found on Saint Simon's? Disappointment, disillusionment, shrouded every day since her grotesque reception in Negroland. Her abhorrence of the theory of slavery deepened and strengthened during every hour she observed its practice.[49] The crisis in these repulsive conditions came when the master refused to consider the complaint of overwork from a group of pregnant women: "How honorable he would have appeared to me begrimed with the sweat and soil of the coarsest manual labor, to what he then seemed, setting forth to these wretched, ignorant women, as a duty, their unpaid exacted labor."[50] With that sickening picture before her, the expectation for mitigating circumstances in this human institution seemed a mockery.

Although depressed by the grotesque and pathetic farewells of the Negroes, Fanny left Butler's Island with a lighter heart than she had carried for many days. After attendants had arranged pots, pans, beds, bedding, tables, other chattels, and passengers in the long-boat, the party rowed down the still stream to the accompaniment of extemporaneous chants devised by the rowers. Among other poetical and musical comments occurred the frequently repeated burden that they were "parted in body but not in mind" from those left behind.[51]

At the end of the fifteen-mile row, the conch sounded the boat's arrival at the famous long-staple cotton island of Saint Simon's. The family took up its abode in an old, half-decayed farmhouse. Here Fanny felt a sense of security which was absent in the rice swamps, where one could never feel quite safe with the water of the Altamaha looking over the dykes.

On the day following their arrival, with Mr. Butler as a guide, Fanny peeped around her immediate neighborhood. The Saint Simon's estate still bore traces of a more prosperous and civilized time when it had been Major Butler's favorite southern residence. To her delight she found stately evergreen oaks, and a tiny would-be garden with several peach trees in blossom, tufts of narcissus and jonquils, bunches of violets, and an exquisite myrtle bush. In all directions thickets of beautiful and various evergreen growth challenged her to explore them, but such anticipations ended abruptly. Mr. Butler remarked that rattlesnakes infested every swamp and thicket and that on no account would she dare go "beating about the bush" in these latitudes.

Suddenly a most extraordinary creature of the Negro species came toward the strollers. He bowed until his hands almost touched the ground, "Massa—your most obedient," and then with a kick and a flourish he drew to the side of the path to let them pass. So sudden, grotesque, uncouth, and yet dexterous a gambado never came into the brain or out of the limbs of anything except a "nigger." That incident occasioned a brief understanding between master and missis such as never came to them again. Together they shouted with laughter which broke out again every time they looked at each other or stopped to take breath. The English actress saw something of the comedy inherent in the associations of the plantation. The man by her side became once again the cultured, aristocratic southern gentleman, dissociated from the injustices of slavery, whom she met and loved in Philadelphia.

On the first day at Saint Simon's she was almost happy and hopeful. Perhaps on Butler's Island she had seen the institution at its worst. Here the Negroes seemed joyous. Throughout the afternoon, they thronged the house to see massa, missis and the little missises. The women, Fanny said, went into ecstasies over her little white pickaninnies. Mr. Butler received numerous, loud and profuse expressions of gratitude for getting married and having children. Although this thankfulness always amused his wife, she realized the earnestness of their rejoicing. The continuance of the family insured the estate and slaves from the hammer, for the owners of the Butler plantations never sold their slaves. These dependents saw in every child born to their owners a security against their own banishment from the only home they knew and separation from all ties of kindred and habit. They naturally anticipated milder rule from masters who were children of their father's masters. A mutual attachment between owner and slave existed under these conditions. So the blacks lauded, thanked, and blessed their master for having married and endowed their children with two little future mistresses.[52]

If the husband could have acted as guide on all his wife's excursions about the island and have received with her the visits of his blacks, she would have carried away a different impression of life there. During those first few days Fanny saw the more favorable aspects of the system. Soon this came to an end. The Negroes on the cotton plantation proved more talkative than those on Butler's Island, and although many were too old to work, they still indulged in gossip. They readily imparted their stories of maltreatment—perhaps missis's reputation as an intercessor preceded her, or perhaps they imposed upon her credulity and elaborated their stories. At any rate, within ten days after his arrival, the master refused to receive any more petitions through his wife. To him, all niggers were liars who kept their mistress in an incessant state of excitement with all the falsehoods which they could make her believe. In turn, the sight of her credulous commiseration only tended to make them discontented and idle and so prepared more chastisements for them.[53]

No doubt now remained as to the final result of Mr. Butler's experiment of taking his wife to observe slavery—he had proved himself unworthy of her confidence. When she came to the South, he had seemed to her the victim of circumstances which made him the owner of slaves. Now she saw him in his true character. He not only acquiesced in his part in the injustice of slavery; he approved of it and refused to assuage any of its miseries. He refused to lend his aid to that enterprise which Fanny believed to be their appointed mission in life, the alleviation of conditions for their own dependents. From this time she counted the days until her departure from the South: "I was not born among slaves," she mourned, "and cannot bear to live among them."[54]

During the remainder of her stay Fanny abandoned discretion. She appealed to the Negroes' sense of truth, duty, and self-respect as never before. She allowed them to feel her compassion and human consideration. They were equal human beings, not slaves. She felt no fear of the Negroes such as haunted the southern white woman. The idea of apprehending any mischief from them never crossed her brain. Frequently she travelled between the two plantations attended only by her Negro rowers.

Aleck, the sixteen-year-old waiter, requested reading lessons. Although Fanny knew it meant breaking the laws under which she lived, she determined that the lad should learn his letters. Perhaps, she said, "unrighteous laws are made to be broken." Anyway, Mr. Butler stood between her and the penalty. A heavy fine would be required to expiate the first offense, but her husband and owner must pay that. A heavier fine would punish the second; and for the third, only imprisonment could atone. What a pity, she thought, that one could not begin with the third lesson because going to prison could not be done by proxy, and "that penalty would light upon the right shoulders."

Only a week of her time in that "blessed purgatory" remained when Aleck presented his request, but much might be accomplished in seven days. If other owners had the fancy, they maimed their slaves, branded them, pulled their teeth, or shot them a little here and there—"all details gathered from advertisements of runaway slaves in Southern papers." Why should she not employ the absolute authority of the plantation and give reading lessons?[55] Such logic prompted the overseer's hint that her existence among the slaves was dangerous to the institution.[56]

Sometimes Fanny feared that the theoretical abhorrence for slavery with which she came South developed during her stay there only into a morbid desire to be delivered from her own share in it.[57] And she did not wish her disapproval to be selfish. Her observation of every detail of the system as a practical iniquity confirmed her opinion of its abomination.[58] Its cruelty and injustice to the Negroes alone would have condemned it, but that constituted only one of its many evils. A perversity of mind and thought noticeable in all persons associated with the system seemed an equal if not more condemnatory result. "Certainly," she said, "the worst of all tyrants is the one who has been a slave." This proved true in the case of Negro drivers. One slave commanded another in the most uncompromising utterance of truculent despotism to which Fanny had ever listened: "You nigger—I say, you black nigger—you no hear me call you—what for you no run quick?"[59] Their insolent tyranny toward each other could be equaled only by their diabolic cruelty to animals, traits which Fanny believed the result of the conditions under which they lived.[60]

A similar perversion touched the whites. "The habitual harsh tone of command" towards those men and women under their direction aroused a feeling of pity for these misguided individuals. Then, too, the disrepute in which every white held honest and honorable labor, because only a degraded class worked, was pernicious.[61] The Georgia "pine landers," lazy, filthy, ignorant, brutal, proud, penniless savages without one of the nobler attributes sometimes allied to the vices of savage nature, were striking examples of the result of this philosophy. Although they were wretchedly poor, they scorned the thought of labor, for that would reduce them to equality with the Negro. To squat, steal, or starve appeared preferable.[62] "Industry, man's crown of honor elsewhere, is here his badge of utter degradation." This observer believed that all the "pride, profligacy, idleness, cruelty, cowardice, ignorance, squalor, dirt, and ineffable abasement" which surrounded her here came from this conception. The northern farmer thought it no shame to work; the southern planter did; there, it seemed to her, began and ended the difference between the two.[63]

Her zeal for the emancipation and equality of the Negro stopped far short of endorsing any ideas which pointed to the amalgamation of the races. A fear of this as one of the ultimate results of the system was one of her reasons for condemning slavery. She saw the menace of miscegenation. Although white men refused to improve the mind of the Negro race by education, they apparently felt no qualms in bequeathing their own qualities, tendencies, and capabilities to it. Numerous mulatto pickaninnies claimed ebony Negro women as their mothers. During her first walk on Saint Simon's, Fanny noticed striking resemblances between several young mulattos and a white man of her acquaintance. When she learned that such relationships seemed to be accepted as matters of course, she said no more about "who was like who."[64] It appeared very evident that no law in a white man's nature prevented his making a colored woman the mother of his children although a law on the statute books forbade her becoming his wife. Why should legislatures have forbidden the marriage of whites and Negroes if an invincible natural repugnance governed the situation? By current reports many southern planters owned a more or less numerous family of colored children. Certainly, Fanny thought, few persons would assert that such connections resulted from the planter's desire to increase the number of his human property or to augment his revenue by intimacy with creatures whom he loathed.[65]

When in April Fanny left Saint Simon's, she believed that she should never return, a premonition which proved true. In the following autumn her brother-in-law, part proprietor of the plantations, settled the matter by stipulating positively that she should never again be taken there. He considered her presence on the estates a source of distress to herself, of annoyance to others, and a danger to the property. Although she questioned the validity of the latter objection, she readily admitted that of the other two.[66]

Years later she understood how ridiculously impossible and impracticable her ideas and expectations were and that their only result could have been "the ruin, danger, and very probably death, of all concerned in the endeavor to realize them." She appreciated in later years what in 1839 she did not even suspect, "the amazement and dismay, the terror and disgust, with which such theories . . . filled every member of the American family" into which she had married.[67] But when she departed from the Georgian plantations, the mists of future years and experiences obscured this understanding. The struggle between love and loyalty to her husband and devotion to the cause of the helpless, unfortunate, suffering slaves was ended. The man from whom she had anticipated much had failed in the crisis. He had forfeited her confidence and respect. She returned to Philadelphia with a new version of the chivalry of the South in her mind, the picture of "an elegant young Carolinian or Georgian gentleman, whip in hand, driving a gang of 'lusty women.' " She admitted this version of the "Chivalry of the South" to be "a little coarse, perhaps," but one which "could not be accused of imaginative exaggeration."[68]

CHAPTER VII

CHAINS AND FREEDOM

FANNY was alone in the deserted drawingroom of Butler Place. Outside, a fierce February gale lashed through the bare branches of the naked oaks. The solitude of the isolated old farmhouse aroused nostalgic longings for distant scenes and absent faces. In the nursery the two chicks, her affectionate designation for Sarah and Fan, slept in snug comfort. Although their pranks and chatter broke the monotony of the daylight hours, their companionship ceased at seven o'clock each evening. All others whom their mother esteemed and loved were far away, in Massachusetts, beyond the Atlantic, or on Butler's Island.

Memories of many friends failed to compensate for their absence. Fanny was lonely, depressed, homesick. She wrote letters to keep up her courage: "It is a strange country, and a strange people; and though I have dear and good friends among them, I still feel a stranger here, and fear I shall continue to do so until I die, which God grant I may do at home! *i. e.*, in England." She addressed the envelope to Lady Dacre, the "Dear Granny" who received her first as the young actress of Covent Garden.[1]

She pulled another sheet of paper from her escritoire: "Your children are very well. Fanny has had not the slightest symptom of croup since our return to the country. . . . I grieve to hear of your low spirits, though 'tis some relief to me to think that I am not now near you to wear and harass you, and produce the depression you complain of. . . . God bless you. Ever your own wife."[2] The clock struck ten. The writer folded her letter and prepared to retire. She lived by rule, and ten o'clock meant bedtime. She closed the desk, picked up the lamp, and departed from the drawing-room. Soon no sound except the howl of the wind broke the wintry silence about Butler Place.

Almost a year had passed since Fanny left the plantations on Saint Simon's—months filled with disappointments and misunderstandings. The years since her marriage in 1834 had been filled with little else. But each year was more trying, more bitter than the previous one. Back in the days when she sat on the green slope in Mount Auburn and listened to an insistent lover, she had pictured herself the mistress of a flower garden at Butler Place. Instead of roses she found cabbages. Years of attempted readjustment left the plat still a vegetable patch.

Most of the other tints had also faded from her varicolored dreams. She had anticipated a home of her own where she would find quiet and contentment. She had dreamed of an appreciation of her intellectual ability. At last, she promised herself, she was to find time and inspiration for the poems and dramas she wanted to write. Instead, she had found isolation, a disregard for intellectual interests, and a selfish, arrogant love, hostile toward any expression of her creative talents.[3]

Perhaps she should have remained faithful to her girlish resolution never to marry, but love had overmastered her conviction that she could never become a sympathetic wife or mother. It obscured, too, her observation, which should have told her that a deep-rooted and unalterable incompatibility existed between her and Mr. Butler. She possessed an active mind and an unbending will; he set little store by intellectual matters. Instead, he prided himself upon an indomitable will and a power to command. He demanded from all dependents such unquestioning obedience as the Dukes of Ormond would have exacted from their serfs, such compliance as the planter demanded of his slaves.

Pierce Butler numbered his wife among his dependents, but she, who had enjoyed economic as well as intellectual freedom, now refused to acknowledge absolute fealty to any man. She believed in the integrity of her own conscience; the surrender of any principle which she felt to be right, seemed to her a stigma of the deepest dye. In her husband's view, a woman possessed neither intellect nor conscience when either conflicted with his will. The handsome, chivalrous, southern gentleman whom Fanny married soon became an obstinate, unreasonable, irritable, autocratic husband; and he found, instead of the beautiful, amiable, English actress, a dissatisfied, fault-finding, self-willed, temperamental abolitionist.

From Mr. Butler's viewpoint, his wife held peculiar and impracticable ideas on the subject of marriage. To her, it meant a companionship on equal terms. Such a conception was ridiculous to him. He steeled himself, determined to remain faithful to the old régime and to demand man's traditional obedience from his helpmeet. Fanny refused to regard his authority, for she considered her own conscience to be her only law and guide. The Unitarian church, to which he belonged and to which she had become a convert soon after her marriage, exacted no promise of obedience as a part of its marriage ritual. His reminders that she was educated in the tenets of the Episcopal church and that its ceremony sanctioned their union fell upon deaf ears. It was not in the law of her conscience to promise implicit obedience to a human being, fallible like herself. No one else could relieve her of the responsibility for her actions before God.[4]

Strict adherence to the doctrines of any sect formed no part of her faith. Religion was a personal matter between herself and her God. She reverenced a Supreme Being, merciful and kind, who spoke to her through her conscience. Not all the creeds of the ages could come between her and that Being's voice. In vain might Mr. Butler din in her ears the "obey" of the Anglican ceremony. The inner voice whispered, "To obey is sin." That whisper came from the Omnipotent; Mr. Butler's "obey" proceeded from a man-made prayer book.

A dictatorial husband and the solitude of Butler Place

oppressed Fanny's restive temperament. Dejection and despondency presented imaginary ills. From her mother she had inherited morbid tendencies and a dissatisfaction with any situation in which she found herself restrained. From her childhood she had rebelled against all except self-imposed discipline. She recognized her own impulsiveness, and she tried to chasten the rebel within herself. Rules directed her daily activities. She carried her scheme of discipline even into the game of Patience. Every evening she played an appointed number of games, conscientiously dealing out destiny to the cardboard men and women.[5] Suddenness was the curse of her nature, and she knew it.

Although she inherited from a thoroughly English father a worship of law and a regard for ancient customs, these characteristics clashed with her innate impulsiveness. Today she was the upholder of dignity; tomorrow she would mortify her friends by walking fully dressed into a lake and then going home, still garbed in the dripping garments, through a crowd of amazed beholders.[6] Fanny disciplined herself, but she resented the interference of other persons. She was morbidly susceptible to reproof or disapprobation;[7] Mr. Butler expected and exacted from his dependents obedience to his every wish. He refused to compromise his selfish preferences; his wife was equally obstinate.

Although their married life had not passed in unbroken harmony before 1838, events and experiences on the Georgian plantations aggravated the question which caused many misunderstandings. Both Fanny and Mr. Butler should have recognized that slavery would doom their happiness as husband and wife. Each protested ignorance of the true circumstances involved. Although her letters and journals supply abundant evidence to the contrary, he claimed that her opinions on the subject were not formed or at least not expressed before their marriage.[8] She said that she knew nothing about Mr. Butler's interest in slaves until she already was his wife. One might look askance at this defense were it not for two circumstances:

she met Mr. Butler in Pennsylvania where slavery was non-existent; he did not become the legal owner of the plantations until the death of an aunt in 1836.[9] Although he had exercised nominal control over the estates for twelve years, he did not legally possess slaves at the time of his marriage. One might suspect duplicity on the part of either or of both. If they were sincere in their allegations, Fanny spoke for both when she blamed her own failure to consider the likelihood of their proving companions to each other.

Naturally enough the winter in Georgia did not pass in uninterrupted domestic happiness. Slavery became a reality to Fanny. Her opposition to the system increased with every sight of its injustices. Mr. Butler denounced all her Arcadian schemes for the improvement of conditions on the plantations, and he then no longer inspired her respect or confidence. She became indifferent, believing herself unessential to his happiness.[10]

When in May, 1839, after their return to Philadelphia he despaired of preventing her return to England, he solicited the intervention of Charles and Elizabeth Sedgwick. The influence which their counsel exerted over her intentions remains uncertain. They were among her most esteemed American friends, and they eloquently presented their arguments against her desertion.[11] Mrs. Sedgwick understood the contradictions in her friend's character. She knew that, were Fanny to embark for England, she would be ready to jump into the ocean as soon as the shore began to recede.

Fanny gladly accepted an invitation from the Sedgwicks and spent several months at Lenox, Massachusetts. Separation adjusted the grievances between husband and wife. Although they were unhappy when together, they were miserable when separated. In October, when she returned to Butler Place, Mr. Butler had decided to spend another winter with his family on the island plantations in the Altamaha. In December they closed the old farmhouse and went to his brother's home in Philadelphia. There, Mr. Butler became ill, and two months passed before he regained his health. When he again felt strong enough for the trip, he thought it inexpedient for a wife and children to endure the hardships of the thousand mile journey in midwinter.[12] Rather than remain in Philadelphia dependent on her sister-in-law's hospitality, Fanny chose to pass the months of her husband's absence at Butler Place. There in lonely isolation she sat on this wintry February night writing letters to keep up her courage.

The week which followed her reply to Mr. Butler's first letter from the plantation brought other communications. The low spirits to which he referred soon became a more severe ailment, and he was seriously ill. She despaired for his health. For the first time the possibility of a future devoid of his existence confronted her. Apparently she realized only then that if she had been unhappy, he, too, suffered because of her discontent. Her remorse was bitter: "When you think of me—*if* you think of me—think of me as one whose love for you has been a source not of joy or delight, but of pain and agony, and now of bitter reproach."[13]

When Mr. Butler returned to Philadelphia in May, 1840, a repentant, contrite Fanny awaited him. She begged him to go to the Warm Springs of Virginia, or Germany—anywhere to regain his strength. She would either accompany him or remain at home as he preferred. She determined to let the slavery question rest more than she had in the past. No words of hers, she concluded, could be powerful enough to dispel from the minds of her husband and his friends the clouds of prejudice formed by early habits of thought.[14]

Although she anticipated a visit to England in the autumn, she almost gave up the plan. Her roots were beginning to spread in her present soil, she said, and to transplant them even for a short time might check the process. Only the thought of her father caused her to hope that her family might make the journey. She lived in constant apprehension lest she should receive a message from across the Atlantic telling her of his death.

During the summer the appearance of Mademoiselle Ellsler and other artists in Philadelphia interrupted the monotony of Fanny's isolated life. Her long absence from theaters, she said, left her impressions of one almost as indistinct as Falstaff's memory of a church. Now she attended every performance.[15] A visiting Scotchman in Philadelphia watched her one evening at a performance of *La Sonnambula*. The small figure "with eyes full of latent fires" engrossed in the portrayal sat beside her husband. At the end of the last scene she arose and threw a wreath at the feet of the prima donna. "I wondered," wrote the discerning tourist, "if she did not regret leaving the stage to pine 'like a dull weed on Lethe's wharf' in the midst of the most unappreciating of all communities."[16] Another interruption, a visit to the friends at Lenox, afforded an opportunity for the intellectual communion which was non-existent at Butler Place. Fanny was happier, and her husband found nothing to complain of.

In November plans for the winter were yet indefinite when a message brought the news of Mr. Kemble's serious illness. Unless his daughter came immediately, there remained little probability of her seeing him again. Aided by the influence of an elderly relative of her husband, Fanny hastened preparations for a return to England. On December 1, 1840, she sailed from New York accompanied by her whole family. On December 22 the travellers reached London.

After several months passed at the Clarendon Hotel, the family leased a house on Clarges Street, Piccadilly. Here in the spring of 1841 Mr. Kemble, who had struggled back to health even after his most sanguine friends had ceased to hope, joined his daughter and her family. In April Adelaide and her aunt returned from Italy. Fanny's two brothers, although not residents of London, frequently made short visits. Friends of her girlhood welcomed her back to England; Harriet Saint Leger returned from Ireland for a lengthy stay; Emily Fitzhugh came from Barristers; Lady Dacre, from the Dacre estate, the Hoo. The social and intellectual circles which she had forsaken years before greeted the returning wanderer. As the descendant of English aristocracy and the husband of Fanny Kemble, Mr. Butler also received a cordial welcome. At last the concurrence of circumstances for which Fanny had often sighed was a reality. She lived with her husband and children among relatives and friends in her own country.[17]

She now tried to compensate herself for all of those jejune years at Butler Place. She frequented the theater and the opera.[18] Adelaide's recent success in *Norma* on the Italian operatic stage made the house on Clarges Street a music center, to which musicians and music lovers came at all hours of the day.[19] Frequently Fanny left London to join a party at Burnham Beeches, the home of George Grote, where political theories and music shared the interest as topics of conversation.[20] Lady Dacre was hostess of other groups at the Hoo. At one of her parties where each guest contributed something to the intellectual pleasure of his friends, Fanny read *Romeo and Juliet*. Other invitations took her to the Arkwrights at Sutton and to the Egertons at Worsley.[21]

Although many hours passed in entertaining and being entertained, Fanny still continued her favorite exercise, horseback riding. On other mornings she posed as Jezebel for Sir Frederick Leighton's painting. She felt rather bewildered by the whirl in which she lived and which sometimes came as a rather trying contrast to her solitary life in America.[22]

The Butler family spent the summer of 1841 travelling in Germany with a party of intimate friends and relatives. The illustrious pianist, Franz Liszt, persuaded Adelaide to appear with him in a series of concerts given in the principal cities along the Rhine. The London party accompanied these two artists, an arrangement which offered, in addition to the tour, the privilege of listening to two of the greatest musicians of the century.

Fanny was disappointed in the Rhine. It seemed less impressive after one had seen the Hudson. But the ruins on the German hills seemed especially excellent because they were ruins and could never again become strongholds of debauchery. Knights and squires no longer interested her as they once had. Instead, the beauty of God's creation, lights and shadows, colors of earth and sky, satisfied her craving for beauty.

Perhaps the journey became more agreeable in retrospect. After her return to England she recalled many incidents for pleasant contemplation. Not the least impressive of these memories were the "tornadoes of sound" with which the piano responded to Liszt's touch. Memories of his vivid charm of manner and conversation and of his commanding expression when he felt the inspiration of music were among the priceless recollections of Fanny's life.[23]

The travellers returned to London in October with the prospect of an entire season in the brilliant society of the forties. The Butlers took a house on Harley Street. Again the winter passed in a series of entertainments until Fanny confessed that she frequently suffered from mind-ache. House parties gathered at Bowood, the country estate of Lord Lansdowne, and at Worsley with Lord and Lady Egerton. These were intellectual groups which included Samuel Rogers, Thomas Macaulay, Tom Moore, Charles Austen, and Charles Greville. Macaulay seemed "like nothing in the world but Bayle's Dictionary, continued down to the present time, and purified from all objectionable matter." Intimate acquaintance failed to diminish the observer's admiration for his vast stores of knowledge or his powers of communicating it.[24]

In the spring of 1842 came a visit to Belvoir, the castled estate of the Duke of Rutland. There Fanny received her first introduction to the ceremony of afternoon tea. On several occasions she received "private and rather mysterious invitations to the Duchess of Bedford's room." There she found a small circle of the feminine guests secretly employed in "brewing and drinking tea, with her grace's own private tea-kettle." At this time the honored custom of five o'clock tea had not progressed beyond such shame-faced, secret practice.[25]

Other house parties followed. Many evenings found the

family at Covent Garden, where Adelaide made her London début in *Norma* on November 2, 1841. At the masqued balls friends met Fanny in her favorite Spanish costume. Finally she returned to the profession of her earlier life in a private staging of *The Hunchback*, in which she appeared in her original rôle of Julia.

Two other significant events found places on her crowded social calendar. When the Duke of Rutland dined at the Royal Palace soon after the party at his estate, the Queen inquired why Mrs. Butler did not have herself presented at court. Such a suggestion was a social command. The expense of a dress for the occasion caused Fanny no slight trepidation, for she had already exceeded her allowance. She referred the matter to her "supreme authority" who decided that she should go. On the appointed evening she appeared in a gown of white satin and point lace trimmed with white Roman pearls. A rented diamond necklace and ear-rings sparkled as she approached her Sovereign lady, kissed a soft white hand, and made a sweeping courtesy to the Court. She "came away with no impression but that of a crowded mass of full-dressed confusion." Although Queen Victoria may have seen Fanny, the latter failed even to glance at her Empress. For once her calmness had forsaken her. Several weeks later she was presented to Dowager Queen Adelaide. Fanny disliked these merely formal demands of social custom. Although, as she said, she "would not go to the end of the street to see a drawing-room full of full moons," she felt obliged to obey the Queen's command and to present herself for her Sovereign's inspection.[26]

Eighteen months had passed since Mr. Butler's return from the Georgian plantations to a wife resolved to forget her own selfish grievances. During these months he voiced but one complaint against her conduct, a contribution to an anti-slavery fair.[27] Apparently they were more compatible than at any other period of their married life. But two such antithetical temperaments could not remain in a harmonious relationship. Her anti-slavery principles again provided the occasion for the disturbance of this congeniality.[28] When the question arose, it dragged with it that other anathema, her refusal to obey his wishes. Her indomitable will again clashed with the stubborn, uncompromising traditionalism of her husband.

In October, 1841, Fanny received a letter from Mrs. Lydia Child, editor of an anti-slavery paper in New York, soliciting portions of the journal kept on the Georgia plantations. Mr. Butler regarded Mrs. Child's procedure as shamelessly indelicate. He remonstrated against any recognition of the request, but Fanny always answered letters. That was a part of her code of honor, for a breach of which she could never have forgiven herself. Apparently she entertained no thought of releasing to the public any part of her journal. She rejected the request but suggested the possibility of substituting several letters written during her journey to the plantations which contained accounts of her observations along the way. According to her custom, she entrusted this reply to her husband for sealing and mailing.

Months later she found the letter in a drawer of the writing desk. Fanny saw no mitigating circumstances in this procedure. He had violated her trust, and any such act of faithlessness deserved nothing except contempt and scorn. With her usual lack of discretion when aroused, she dispatched another letter detailing the whole circumstances to Mrs. Child, perhaps in terms none too complimentary to Mr. Butler. Although neither her letter nor any other contribution from her pen found its way into the abolitionist journal, this request led to circumstances which helped to force asunder the southern slave owner and his abolitionist wife. It recalled those miserable experiences on the plantations and rekindled all the resentment she felt against the man who failed her in fulfilling her life's mission.[29]

One galling circumstance of Fanny's married life was the fact that she derived her support from the labòr of slaves. She felt that she made a daily and hourly sacrifice to her husband's conception of right. While on the plantation she sometimes refused to eat because the food had been earned by the unrequited Negroes. Also, after having spent her own money for several years, she resented the thought of being supported by anyone else's. She felt that no part of her husband's funds was really hers, not even her yearly allowance.

In the spring of 1842 Fanny owed a milliner's bill of £97 sterling, and this, she decided, she must pay by her own efforts. She therefore began a translation and adaptation for the English stage of Dumas's *Mademoiselle de Belle Isle*. Scarcely had the work got under way when she was reminded that her writing was not her legal property. A contemplation of the position of women with regard to their earnings awakened a wrathful though vain indignation. That a man whose wits could not keep him from starving for half a week should be able to claim as his own the results of his wife's mental processes seemed most unjust. Why should Madame de Staël not have demanded of Rocca, "If my brains are indeed yours, why don't you write a book like 'Corinne' with them?" Fanny could not persuade herself that anything which she created really belonged to anyone else. What her brains earned seemed hers regardless of the legality of ownership.[30]

In April, 1842, she left London for Liverpool, intending to return to America. Mr. Butler could assign no particular reason for this desertion. He attributed it to a recurrence of her moral disease, his designation for that morbidity which made her miserable in America. She omitted all references to their marital difficulties, and so his version remains unqualified by the proverbial other side of the misunderstanding. Whatever the cause for this strange procedure, she returned with her husband to London after he had pointed out the mortification which her sudden departure must bring to her father and sister.[31]

Other desertions, equally indefinite in circumstances, followed during the summer and fall. The cause seemed again to be her refusal to obey his will: "The other day when I asked you what it was you required from me when you rejected the attempt at a reconciliation, that my affection and conscience both prompted me to make, you replied, that until I *obeyed your will*, you would not be reconciled to me."[32] Fanny could tax herself with no disobedience except a refusal to answer a question about some money borrowed from her sister. This refusal resulted from his mode of interrogation, which aroused her pride, resentment, and resistance to a demand which she thought he had no right to make.

Mr. Butler thought that it was absurd to attempt to prove such a generally acknowledged point as the necessity of a woman's subjection to her husband. No one unless morally or intellectually astray could fail to see the heartlessness and falsity of her contention for equal rights.[33] With perfect self-complacency he phrased his reply: "On my soul and conscience I have done everything in my power to make you happy and contented as my wife. I have not succeeded, God knows: but if I have not, at least I can console myself with the knowledge of having done all that I could and the firm conviction that the fault is not with me. The fault has been entirely your own. . . .If you will govern your irritable temper, and if you can consent to submit your will to mine, we may be reconciled and may be happy."[34]

Fanny replied that she already had promised to endeavor to control her temper; to promise more with her nervous, excitable temperament and the temptations to irritation which naturally sprang out of their differences of disposition was unwise and unwarrantable. The second condition, that she submit herself to his control, she could not consider for a moment. Duty demanded her not to submit her conduct to the dictates of any other human being.[35]

Her refusal to accept his terms put an end to immediate attempts at reconciliation. Fanny remained with her sister, who finally attempted to act as mediator. Although Mr. Butler expressed his willingness to receive his wife on his previously stated terms, he refused to allow her return on any others. During eight years he had listened to the claims of a wife who contended that she had a husband who was not a husband but an automaton of companionship, friendship, and love without any rights. He had suffered too many trials again to risk going through that frequent sequence of events: quarrel, separation, reconciliation, and another quarrel.[36]

A letter from Fanny followed Adelaide's visit. She again implored pardon for past offenses. No self-righteousness blinded her to her past shortcomings. She offered every assurance which a fallible human being dared of her desire and purpose to fulfill her duty. If reflection upon his own share in the wreck of their peace suggested no terms of reconciliation except those which her conscience forbade her accepting, she requested some arrangement which would restore her to their children.

Should he refuse any compromise, she proposed separate establishments in the same house: "You have apparently lost all affection and regard for me," she wrote, "and have attained such a state of indifference towards me that you see me, meet me and speak to me as you would to one of your servants or a common acquaintance. . . .Having loved you well enough to give you my life, when it was best worth giving . . . you can never be to me like any other human being, and it is utterly impossible that I should ever regard you with indifference." If he refused to accept either proposition, but one alternative remained to her. She would hire a lodging in the same house with her father or near him and remain there.[37]

When she received no reply to this appeal, she took matters into her own hands. At twelve o'clock one night Mr. Butler answered a loud knock at his front door. Fanny had returned.[38] Either his chivalry or his fear of the scandal which would result from a man's turning his wife into the London streets at midnight gained her admittance.

The two disagree as to the relationship which followed her strange return. Mr. Butler said that for some time they maintained distinct establishments even at their meals. They received and answered invitations separately. Friends who noticed this unusual procedure finally brought about a reconciliation in February, 1843. They then continued to live as husband and wife during the remainder of their stay in England and for a short time after their return to the United States.[39] Fanny said that from the autumn of 1842, they lived separately and with a general discontinuance of all the relationships of husband and wife. His treatment of her, she continued, was such that she would have been warranted by the laws of God and of the land to depart from his house without incurring the charge of desertion or any other breach of her duty.[40]

That gossipy diarist—Clerk of the Privy Council, Charles Greville, characterized Fanny's life as a domestic tragedy without any tragical events. She married a weak, dawdling, ignorant, violent-tempered man utterly unsuited to her as she to him. With all her prodigious talents, fine feelings, noble sentiments, and lively imagination, she possessed neither tact, judgment, nor discretion. She acted like a fool—her detestation of slavery seemed the principal cause—and he became a brute. After becoming aware that he had outlived his liking for her, as she, her esteem and respect for him, she remained in perpetual fear lest their alienation should at last prevent their living together. She would then be separated from her children for whom alone she desired to exist. Meanwhile she saw her husband, brutal and unkind to her, ruining himself and the children by the stupid management of his affairs.[41]

The family had left Philadelphia in November, 1840, for a visit of several months. Two and one-half years later the Butlers were still in England. This long absence seems unusual when one recalls that all of Mr. Butler's interests were in the United States. Neither he nor his wife voiced any explanation. In April, 1843, Fanny said that for a year and a half she had been perfectly wretched at the protracted stay in Europe. As often as possible she protested against their long sojourn.[42]

During October, 1842, the family gave up the house on Harley Street, but instead of sailing for America they took apartments at the Clarendon Hotel. After another postponed departure they rented a house on Upper Grosvenor Street.

Mr. Butler's only comment on the delay was that although he designed to return to the United States late in the autumn of 1842, he changed his intention and determined to continue in London until the following spring.[43] One wonders whether any relationship existed between this protracted stay and Fanny's desertion. A year later a friend of hers, then acting as an attorney, instituted an investigation into Mr. Butler's life in London either to verify or to unearth proof of irregularities.[44]

The family landed in Boston on May 19, 1843. Instead of returning to Butler Place, Mr. Butler decided to remain at a boarding house in Philadelphia. Although acquaintances assured Fanny that she was comfortably situated, she felt a tightening about her heart when she thought of the only place in America which she had known as home.[45] During the years in the country, she had often imagined that she would be able to find some congeniality in the society which she could gather around her in Philadelphia. Now, although there, all such interests were denied her. She inhabited a bedroom in a boarding house, and the public rooms offered the only space available for the entertainment of visitors.

In Philadelphia she endured all of the unpleasant features of life at the farm without any of its few compensations: hot pavements instead of gravel walks, a public living room in place of her own parlor, and public parks instead of green fields. One could scarcely expect these unpleasant surroundings together with continued ill health to steady her excitable temperament. According to Mr. Butler's account, she soon relaxed into her old waywardness and irregularity. His obstinate demands and her stubborn resistance destroyed all vestige of happiness or compatibility.[46]

From her girlhood, riding had been her favorite exercise. Although Mr. Butler had galloped willingly with the English actress, Miss Kemble, even in sub-zero weather, he objected now to his wife's lonely trips around Philadelphia. In the summer of 1843, he sold her riding horse. In desperation she

9

sought for some means to re-purchase it from the livery-stable keeper. She gathered together ninety-four short poems, several of which she wrote almost twenty years before, and sold them for the necessary amount.[47]

Before publication of this small volume in 1844, her claims to recognition as a poet rested on her two dramas, on the short snatches of verse scattered through the journal published in 1835, and on occasional contributions to magazines. This volume raised the estimate of her poetic ability although the book contained no piece of length nor any ambitious poem. Never before had she written so simply and strongly, dealt so boldly with the realities of life, nor displayed an equal richness of imaginative power.[48] Her verses showed a remarkable masculine strength and vigor for an age when men were proud of the ability to write effeminate poetry.[49]

The lyrical, descriptive, and didactic poems, together with the few sonnets which made up the collection, showed in the tone and temper of their development their author's indebtedness to Dante, Shakespeare, and Milton. The melancholy and sorrowful spirit pervading and shadowing many of these productions especially suggested the influence of the Italian poet.[50] The author made no attempt to conceal the sources of the poems as fragments of her own experience. Many of them were autobiographical. Although some celebrated the heroic, many expressed feelings of dejection, melancholy, weariness of life, and almost despair.[51] Life conspired against man from the beginning of time. His struggle was futile, for sorrow and disappointment were foreordained as his lot. The best which he dared anticipate was the silence of death or a future life more favorably disposed to his anticipations:

> Struggle not with thy life!—the heavy doom
> Resist not, it will bow thee like a slave:
> Strive not! thou shalt not conquer; to thy tomb
> Thou shalt go crushed, and ground, though
>   ne'er so brave.

Fanny cared little what any one thought of her writings. To her they were excellent poems, because they provided the necessary number of dollars which she needed for the re-purchase of her horse.[52]

Even from the few indirect references which remain in her published letters, it is apparent that the summer of 1843 was most unhappy.[53] She had returned to America with the conviction that duty and not happiness was the purpose of life. While in Boston she had made a pilgrimage to the spot in Mount Auburn where she had left Aunt Dall nine years before. From the grave that companion's self-forgetfulness seemed to bid her niece be of good cheer and forget selfish interests.[54]

Fanny tried to crush her own preferences and to discipline her temperament. She wanted happiness for herself, for her husband, and, most of all, for her children. But she would not accept it at the sacrifice of what she conceived to be right. The ideal which she demanded was, perhaps, as her husband said, visionary and unpractical. But she had envisioned it. Although she might chasten herself for awhile, she could be satisfied with nothing less than the realization of her dream. The spirit was at last to burst the restraining bonds and to grasp, if not what it desired, the freedom which most nearly resembled that for which it struggled. In the summer of 1843 she was not yet ready to accept this alternative. She trusted that her situation might remain endurable. She overlooked many injustices because of her children. When no other bond could have held her, she remained with her husband performing such duties of a wife as he would accept and all the duties of a mother which he would permit. This state of affairs suddenly ended in October.[55]

During her husband's absence in New York Mrs. Butler found among the papers of his secretary two unsigned letters in feminine handwriting. Mr. Butler claimed that he had never opened either letter, but he refused any explanation of them. Instead, he delivered his wife a lecture upon the indelicacy of breaking seals on letters addressed to him and upon her unjustifiable conduct in looking among his papers.[56] These letters convinced her that he had been guilty of a breach of the primary obligations of the marriage contract at an early and less unhappy period of her married life.[57] Although six years had elapsed between the imputed moral irregularity and her knowledge of it, this discovery ended the last hope of reconciliation. His being an "antique adulterer" rather than a modern transgressor did not diminish the wrong.[58]

She consulted a legal adviser, Mr. Gerhard, who called Mr. Meredith to his assistance. On October 27, she informed her husband: "In consequence of your infidelity towards me, and your ill-treatment of me, I have come to the determination to be separated from you."[59] Theodore Sedgwick also came to her assistance. Through him the husband and wife reached a temporary agreement.

Mr. Butler refused to be a party to any formal contract of separation. No necessity existed for the interference of lawyers, he said, for he would make an arrangement which would secure his wife an independent residence. He offered two thousand five hundred dollars a year for her support. Since they then lived at a lodging house, she might maintain a separate apartment under the same roof, which would permit constant intercourse with her children. In return, he demanded that she conform to three indispensable conditions: not to go on the stage, not to advocate in print the abolition cause, and not to publish any writing which he disapproved of. Fanny accepted the offer with the understanding that the allowance be paid monthly or quarterly through Mr. Sedgwick.[60]

At an earlier period of his marital difficulties, Mr. Butler had appealed to members of the Sedgwick family for counsel. Now he denounced them bitterly for believing his wife's exaggerations and for assisting her. They were her allies in disseminating scandalous reports and in assisting her in a search for proofs of supposed infidelities. They accepted her word, he said, without seeking his explanation or contradiction.

Certain other happenings during the winter may have dis-

PIERCE MEASE BUTLER

From a daguerreotype. Reproduced through the courtesy of Dr. Owen Wister and Miss Florence B. Kane.

posed her friends to an unquestioning acceptance of her story. On April 15, 1844, Mr. Butler answered the challenge of Mr. James Schott of Philadelphia in a duel at Bladensburg, Maryland.[61] Mr. Schott branded Mr. Butler as one who under the mask of friendship had ruined the peace and happiness of an unoffending family.[62] He demanded satisfaction in a duel, which ended in a fiasco. After the exchange of two shots without damage to either party, the seconds withdrew the challenger.[63]

Such an occurrence must have been known to Fanny's friends and have influenced them to a ready acceptance of her allegations. Mr. Butler blamed her for all the unsavory gossip against him. Although society rang with his monstrosities of conduct at this time, he remained perfectly silent, he said. His assailant was his wife, and he was content to bear all the injury which she chose to inflict.[64] Apparently he forgot that Mr. Schott possessed a tongue and a grievance. This duel also militated against Mr. Butler's charge that his wife was accepting the compromise only as a temporary arrangement until she could gather the requisite testimony for a divorce on the charge of infidelity.[65] Although she demanded a separation, seemingly she never desired a divorce.

She acceded to her husband's arrangements in order that she might remain near her children. The agreement stipulated that her intercourse with them should be unrestricted, but soon this relationship was constantly interfered with.[66] In May, 1844, Mr. Butler tired of boarding house life and engaged a house of his own. This ended the plan for the maintenance of separate apartments. When she inquired about possible arrangements which would enable her to remain near the children, he dictated terms upon which she might accompany them to their new residence. All communication whether by word or letter must cease at once between her and every member of the Sedgwick family; she must continue no acquaintance with any person whom he disapproved of; she must not mention to friends any happening which might take place in his home; she must cease speaking of him in terms of reprobation and reproach. To him, these conditions seemed not at all unusual. They required merely what was essential to the well-being and right government of every family. If Mrs. Butler considered her duty to her children paramount, she would readily accede to the proposal.[67] He allowed her two days for a decision. When she failed to accept during that time, he said that she had abandoned her children and deserved no further consideration.[68]

She then took rooms in a boarding house nearer their home. Although Mr. Butler promised that she might see them daily, she was barely settled in her new apartment when he took them to Newport. After their return, he curtailed at his own pleasure the seven hours each week allotted as her portion of their time.[69] In December, 1844, she again sought a different adjustment of relationship with her children.[70] Mr. Butler reiterated his propositions of the previous spring with renewed emphasis on his first requirement, "to renounce at once and forever all communication with those low-bred, vulgar meddlers, the Sedgwicks."[71] When no other chance to remain near her children and to exercise a mother's privileges seemed possible, on December 18 she accepted these conditions. He excused the harshness of his terms because, he said, they were dictated not to a wife or even to a friend.[72] Although she complied with all demands in December, she did not receive permission to enter the children's home until March 3, 1845. Painting, papering, and re-furnishing necessary to her comfort served as pretexts for this delay. This indeed seemed an elaborate preparation for the advent of one neither wife nor friend but calumniator.[73] Once there she soon realized the futility of her sacrifices. She was represented to the children as the cause of all their inconveniences and disappointments. She was still deprived of her rights of their guidance and care.

In April after her return, Mr. Butler received a letter from Miss Sedgwick which contained an envelope addressed to Fanny. He delivered the letter, expecting her to return it unread. She interpreted his delivery as permission to receive it. But he intended otherwise: "You have lived in this house a little over a month, and you have already violated the principal condition which you bound yourself to observe while living under my roof. I will hold no intercourse with a person so utterly wanting in truth and good faith." When this aspect of the affair became known, she believed he had used the letter as a trap deliberately set to ensnare her.[74]

About this time Mr. Butler learned that the tongues of various gossips were wagging about the governess, Miss Hall. Without any proof as to the origin of the reports except a far travelled suggestion which pointed to Mrs. Butler as the source, he demanded that she acknowledge or deny having originated the imputations. He had failed to learn that she would not be driven by force. His method of approach aroused her stubborn resistance.

She addressed a note to the governess denying ever having spoken, written, or thought the injurious things attributed to her. Then she reminded Mr. Butler that in bringing such an accusation he must prove his charges otherwise than by suspicion or by the affirmation of a stranger. The guilt of propagating malignant falsehood was in her opinion greater than a breach of chastity. She demanded indisputable proof of his allegations.[75]

With the coming of summer Sarah and Fan went to the country again with no arrangements for her accompanying them.[76] Before their return in September she requested a re-ordering of circumstances which would place her in her rightful relation with her children. The experiment of the past six months sufficed to show that nothing except disorder and serious disadvantages could result from the existing state of affairs. She exercised no authority in their care or management. Such a situation she thought detrimental rather than beneficial to their development. If her remaining was not for their good, she could not consider a longer residence there.

When after ten days she received no reply to the requests

of her petition, she left the house, convinced that her longer sojourn was prejudicial to the children's welfare: "Should you at any future time see fit to restore to me my proper position towards my children, be assured that *nothing* will prevent my resuming it." With this promise she departed from Mr. Butler's home on September 10, 1845. Six days later she sailed for England, a friend having furnished the means necessary for the journey.[77]

At last Fanny disregarded convention and threw aside its imposed restraints. The society in which she lived, her own training, and her ideals insisted that a marriage endured as long as both parties to the contract lived, but no vows made her a slave. She remained an individual with a mental and spiritual life of her own. This individualism refused to be crushed. Although a proud will endured many humiliations because of its love and devotion to two little girls who needed a mother's guidance, it revolted when too fiercely assailed. When Fanny became convinced that the environment which surrounded her children was detrimental to their mental development, no tie remained to assuage the personal misery of her existence. She determined to make her life and that of her children, if not what she desired, the most wholesome which circumstances would permit. The inner voice again told her that she was acting wisely. She left her children's home with a sad heart—every vision of her youthful dreams lay in charred ruins—but she left with a clean conscience and a free will.

CHAPTER VIII

FOOTLIGHTS FOR HEARTH

WHEN Fanny reached London, she went immediately
to Mortimer Street, Cavendish Square, where her
father resided. Friends hastened to welcome her
home and to offer infinite suggestions as aids in her perplexing
affairs. Although even the wise Solomon believed in the safety
of numerous advocates, she found only bewilderment in their
opinions. Many suggestions were worldly, false, or full of
compromise between right and wrong for the sake of expediency, peace, profit, or social considerations. Fanny sat
listening to these friendly importunities, half the time shocked
at those who uttered them and the other half, shocked at
herself for being astonished at people so much her betters.

She had come to England upon Mr. Kemble's advice, and
his counsel guided her. He intended to return with her to
America. There, in addition to protecting her interests, he
planned for their return to the stage. If that seemed impracticable, he would substitute Shakespearean readings such as
he was then offering to English audiences.[1] True to the family
tradition he could not remain away from the stage very long.
Although he made several farewell appearances, a few years
at most found him again engaged in some theatrical activity.

The two meant to sail for America in November, but threats
of war growing from the agitated Oregon question made this
plan inexpedient. After they had decided to postpone this
journey indefinitely, her father suggested that Fanny spend
the winter in Rome. Adelaide now lived there, and she urged
her sister to come for a long visit.

From her girlhood Italy was the country of Fanny's dreams. During her prosperous years on the stage she had hoped to save enough money for the purchase of a modest home there. Now that Southern mania, as she referred to this aspiration, returned after many years of dormancy. When Mr. Kemble suggested her going, she was overjoyed; nothing else could give her so much satisfaction, she assured him. Since she had returned dependent upon his generosity, it remained for him to decide in what manner the burden would be least grievous, costly, and inconvenient. She now doubted whether she could live there continuously. Travellers depicted the state of the Italian people as one of social and political degradation. The contrast between these inhabitants and the remains of a past glory and beauty must grieve all who appreciated that lost grandeur. She clung to the feeling that some day she would return to her favorite Lenox by the side of the Bowl, the beautiful little lake among the Berkshires, where, she said, "selfishness and moral cowardice and worldly expediency exist in each man's practice no doubt quite sufficiently; but where they are not yet universally recognized as a social system, by the laws of which civilized existence should be governed."[2]

On December 20, 1845, Fanny set out from London for Havre. Friends described to her the picturesque beauty of the forest and mountain regions of the Nivernais. The rigor of the winters which she had experienced in Philadelphia should have warned her that in December the traveller must meet unexpected difficulties on such a journey. But her desire to see the natural beauty of this mountainous district and to return to Paris after an absence of twenty years prompted her to abandon discretion and to choose the route from Havre by Rouen to Paris, Orleans, Châlon-sur-Saône, Lyons, Marseilles, and Rome.

Although the scenery among the hills and mountains merited all the words of praise which it had received, other less inspiring circumstances marred the satisfaction of this route. A snowfall imprisoned the diligence at the miserable little village of Château Chinon. There Fanny and her maid passed the night in such a cut-throat looking place as neither had ever seen before. When it seemed likely that no stage would arrive for several days, they hired a rickety gig for sixty francs and trusted themselves to the care of a one-eyed, villainous looking driver who conducted them to Châlons. Although appearances belied his true character, Fanny regretted the venture after they were on the way. She feared that somewhere among the snow-covered gorges he meant to rob and murder them.[3]

In retrospect the mountain wildness, the romantic Rhone, the clay-colored towers of Valence, the Mediterranean by moonlight—a silver shield set in ebony—and the dazzling orange light of the evening sky at Leghorn compensated for the annoyances of filthy rooms, freezing diligences, unsavory meals, and rascally inn-keepers. As always the beauty of nature held supreme charm for Fanny.[4]

Before arriving in Rome on January 9, 1846, the traveller apologized many times for her earlier strictures upon Americans and their crude customs. If she had travelled more on the Continent before her journey to America, she would have been less surprised and amazed by the various unpleasant peculiarities of its inhabitants. When she observed and compared smoking and spitting on the Hudson to the same offenses on the Rhine and Rhone, she scarcely knew where to award a preference. Cuspidors were the bane of her life in the United States. Aboard the boat on the Rhone, an ordinary spittoon would have been a delight to her eyes. Frenchmen apparently had lost their natural grace of politeness without acquiring in compensation any decorum or decency of manners. They made unpleasant travelling companions. Their language frequently exceeded decency, and the tone of it bordered upon what Englishmen would have considered unwarrantable freedom.

After having censured many American inns for their insufficient ablutionary privileges, Fanny found herself in one of the best hotels in Paris with a thing like a cream jug for a water vessel and a basin the size of a small pudding-bowl. When she requested warm water for a morning bath, she received a little copper pot with an allowance such as a young gentleman shaving the faintest hopes of a beard would have found insufficient. England seemed the only place in the world where people were not disgustingly dirty, and the traveller sometimes doubted whether many were clean even there.

Experiences of the journey recalled, too, the security with which a woman might travel in America certain of assistance, attention, respectful civility, and humane protection, screened by sacred and universal care from every appearance of neglect or impertinence. The deference paid to women in the United States seemed almost too profuse, for it made young American women presume on their privileges. They were becoming saucy in their supremacy and unblushing in their mode of claiming and receiving it. While Americans pushed their courtesy toward the weaker sex to the verge of injustice, the French erred in the opposite tendency. After Fanny had travelled alone on the Continent, she truly appreciated the American deference to woman.[5]

In early life, the English girl had often thought of Italy, the treasure house of art and the trophy-laden temple of the past, but destiny led her elsewhere, to a land where hope beheld all things unshaped—America. There a fairer dream than the imaginations of youth entranced her for awhile and, then, lightning-like, departed. Now in the bankrupt days of her life, the vision of southern splendor again beckoned. This time she answered its summons and came to seek consolation in its art and nature. In associations with her sister, in the study of unusual customs, in the admiration of treasures of art, and in the contemplation of the past glories of Rome, she hoped to find something to assuage the loneliness of a disappointed life.[6]

Soon after her arrival came one of the most unusual celebrations of the year. The nine-day carnival which began on Saint

Valentine's day showed her an Italian non-religious celebration. Horse racing, masquerades with showers of confetti, and masked balls ended only with the grim entrance of Lent.[7] Then during this religious period she turned to the art galleries until the sacred celebrations of Easter claimed the attention of every inhabitant of Rome.

When she visited the various collections of paintings and sculpture, the traveller found many productions which exceeded her expectations. In others she felt a keen disappointment. The sickly coloring and feeble expression of Guido's paintings seemed weak and affected.[8] She felt an unconquerable aversion to all representations of physical pain. The sufferings of the nobler part of human nature, heart and mind, she believed the only ones which artists should portray. "Laocoön" was an intolerably painful miracle of art. "The Dying Gladiator" and the "Wounded Amazon," in whose pathetic gestures neither shame, sorrow, nor pain predominated but all blended, were almost the only works of art where the admixture of physical suffering was so treated as to be endurable.[9] She especially denounced all portrayals of the physical suffering of Christ. She preferred a fine landscape to a fine portrait. The copy of the human countenance, like the countenance itself, suggested the nature of man, unrest. The copy of nature, like nature itself, suggested God, repose.[10] The "Apollo of the Vatican" and Raphael's "Suonatore" were to her the consummations of man's achievements in sculpture and painting.

In May Fanny accompanied Adelaide and her family for the summer to Frascati, where they took a villa, formerly a favorite residence of the Borghese.[11] Early morning walks through the dewy vineyards, reading, music, and evening rides over the wide campagna to Lake Regillis or at the base of Monte Cavo succeeded the days in the art galleries and the morning walks through the markets of Rome. It was a perfect life, and to have led it for several months was a miracle. She found consolation but not forgetfulness. Memories of two little girls beyond the Atlantic intruded themselves into every hour:

> If there were any power in human love,
> Or in th' intensest longings of the heart,
> Then would the oceans and the land that part
> Ye from my sight all unprevailing prove,
> Then should the yearning of my bosom bring
> Ye here, through space and distance infinite.[12]

Nowhere else had the mutability of all things impressed her as here in Italy. All its past glory could not atone for the present shame of the people. The loveliness of external things failed to compensate for the ugliness of human souls without truth or honor: women without chastity, men without integrity, and a whole country without religion.[13] According to the Italian theory, women could not be trusted on any occasion. At night an Italian locked up his women servants and barred all the windows of their rooms. Want of honesty prevailed in both city and country. No matter how explicit one made the terms of any arrangement, when the moment to pay arrived, misunderstandings, misrepresentations, or misstatements always served as pretexts for extra claims. Beggary appeared incessantly.[14] The ruined aspect of outward things seemed cheerful when one compared it with the degradation of wretched, shameless paupers.[15]

The chief diversions of the people, and almost the only one in the rural districts, consisted of religious festivals. These occurred with a frequency which broke up all habits of industry. No one worked on a fiesta, and, on an average, every third day of the week was sacred to some saint, or rather to laziness, the great god of the Italians. Horse races, donkey races, foot races, the firing of guns, and the display of fireworks superseded the devotional character of these celebrations.[16]

Roman Catholicism in Italy was different from what Fanny had found it in the United States, where she had seen this faith of implicit obedience and absolute subserviency encountering the political spirit of unbridled democracy. There it thrived, spread, and flourished because it was separate from political affairs, for it was a religion and not a government. As a religion it remained the most pliant, malleable, insinuating, pervading, and powerful yet to exist; as a government it was rigid, uncompromising, despotic, and incapable of either receiving or accepting the impulse towards universal freedom which the world at this time obeyed. The Bishop of Rome might some time be head of the most powerful sect of Christendom; it seemed impossible that he could ever be the enlightened sovereign of a people with free institutions. When it attempted a double rôle, Catholicism failed in both.[17]

Even with all the pauperism, dishonesty, and irreligion of the country, prescience suggested to this observer that the great field of Roman glory was but lying fallow. For the full ripening of such a power as that colossal empire had been, hundreds of years were necessary. A proportionate time of rest must follow before the people of those lands could reproduce the elements of political greatness: "The priest-ridden ignorance and superstition, the laziness, the imbecility of the present government, are but like dung spread over the soil; the seeds ferment below that shall again cover these glorious countries with the noblest harvests of humanity; for in the moral, as the physical world, corruption is the cause of regeneration, just, unfortunately, as in civilization, ripeness has hitherto preceded rottenness but by a little space."[18]

On December 8, 1846, Fanny left Rome for England. She refused to accept the further generosity of her father or to deprive him of funds necessary for comfort in his old age. Distasteful as the profession of her early life had been, she now determined to return to the stage. Although most aspects of this undertaking were painful, it presented at least one encouraging feature. It provided a means through which she could work and support herself instead of living dependent on others.[19] Perhaps, too, the prospect was not as unpleasant as she imagined. Unconsciously, imperceptibly even to herself, the theater lust of the old stroller, John Ward, or of the young hairdresser, Roger Kemble, again may have stirred in her blood. When depleted finances necessitated her turning to some livelihood, no other vocation except the stage received consideration.

After she left America, Mr. Butler offered to secure an annuity of £200 sterling to her during her life and at her death to her children. In return she agreed to release her dower rights and to convey to him a fee simple title to his real estate. For this pledge she named Charles Sumner as trustee,[20] but Mr. Butler failed to secure the mortgage guarantee. Although he paid the allowance irregularly until February, 1847, she felt no surety of its continuance.[21] She thought it wise to find a dependable means of livelihood.

Upon her return to England, Mr. Moxon immediately accepted for publication *A Year of Consolation*, the record of her observations in Italy. This diary was not primarily a record of her own life, for she suppressed almost every reference to personal matters. She kept a record only because it suggested a possible means of earning something towards her support.[22] She was not disappointed, for the publisher offered more than she had anticipated for the manuscript.[23]

With all its occasional faults of petulance and recklessness, *A Year of Consolation* was a book such as no one but a woman of genius trained in the hard school of suffering could have written. Its style to all intents and purposes seemed Byronic. Every page was strongly colored by the author's own individuality and intense consciousness. Occasionally she startled the reader with a fearless, too-confiding frankness;[24] but her introduction of unfamiliar parallels attested to the truth of her impressions. One felt a sincerity which distinguished it from the usual books of travel.[25] The really valuable portions of the journal were accounts of her residence among the peasantry at Frascati and her trips into parts of the surrounding country seldom frequented by tourists.[26]

Although she possessed quick perception and shrewdness of

observation, she frequently spoiled vivid impressions by a careless and slovenly style. Some expressions and descriptions seriously offended the sensibilities of her countrymen. It seemed a pity, they said, that an author who could think and write well should often be utterly reckless in what she thought, wrote, and published.[27] As usual Fanny cared little what reviewers thought. Years before she had determined never to be reasoned into proprieties by the press gang.

The proceeds from the sale of this writing could not supply necessities for long unless increased by other resources. A second time the need of money drove her to the theater. On the evening of February 16, 1847, she returned to the stage of the Theatre Royal, at Manchester in the rôle of Julia.[28] She approached this return to a profession almost forgotten for thirteen years with a trepidation which the youthful débutante of Covent Garden had not experienced. During the years of retirement in private life, she had not improved her ability for acting by either study or experience. She had seldom entered the theater, and her thoughts had rarely reverted to anything connected with her former vocation. She had lost the personal qualifications for the younger heroines of the drama. "A stout, middle-aged, not particularly good-looking woman" seemed not a very attractive impersonator of Juliet or Julia.

A new use of stage makeup was one of the various changes which she now encountered. "The inevitable rouge, rendered really indispensable by the ghastly effect of the gaslight illumination of the stage, had always been one of its minor disagreeables" to her. Now she found that in addition to rouged cheeks, her fair theatrical contemporaries "literally white-washed their necks, shoulders, arms, and hands." She declined to adopt the practice. Her zealous friend, Henry Greville, indignantly insisted that what so beautiful a woman as Madame Grisi condescended to do should not be disdained by a comparatively ugly person, but Fanny remained unmoved. She "refused to make a whitened sepulchre" of herself, and "con-

10

tinued to confront the public" with her own complexion
although she looked "like a gypsy, or, when in proximity with
any feminine coadjutor, like a bronze figure arm-in-arm with
a plaster-of-Paris cast."[29]

Manchester audiences either overlooked her personal dis-
qualifications or were willing to excuse them. The name of
Kemble still held its charm for patrons of the English theater.
The warmth of the applause assured her that she stood before
an audience disposed to make allowance for any wrong that
time might have done to her person or any injury to her
style induced by long absence from the boards. Competent
judges soon perceived that the actress was mistress of herself
as well as of her art. She still depended on intellectual rather
than on physical force in her interpretations. For this first as
for the five succeeding performances people thronged to see
the last of the Kembles. Her stay became "a banquet of taste—
a holiday of intellect."

The actress's attention to attitude and gesture and her
dependence on these rather than upon declamation gave an
unusual dignity to such characters as Lady Macbeth. Although
her long absence from the stage made her self-conscious and
caused her to guard against inspiration as though she feared
it might lead her into extravagance, she came armed with
learning, style, and elocution. The English stage at this time
was lamentably deficient in all three.[30]

The proprietor of the theater raised the price of admission,
assigning as the reason Mrs. Butler's exorbitant terms, reported
as £500 for six nights.[31] Whatever the immediate remuneration,
Fanny felt satisfied with the experiment. It proved that her
theatrical strength still remained and perhaps would continue
to endure for several years. She hoped that by moving from
place to place her attraction would continue to be sufficient
to secure for her a small capital upon which she might live
independently.[32] She found that her power of voice and
delivery, which was favorable for tragedy, had not diminished;
her self-possession had increased, and that ought to be good

for comedy. The company provided to sustain her was commendable. It might have been excellent had all its members not been too great geniuses either to learn or to rehearse their parts.[33]

From Manchester, Mrs. Butler went to Birmingham. Although the management charged double prices for the performance, she played Julia to a full house.[34] From Birmingham she journeyed to the Theatre Royal at Liverpool. Here, assisted by Mr. Creswick, then at the zenith of his powers, she repeated the successes of Manchester. Although some critics thought that the art of the actress was too apparent in her mode of reciting the words, her actions and facial expressions were illustrative and appropriate. Her acting and declamation were of high order especially in passionate scenes.[35]

The self-consciousness noticeable during her first performances at Manchester rapidly diminished. She began to allow impulse to become a part of her interpretations. On one occasion she was busily engaged in conversation with a friend and almost missed her entrance in the third act of *School for Scandal*. On the spur of the moment she failed to recall just what tune Lady Teazle intended to hum. An astonished audience saw the actress rush into view to the words of

> Oh! Hi! Ho! the boatmen row
> Going down the Ohio,

the most popular Negro melody of the day. The unexpectedness, originality, or absurdity made it the hit of the evening.[36]

Accompanied by Mr. Creswick, the actress went from Liverpool to the Theatre Royal at Dublin.[37] Then followed appearances at Bath and Bristol[38] and a benefit performance for the stage manager of the theater at Manchester.[39] On April 26 she came to Princess's Theatre, London, with Mr. Creswick still as supporting artist.[40] Mr. Bunn, lessee of Drury Lane, had tried to stage Mrs. Butler's return to the boards in his theater. He failed, he said, because of her exorbitant terms, and that honor went to Mr. Knowles of Manchester.[41]

Perhaps circumstances favored her in necessitating the return elsewhere. She had an opportunity to re-acquire that practice which long absence from the stage rendered expedient before she appeared in London.

As usual *The Hunchback* was selected as her opening piece, probably because she originally created the rôle of the heroine in that drama.[42] Her main qualification for the performance of such characters now was her ability to give them the appropriate form and expression. Although her interpretations still lacked something of the spontaneity and the impulsiveness which produced strong natural effects, her style of acting was full of subtlety. It was suggestive in its by-play, in the space allowed for the progress of mental action, and in the judicious prominence and emphasis given to particular passages. To her succeeding character, Juliet, one critic paid the supreme compliment of saying that in the more tragical scenes it displayed much of the Siddonian feeling and expression.[43] Her conception of the character was vivid, her execution highly finished, and her judgment, clear. If she were not the greatest actress on the English boards, she at least was inferior to none.[44] Deep tragedy was now her forte.[45]

During the month which followed, the actress appeared in other of her once well known rôles: Mrs. Beverley of *The Gamester*, Mariana in Knowles's *The Wife*, and Mrs. Haller in *The Stranger*. The new generation of histrionic critics continued to discuss her ability and her acting. She united the study and elaborate conception of the Kemble style with the ideality and subtlety of the new school. The poetess and the woman were both conspicuous in her conceptions. To her, the highest point of acting was not the exciting of feeling but the awakening of the intellect, and the intriguing of the imagination. This idea could scarcely make her popular. If she were less fastidious in taste, she would be more loved even if less admired.[46]

This characteristic accounted for a public more apathetic towards her reappearance than the manager had anticipated.

FANNY KEMBLE AS JULIET

*From the Illustrated London News (1893). Courtesy of the Library of Congress,
Washington, D. C.*

While the critic of dramatic art found her portrayals surpassing his expectation, the public mind was less impressed.[47] Although the theater was comfortably filled at each performance, it was not until near the conclusion of her engagement in London that the houses were crowded. English patrons of the stage hailed her as their only legitimate actress. Even with her incapacity for juvenile tragedy, they hoped for the formation of a company selected to act the poetical drama with her as the leading actress.[48] Her return to the London boards again came at a time when devotees of the legitimate drama were deploring the fashion which induced the public to forsake Shakespeare for foreign art. Music performances and the importation of foreign artists such as Jenny Lind were usurping the places of the drama and of native actors. They hoped that Mrs. Butler might revive interest in the native poetical drama just as the youthful Fanny Kemble had done almost twenty years before.[49]

Fanny allowed herself only a short vacation during the summer of 1847. She could not afford to remain idle. Even though audiences during the warmer months were frequently small and the gains permitted her to lay aside only small sums, they prevented her being in debt. A few weeks, passed at a friend's home just beyond the Border in Scotland near Ercildown (Earlston), were her only vacation. No place could have been more inspiring to the actress. She revelled in the wildness and the romantic surroundings of the region associated with Burns's songs and Scott's *Border Minstrelsy*. Old superstitions dating from the days of Thomas the Rhymer pervaded the neighborhood. The Leader, a sparkling trout stream, famous in song, ran across her friend's lawn. Melrose and Abbotsford were only a few miles distant; "the bonnie broom of Cowdenknowes" bloomed in the neighborhood; the Gala, Tweed, and Yarrow ran through the lovely region. The Eildon Hills were the scenes of many walks, rides, and drives. After this visit and a few days with cousins in Edinburgh, she returned to her theatrical engagements.[50]

On February 21, 1848, Mrs. Butler returned to Princess's Theatre, where until March 17 she appeared as co-star with Mr. Macready.[51] Exponents of two opposing schools of acting clashed in these performances. The quiet, subtle, studied, intellectual style of the Kembles contrasted with the violent and "natural speaking" school which Macready represented.

Rehearsals as well as performances occasioned moments of both merriment and embarrassment for the stage manager. Actresses who appeared with Mr. Macready always feared for their safety whenever he approached them. Black and blue bruises were marks alike of his rage or tenderness. The actor was quite aware of his unpopularity. While the negotiations for Fanny's contract were pending, he alluded to his reputed irritable temper and violent efforts. The devil was not nearly as black as he was painted, the tragedian said. Fanny thought that he really tried to prove his contention. She finished the series with nothing more serious than a crushed finger and numerous bruises. Those who had observed his previous performances assured her that he was most considerate of her feelings and safety. She could not believe that he meant to be unjust to his fellow-actors. He was too much absorbed in himself and in his own effects to remember anyone else.

Acting with him was unpleasant. He kept no specific time for his exits or entrances but went off in the middle of a speech addressed to him or entered during a soliloquy. He stood two feet back of the person who attempted to address him, and growled and prowled around the stage until fellow actors never knew when he had finished speaking or where he would place himself. His lack of a musical ear made his delivery of blank verse defective and painful to persons better endowed in that respect.

The actress rejoiced when the engagement came to an end. Perhaps both felt relieved. He said she had no conception of the fundamental principles of her art. She retorted that his coarse and merely technical acting estimated success only by the violence of the stage effect produced. He scorned her willingness to play the rôle of Desdemona, because, he said, nobody could make anything of it. She replied that any rôle which Shakespeare created was too good for her to attempt to interpret.[52]

She did make something of Desdemona, something different from the conventional impersonation. Instead of the traditional white satin, she fashioned a black and gold gown which looked like those of Titian's pictures, the only habit of the noble Venetian ladies. She decided, too, that Desdemona must not have wanted to be murdered. All English actresses had appeared to "acquiesce with wonderful equanimity to their assassination." Fanny struggled and at last threw her arms tightly around Othello's neck—she had previously warned Mr. Macready and begged his pardon for the liberty—that being her conception of the poor woman's last appeal for mercy.[53]

Ophelia, too, received a rendering different from the conventional one. She became an important character instead of the sentimental young lady usually presented. Lady Macbeth and Queen Katherine showed perfect identifications of the actress with the characters. The Kemble voice and manner again ruled the London stage.[54] No representative of the histrionic art on the English boards, man or woman, according to one patron, equalled the performance of Mrs. Fanny Kemble Butler.[55]

These revivals of Shakespearean drama in London failed to achieve the prolonged success which the managers of the Princess's anticipated. Before the conclusion of the series Mr. Macready informed friends that he intended to retire from the stage at an early date because of the deplorable conditions of the national drama.[56] Almost all English theaters complained of a lack of patronage,[57] and the same tale of theatrical ruin came from every corner of Europe. With few exceptions the renowned singers of the time were in London.[58] After Easter, opera succeeded the drama at the Princess's because the legitimate stage failed to attract.[59] With her engagement in

London Fanny bade another and final farewell to the stage except for an appearance at a charity performance a week later.[60]

On March 25 she attempted her first public Shakespearean reading at Highgate.[61] She considered the possibility of dramatic readings before she decided to return to the theater, for they had proved a source of rich compensation to her father. While he still practised that art, she was unwilling to deprive him of any opportunity for profit, but when he definitely renounced all idea of continuing his appearances, she immediately began her study for this work.

In many details his successes were the models of hers. She followed his example in making one play the subject of each reading completed in two hours with an intermission of ten minutes. Although she desired to make a thorough study of each drama in its entirety, she soon realized, as her father had also, the inexpediency of such an undertaking. She therefore did as he had done—cut each play so as to conserve the entire story and as much of the beauty and wisdom of the production as the time limit would permit.

Although Mr. Kemble had limited his interpretations to the few most theatrically popular of the Shakespearean dramas, she included twenty-four, all the plays which could be read with any hope of attracting or interesting an audience.[62] This repertoire she invariably completed once before repeating any one of its items, because she wished to familiarize the public with those plays seldom or never acted, and because this scheme prevented her interpretations from becoming mechanical or hackneyed by frequent repetition. She persisted in this system, she said, in order not to debase her work.

The resulting loss to her proceeds was considerable. Large audiences always attended the reading of the better known plays, but fewer came for those which were unfamiliar. This procedure was one of the instances where Fanny's convictions decided the matter, and all her counsellors on two continents could not change her determination. Man did not live upon bread alone, she said. During the more than twenty years that she "followed the trade of a wandering rhapsodist," she never consciously sacrificed her sense of what was due to her work for the sake of profit.[63]

After a short tour of several smaller towns, she began her first London series at Willis's Rooms, King Street, Saint James, on April 3, with *The Merchant of Venice*.[64] The critical estimate of character and passion that distinguished her acting proved of excellent service in the more subjective interpretation required by dramatic reading.[65] Crowded audiences gathered to hear her presentations. Fanny Kemble had found her vocation for the following twenty years of her life.

While she was busily engaged in this work, on March 29, 1848, Mr. Butler filed an application for a divorce before the Court of Common Pleas in Philadelphia. He charged that on September 11, 1845, his wife wilfully, maliciously, and without reasonable cause deserted his habitation.[66] Mrs. Butler returned to the United States in May.

On October 9, 1848, she filed an answer to the allegations of her husband's application. Although she admitted that she left his house on September 10, 1845, and since that time had not returned, she denied that her absence had been wilful or malicious within the true intent and meaning of the Act of Assembly. The libellant, she said, for a long time previously absented himself from her as a husband; he gave his assent and license to her quitting his habitation; his conduct for some months previous was designed and calculated to force her away; his cruel treatment and personal indignities would have justified her departure even without his acquiescence.[67] Mr. Butler never invited her to return although her final note to him expressed a willingness to do so should he restore her to her proper relationship with her children. She now petitioned that the cause be tried by a jury on the issue or issues formed according to the Act of the Assembly.[68]

In October the application for divorce came before the Court of Common Pleas in Philadelphia.[69] On November 27

attorneys began their arguments before Judges King, Campbell, and Kelley. The prosecution contended that Mrs. Butler's
desertion had been wilful. Her countercharge of cruelty could
not enter into the case, they said. Cruelty in a legal sense
meant danger to life or limb, and the defendant brought no
charge of such hazards. Defense attorneys sought to prove
from Mrs. Butler's *Answer* that she was innocent of wilful
desertion. They contended that cruelty might be a mental as
well as a physical hazard. The arguments centered about these
two conflicting definitions of cruelty. Mr. Butler admitted that
his wife's conduct had been pure and her reputation intact.
His counsel did not deny the particular incidents detailed in
her *Answer*. They objected to an issue and called upon the
Court to decide upon the facts without the intervention of
a jury.[70]

In January, 1849, Judge King delivered the opinion of the
Court. It refused to decree a divorce and referred the case
to a jury for trial of the facts. Mrs. Butler's long answer submitted in the case was contrary to practice. All except her
mere denial of Mr. Butler's allegations were extraneous
surplusage and must be stricken from the record. The judges
gave it as their opinion that neither party could claim desertion
in a separation by common consent. Either party might
terminate the agreement by recalling the other. In that case
the party who remained absent from the time of recall was
guilty of desertion unless some previously sufficient cause
justified a refusal to return. Cruelties warranting the with-
drawal of an injured party need not be bodily injuries. The
refusal of the husband to furnish necessities, or a course of
humiliating persecutions, annoyances, and indignities also
amounted to legal cruelty. Through this decision Mrs. Butler
gained the point for which she petitioned, trial by jury.[71]

Although the case was docketed for April 16, 1849, it was
postponed.[72] Before September 3, when the application for
divorce again came before the Court of Common Pleas, Mrs.
Butler had agreed to a compromise in preference to further

litigation. Mr. Butler offered her an annual allowance of $1,500 with the privilege of her children's society during two months of each year. She, in return, withdrew her application for a trial by jury.[73] After this agreement, on September 22, 1849, the Court decreed a divorce which permitted both parties to remarry.[74]

More than a year had passed since Fanny's return to America. The friends of the Berkshires welcomed her back, and she had made her home there. When the details of the litigation demanded her presence in Philadelphia, she stayed at Washington House.[75] During the remainder of the months she dispensed her free hospitality at her cottage at Lenox, where her masculine costume and her skill in the management of a fleet steed attracted almost as much attention as her presentations of Shakespeare did elsewhere.[76]

Contentment and tranquillity if not happiness attended the granting of the Court's decree. The most painful and humiliating chapter of her life was closed. She could forget its cruelty now, and recall only the moments of felicity. Sometimes in her musings it seemed that these implacable years had never been. She was the young actress again, sitting under the trees on the velvety slope of Mount Auburn planning a rose garden for Butler Place.

CHAPTER IX

YEARS OF CONSOLATION

THE AUDITORIUM of the Masonic Temple in Boston overflowed with would-be listeners to another Shakespearean reading. Many, who had failed to procure tickets before the supply became exhausted thirty-six hours previously, now lingered near the entrance with the hope that seats might be crowded into the aisles or on the platform. When an elderly gentleman placed a chair behind the small, red desk and laid two large volumes on the crimson covering, the hum of conversation ceased. A moment later Mrs. Butler appeared from a door near the platform escorted by Charles Sumner, who sixteen years before had neglected his Harvard law studies to attend the young English actress's performances at Tremont Theater. After a gracious bow she pushed back the dark hair from her forhead—perhaps an unconscious expression of nervousness which she sought to conceal—and said with slightly affected emotion, "I have the honor to read the *Merchant of Venice*." She seated herself behind the desk, reviewed the characters, and then began the presentation of the play.

It seemed unbelievable, said a listener, that a single voice by reading of a play could produce the effect which followed her simple introduction. The power and genius of the reader held her audience for two hours in a silence interrupted only by spontaneous outbursts of applause. Her voice, expression, manner, and gestures portrayed the feelings of each character. One moment the fiendish rage, hate, and vengeance of Shylock ruled in her countenance and voice; the next Christian Antonio's submission to his fate. Then sweet Portia described her lovers, acted the judge with dignity and wisdom, or tantalized her husband with the loss of his ring.[1] At the close of the interpretation the audience called loudly for the reader. Finally she responded with a courtesy: "I can't make any speech not in my book, but I thank you with all my heart."[2]

In one of her sonnets she perhaps disclosed the secret of her own power:

> Oft, when my lips I open to rehearse
> Thy wondrous spells of wisdom and of power
> And that my voice and thy immortal verse
> On listening ears and hearts I mingled pour,
> I shrink dismayed—and awful doth appear
> The vain presumption of my own weak deed;
> Thy glorious spirit seems to mine so near
> That suddenly I tremble as I read—
> Thee an invisible auditor I fear:
> Oh, if it might be so, my master dear!
> With what beseeching would I pray to thee,
> To make me equal to my noble task,
> Succor from thee, how humbly would I ask,
> Thy worthiest works to utter worthily.[3]

Such sentiment explained the introduction which invariably preceded every presentation, "I have the honor to read . . ."

When in 1848 Mr. Butler's suit for divorce necessitated her return to America, Mrs. Butler cancelled six weeks' engagements at a loss of more than six hundred pounds.[4] After a summer with friends at Lenox she decided to redeem this forfeit by a series of readings in America. She chose Boston for the experiment, because that place was famed for its intellectual interests. She recalled her triumphs on the stage there sixteen years before. In no other city had she found social position determined by mental cultivation.[5] Friendships also drew her there, and sentiment as well as the possibility of greater financial return suggested its expediency. An appearance in Philadelphia would have savored too much of appealing to cheap publicity or of bearding the lion in his den. She would not embarrass the man still her husband by a return to the stage in his own city.

One gossipy newspaper proposed the protection of her money bags from Mr. Butler as a reason for her avoiding Pennsylvania. A man ought at least to have the gallantry of a sultan of the barnyard and to scratch for the weaker vessel, said the scribe. Since Pennsylvania did not insure a wife's property and earnings against despoliation by her husband, Mrs. Butler deserved to be complimented for taking refuge in a state which did.[6]

Another newsmonger denied any such motive, saying that, fully recognizing to the last moment Mr. Butler's lawful claims upon her as his wife, she sent him a check for twenty thousand dollars, the returns from her Shakespearean readings. He, of course, declined to receive it.[7] Although both stories were only gossip, they indicate the public interest in her affairs at this time. Such concern was more acute in Philadelphia than elsewhere. She wanted success or failure to depend upon the merits of her work itself. In order to eliminate in so far as possible a result determined by publicity, she decided to make the attempt in the recognized intellectual center of the country.

Her faith was rewarded. When she took her place on the stage of the Masonic Temple on the evening of January 26, 1849, an enthusiastic audience awaited her. Her interpretation pleased her listeners. Contrary to what many expected, she did not concentrate all her powers upon some few grand and striking parts. Instead she preserved the entire story of the drama and its finer poetical passages. Although the partiality for definite portions was not pronounced, she slightly favored those of a tender and pathetic cast.[8] She convinced her hearers that even though "the fire of true genius had been hidden for many years, and, seemingly, had burned low for want of fuel, it was still undimmed."[9]

That evening was but the beginning of her success. Every

reading increased the demands for admittance to each of her four weekly presentations. Seats sold for one dollar, but some listeners gladly paid five dollars for a place.[10] Many had feared that the legitimate drama again was losing its hold upon the public because of the inefficient mode in which the old dramatists were presented. Then Mrs. Butler appeared and turned the heads of the sober-minded and fastidious Bostonians by her interpretations of Shakespeare.[11]

One month after her first appearance she still read in Boston to overflowing audiences, which obtained the coveted tickets as much as forty-eight hours before the opening of the auditorium doors; and she had received invitations to appear in other cities, including New York. Although a little extra enthusiasm resulted from her peculiar circumstances and from the fact that to praise her presentations became fashionable, opinion agreed that the readings were performances of great excellence and beauty.[12]

The poet Longfellow's enthusiasm took him to almost every drama of the series and afterwards to the "charming little gay suppers" at the Revere House. There the reader entertained such other friends as Mr. Hilliard and Charles Sumner with descriptions of the cold evenings at Pittsfield, where "the pitiless sky at night was like an armory hung round with steel weapons" and the crackling ice seemed like the "breaking of the great bass strings of a harp."

Evening after evening the poet jotted down incidents of these congenial gatherings and his impressions of the readings which preceded them: "Mrs. Butler read *King Lear* and wonderfully well; too tragic a play for those who have any sorrows of their own. . . . *Hamlet* sublimely read; with the only true comprehension and expression of the melancholy Dane I have ever had the good fortune to hear. What nights these are!— with Shakespeare and such a reader":[13]

> O precious evenings all too swiftly sped!
> Leaving us heirs to amplest heritages

> Of all the best thoughts of the greatest sages,
> And giving tongues unto the silent dead!
> How our hearts glowed and trembled as she read,
> Interpreting by tones the wondrous pages
> Of the great poet who foreruns the ages,
> Anticipating all that shall be said!
> O happy Reader! having for thy text
> The magic book, whose sibylline leaves have caught
> The rarest essence of all human thought!
> O happy Poet! by no critic vext!
> How must thy listening spirit now rejoice
> To be interpreted by such a voice!

concluded that appreciative poet.[14]

In March Mrs. Butler went to the Stuyvesant Institute in New York, and the month which followed brought a repetition of her success in Boston.[15] On three evenings and one morning each week, the Institute was crowded almost to suffocation with the élite of New York. Here, too, Shakespeare regained his influence at the nod of fashion. The same potent dictum, said one partisan, installed Mrs. Butler as High Priestess of the inspired Bard and the only true interpreter of his divine imaginings.[16] Many persons who had attended Macready's readings preferred hers; her presentations smacked less of the stage.[17] Although they revealed less philosophical dissection, she clothed them with an almost indescribable charm and fascination. Her interpretations were more effective, picturesque, and popular; Macready's, more philosophical, suggestive, and acute. Her style was adapted to the world; his to the college.[18]

When Mrs. Butler announced that she would read *Measure for Measure*, fastidious New York set her down as the boldest of her sex. Apparently none of the scandalized inhabitants who were fortunate enough to obtain tickets missed the performance. After the presentation they felt half inclined to rank her as the cleverest rather than as the most audacious of women. Even those who still regretted her choice admired

the tact and skill which carried her through this drama never
before attempted on an American stage.

Many congratulated her upon her failure in Falstaff of the
Merry Wives of Windsor. That a cultured lady could interpret
his coarseness seemed an impossibility. Had she succeeded
with this lout, said an admirer of her characterizations, she
must have suffered the loss of some of the high regard which
she enjoyed.[19] Beatrice of *Much Ado About Nothing* with wit, the
overflowing of a joyous spirit, instead of sarcasm as her predominant characteristic, was acclaimed the reader's most
brilliant effort.[20]

New York revived an interest in Shakespearean drama.
Although the auditorium was uncomfortably crowded, large
numbers still turned away unable to obtain admittance.[21]
Mrs. Butler had found a pocket of gold. Her receipts for the
month at Stuyvesant were estimated at $8,000.[22] She must
have felt no inclination to regret the exchange of the six
hundred pounds foregone in England for the two months'
income from her Boston and New York appearances.

On April 2 she began a series with *The Tempest* in the chapel
of the Female Academy in Albany,[23] followed by three readings in Brooklyn,[24] which netted $2,000.[25] Then came a return
engagement at Stuyvesant Institute.[26] While there she donated
the use of her talent to a public charity. At about the same
time she gave $300 to a fund for the relief of the family of
Edmund Simpson, an actor who died leaving his wife and
children in destitute circumstances.[27] Generosity distinguished
her whole career.[28] The sight of suffering or poverty was
unbearable to her. The beggars of Rome spoiled her year
there; the suffering of the Negroes on the plantations was
unendurable. She always alleviated physical misery when
possible. When opportunities came for the exercise of her
dramatic ability in philanthropic enterprises, she never refused.
Whatever an appearance would earn found its way to the
relief fund of the organization requesting her aid.

Although she returned to dramatic interpretation because

11

of the rich profits which it offered, she did not hoard her earnings selfishly. Neither was she willing to rest upon the recognition of past endeavors. When an assembly paid to hear her read, she gave the best of which she was capable. She studied and planned how to make her interpretations more attractive and more worthy of the great poet whose creations she read. In a few years she developed an original technique, a type of presentation which critics found it impossible to describe and analyze, or disciples to imitate.

After the conclusion of the second engagement at Stuyvesant Institute, Mrs. Butler spent the month of May in touring the State of New York, where engagements took her to Auburn, Syracuse,[29] Buffalo,[30] and Rochester.[31] Then she returned by New Bedford[32] to Boston, where for the first time in America she read to a thin house. The hot weather, one scribe reported, "played the deuce with all theatricals in the city" and made the so-called benefits of the actors anything but beneficial.[33] After this appearance she departed for Lenox, where she took rooms for the summer at Wilson's Hotel.

Fanny first went to the Berkshires in 1834 to be near her friend Catherine Sedgwick. When she had once seen their natural grandeur, they became the object of her annual pilgrimages. To her, nothing else could be compared with the sight of the valleys dotted by small lakes, the uplands clothed with grain fields, and the orchards studded with farm-houses. She liked to wander among the hills covered from base to brow with every variety of forest tree; to follow the clear, mountain brooks bordered with masses of granite rock; to ride over the mountains canopied by a cloud-varied sky.[34] Almost every summer spent in America found her for at least a few months among these surroundings.

Visitors as well as permanent dwellers formed a congenial society. The Sedgwicks remained the constant center of the group, and their home became the meeting place of many notables. Two miles west of Lenox on Stockbridge Bowl, Hawthorne came in 1850 to reside in the Red House and to write *The House of the Seven Gables*, *A Wonder Book*, and a part of *The Blithedale Romance*.[35] Mrs. Kemble often rode up to the door on her strong black horse and conversed in heroic phrases with the inmates of the Red House. Sometimes she asked little Julian whether he would like to take a ride. Upon his emphatic affirmative she swung him astride the pommel of her saddle and galloped off. When they returned, she reined up with one hand and grasping her cavalier with the other held him out at arm's length: "Take your boy!—Julian the Apostate!" she called to his father.[36]

In the autumn of 1851 Hawthorne moved from the Bowl to Fanny's own little cottage on Kemble Street, Lenox, which she bought and named The Perch. Although he regretted the loss of the view from the Red House, her rooms were larger and more convenient, and she offered her furnished cottage for the same price as he paid for the smaller place.[37] Several miles away Herman Melville resided at Arrowhead, fed hay to his horse and pumpkins to his cow, and wrote *Moby Dick*.[38] At intervals during the summer months Bryant, Longfellow, Holmes, Dr. Channing, Charles Sumner, Henry Ward Beecher, Bret Harte, and Harriet Hosmer came to Lenox.[39]

Some enthusiasts claimed that Fanny made her first attempt as a Shakespearean reader with Catherine Sedgwick, Melville, Longfellow, and Hawthorne in her audience.[40] Be that as it may, Lenox remained to her the most beautiful and congenial spot in America. Although the town did not receive her very kindly at first, as the years passed she became a tradition. At first the mimic world behind the footlights to which she belonged was in too great contrast with the stern realism of New England for her coming to be entirely welcome. The plain townsmen saw only the features of a great adversary behind the mask of comedy. One of the village papers said that Miss Kemble had lost all delicacy of sex strolling about the country as an actress. But time softened this rigid estimation, and she became one of the most popular women of the community.[41] She gave readings in the halls for charitable purposes, made donations to the library, and presented the village with a clock for the Congregational Church.[42]

Fanny yielded herself to an unconventional recreative life among the Berkshires. She often rode ten or twelve miles— tradition said *à la chevalière*—before breakfast.[43] With a few friends or sometimes with a group of young ladies from Mrs. Sedgwick's school, she rode or rambled over the mountain tops where each member of the party tried to spy out the finest view and to excel her companions in the use of descriptive adjectives. One popular excursion led to Monument Mountain, where Fanny ascended to the topmost crag and declaimed the vain struggles of the Indian girl celebrated by Bryant. Other trips led to Greylock, to Salisbury Twin Lakes, to Mount Washington, or to the wild gorge of Bash Bish.[44]

Next to mountain excursions, Fanny preferred angling. Often from eight in the morning until sunset she might be seen on Laurel Lake or Stockbridge Bowl accompanied by a young boy of the neighborhood hired to row the boat. The former actress had her own ideas about dress, and for fishing trips she appeared in blouse, trousers, and boots. Mrs. Sedgwick, with the New England woman's regard for the conventional proprieties, questioned: "Fanny, how can you bear to make yourself so conspicuous?" "Elizabeth, I won't listen to moralizing on this subject. When I go on the stage, I dress for the occasion; and when I go a-fishing I dress for the occasion."

One day this lady accompanied her. The water ran into the boat; Mrs. Sedgwick's long skirt was saturated with the dirty water. Fanny called attention to the superiority of her own costume. As they rowed ashore, she clinched the argument with the crushing remark that her companion was the most bedraggled creature whom she had ever seen.[45] Archery was another form of recreation in which she excelled. Charles Sumner recorded with elation that he witnessed a contest at which Mrs. Butler hit the target in the golden middle.[46]

During more than forty years, Fanny continued to spend

her vacations among these mountains and gorges where she had found her dearest friends in America. After she sold The Perch she rented the Kneeland place and superintended farming activities during several summers. Here upon one occasion she decided to serve beer to the men who were cutting hay. Charles Sedgwick remonstrated earnestly. She was introducing among the laborers "a mischievous need and deleterious habit" until then unknown at Lenox, he protested. She listened to his scolding and cancelled the order for the beer, saying, "My meadow was mowed upon cold water from the well."

Later in life she again took rooms at the hotel: "Your American people are very stupid not to come and see all this," she said as she looked at the Berkshires. "Some day they'll find it out, and Lenox will be a great place."[47] When she walked by the village cemetery, she added, "I will not rise to trouble anyone if they let me sleep there. I will only ask to be permitted once in a while to raise my head and look out upon this glorious scene."[48]

With the end of summer Fanny's thoughts again turned to her readings. When autumn came, the actress felt a restless stirring in her blood until the footlights were again in view. She now felt at liberty to accept invitations whenever they were offered. She was no longer Mrs. Butler, for the divorce granted in September severed the marital tie. She decided at last to gratify the importunities of Philadelphia friends by a series of interpretations there. On October 1, 1849, as Mrs. Kemble, she resumed her dramatic readings at Sansom Street Hall with *As You Like It*.[49]

The attitude of the Philadelphia public must have caused Fanny some concern. Would it welcome her or resent the unsavory publicity which her departure from England four years before had brought to one of its prominent citizens? On Saturday before her first appearance an editorial comment in part allayed her anxiety. The writer assured Mrs. Kemble that she held a holy place in the hearts of Philadelphians.

For a long time they had desired the opportunity to testify to their appreciation of her talents and at the same time to indicate their sympathy for her.[50] This editor voiced the sentiments of at least a number of the inhabitants, for during five weeks audiences filled the lower salon of Sansom Street Hall to listen to her interpretations.[51]

Such entertainments were extremely popular throughout the country at this time. During the autumn of 1849 almost a score of persons read Shakespearean dramas in various cities of the United States.[52] Several considerations aided in their winning general favor. These readings presented an opportunity for persons opposed to the theater to enjoy some of its entertainment without violating their scruples. Many people, partly Puritan and partly Grundyish, wanted to go to the theater, but they let, "I dare not wait upon I would." They compromised the matter by shaking hands with his Satanic Majesty in kid gloves at the lecture hall.[53] Another determining factor was the ability of the dramatic reader to present his art under conditions which would have made the staging of the drama itself an impossibility. A small stage or lecture hall sufficed as a setting. No large cast increased expenses beyond the patronage of the smaller cities. Some lovers of Shakespeare preferred the talented reader to the average theatrical company which presented one or two competent actors for the leading rôles but provided incompetents for the remaining characterizations. This combination of circumstances presented a situation which liberally rewarded skilled interpreters of dramatic literature.

After her success in Philadelphia, the artist for the first time sounded the dramatic temper and interest of the West. She read in Pittsburgh,[54] continued on to Cincinnati where six interpretations netted $1,600,[55] and then returned to Pittsburgh for a second series.[56] Although she received invitations to appear in southern cities, she persisted in her determination not to give readings for pay in the slave states.[57]

Although she appeared in Baltimore for the benefit of the

Commercial Library Association, she refused an invitation to give a series of readings there. People of the South, said a reviewer, might charge their "peculiar institution" with depriving them of her interpretations. They could console themselves by listening to Miss Kimberly, who was not so fastidious as to scorn their money and who perhaps was inferior to Fanny only in name. One facetious commentator thought Mrs. Kemble's conscientious scruples were subject to a sort of Wilmot proviso. She received money from a divorced husband who derived his revenue chiefly from slave property in a slave state. Her only objection in this case seemed to be the smallness of the amount. Genius sometimes unfortunately appeared ridiculous.[58]

By December 17, she returned to New York in order to lend her assistance at a benefit entertainment of the Saint George's and British Protective Emigrant Association.[59] Here almost twenty-seven hundred persons listened to *As You Like It*. One characteristic of the reader could not have been more vividly portrayed than in her reply to the organization's words of appreciation: "I am an English woman—why should you thank me?"[60]

Fanny observed that each member of the management committee wore a handsome silver badge of Saint George and the Dragon on the left breast of his coat. The well known symbol touched a patriotic chord in her heart. Although she resisted, she felt tempted to ask one of the gentlemen to lend her a badge for the evening. Some days later a number of the members presented her with a gold emblem similar to those which she had coveted. The charter prevented their making her an honorary member of the organization, they explained, but they desired to express their thanks for her aid.

Always after this the ornament appeared as part of her costume for the historical plays. Its peculiar character excited many comments. A friend reported a comical discussion between two gentlemen, one of whom maintained that it represented a foreign order given by some royal or princely personage: "I'll tell you it isn't," was the rather testy reply; "she never was *ordered* abroad or at home by anybody." The listener thought the gentleman must have known Fanny.[61]

Upon one occasion the badge dropped into the crack of an old oak wardrobe. When weeks later a maid found it by chance, Fanny had given up all hope of ever seeing her knightly insigne again. Although she was glad to regain possession of her patron saint, she felt half inclined to resent its coming to light for a least a hundred years. Then, she knew, it would have occasioned pretty speculations and wise disquisitions concerning the who, how, why, where, and when, and what women were or were not entitled to belong to the orders of knighthood.[62]

Fanny spent the Christmas holidays with friends at Lenox and then resumed her interrupted readings.[63] Her philanthropic interest again found expression in benefit readings for Hungarian refugees, for invalids in New York, and for the Saint Joseph's Hospital, an institution at Green Hill. Her generosity knew neither race, color, nor creed. That a person or group needed assistance was sufficient to gain her sympathy. Mr. Bass of the Astor Place Theater tendered her an offer to return to the stage, but she refused to resume a profession which always had been distasteful to her.[64] Her readings offered a lucrative prospect, and perhaps the greater freedom which she enjoyed in her new vocation also militated against her return to this less congenial atmosphere.

On April 29, 1850, Julia Dean appeared at Astor Theater as Gabrielle in Mrs. Kemble's *The Duke's Wager*, a translation of Dumas's *Mademoiselle de Belle Isle*.[65] Apparently the play was advertised as her creation, and some confusion followed. Some critics reported that the management bought it as an original production, and the price paid, $500, created a sensation. Many thought that this was an extortionate demand even for an original play. Some felt that she could have written the drama; others refused to reconcile the idea of any woman's writing on an incident so foreign to female delicacy. Those better versed in dramatic literature recognized the situation as one which presented excellent dramatic possibilities utilized by writers since the time of Shakespeare.[66] The translation evidently possessed some merit, for the play did not disappear immediately from the repertoire of American theaters. In 1858 Julia Dean Hayne presented it in Boston.[67] Fanny probably took little interest in its success or failure. She had fulfilled her obligation with the translation. If Americans received a shock from seeing the Duke enter a lady's room, that was a reflection on the prudery of the audience and not on the drama.

In the summer of 1850 Fanny returned to England for an indefinite stay. She hàd not quite finished making her fortune in spite of the newspaper accounts of her fabulous wealth. She preferred, she said, to put the finishing strokes to it among her own people.[68] After readings in several provincial towns, she gave a series at Saint James Theater, London. She spent another year in the smaller cities of the United Kingdom[69] and then returned to London on February 3, 1852, where she read *Midsummer Night's Dream* to the accompaniment of Mendelssohn's music.[70] Although this became a popular production, London audiences desired to hear other plays. She seemed obstinate in her refusal to read *Antony and Cleopatra*, as though her "Egypt" were not one of her most excellent pieces in conception and execution.[71] Those more familiar with her procedure knew that she recently had read this drama elsewhere, and it must wait until all others of her repertoire had their turn.

In January, 1853, Fanny went to visit Adelaide in Italy. She neither loved nor liked Italy as she did Scotland. She gladly would have exchanged the sight of its shores, world-renowned for beauty though they were, for a glimpse of the bleakest stretch of the howling wilderness between Moy and Inverness. The natural loveliness of Italy was of the type least attractive to her. The severe, the stern, the wild, and even the savage were far more congenial to her taste than a profusion of shining, glittering, smiling, sparkling, brilliant prospects.[72]

After a summer at Sorrento, the Sartoris family again took a house in Rome. There the sisters found an agreeable society. Thackeray and the Brownings made it both witty and poetical. With these and other intimate friends, Mr. Leighton, the artist, Mr. Ampere, the philologist, and Harriet Hosmer, the sculptress, Fanny enjoyed riding over the campagna and lunching in the midst of the lovely in nature or of the picturesque, ruined remains of Roman power.[73] Mrs. Browning thought Adelaide more lovable and sympathetic than Fanny. Still she enjoyed the renewed associations with her former friend, who looked magnificent with her black hair and radiant smile: "A very noble creature, indeed, somewhat unelastic, unpliant to the eye, attached to the old modes of thought and convention, but noble in quality and defects; I like her much. She thinks me credulous and full of dreams, but does not despise me for that reason, which is good and tolerant of her, and pleasant, too, for I should not be quite easy under her contempt."[74]

Fanny returned to England in July, 1854. Incessant dyspepsia and other unfavorable Italian influences, she said, sent her home "as thin as a lathe and as light as a feather." After several months spent with friends sight-seeing in Ireland, she went to her father in London. When after a brief illness he died in November,[75] she lost the strongest personal tie which held her in England. Those last weeks with him were the source of much satisfaction to her. The fear of hearing of his death haunted all the years passed in America. Now she could leave England knowing that another crushing message such as that which told of her mother's death would never follow her to her adopted country.

In May, 1856, Fanny returned to the United States.[76] Once again she spent the summer at Lenox with her daughter Sarah as a companion. The girl felt the charm of Lenox just as her mother always had. Together they passed many afternoons reading and evenings with Sarah at the piano playing from her mother's carefully selected music.[77] With winter came the dramatic readings. When she counted the proceeds of a hard winter's work, she thought she might become a rich woman some day. Her tour again took her as far west as St. Louis and the western shore of Lake Michigan.

The hurry of life in that part of the country, the rapidity and enterprise which carried civilization forward, baffled description and seemed unbelievable. Cities of magnificent streets and houses, wharves, warehouses, storehouses, and shops full of Parisian luxuries existed where a few decades before forests grew and savages wandered.[78] An experience in Milwaukee vividly impressed upon her the thrift of the tradesmen in this rapidly growing section. An extortionate hotel bill elicited a communication to the editor of the *Milwaukee Sentinel*. The charges for one week's stay of herself and maid at Walker House totalled $91.50. The landlord claimed $10.00 for the use of his piano, $7.00 for fires, and $42.00 for an extra parlor. Although she suspected that any person who made such charges was insensible to shame, and that the publication would not affect him, a statement of the facts might afford amused astonishment to some citizens.[79]

Living in America was irksome to Fanny. She was often sad when she reflected that it must be her home for the remainder of her life. She desired to live beyond the Atlantic, but her children held her in America. This enforced habitation made them *dear*, she said, in more than one sense of that word. Expenses were extravagantly high. The discomforts, which one obtained for an amount which would have purchased a liberal allowance of luxury in Europe, were by no means the only annoyance.

In New York, where she remained during part of the winter, she paid sixteen guineas a week for lodging and board for herself and maid. For this sum she inhabited a good-sized drawing room burdened with three looking glasses set in superb frames, green and gold satin curtains, and carpet and rugs of the most resplendent rainbow colors. The bedroom attached to this "magnificent trumpery" was no larger than a small closet. It had no curtains at the window or bed, and no fireplace. The bed was pushed against the door so that it could not open wide. A washstand, a sunk marble basin without any substitute for a towel horse, completed her quarters. This juxtaposition of drawing-room and bedroom spoke volumes for the love of finery and the ignorance of all decent comfort which seemed alike semi-barbarous.[80]

The first of December ended the best part of the year for Fanny, for at that time Sarah returned to Philadelphia for the winter months. Soon after her departure, the reader returned to her vocation. She labored industriously so that the time until summer returned bringing the one happiness of her year, the months with her children, might seem shorter.

When she went to Syracuse, a worthy clergyman of that city importuned her to bestow an hour's reading on a convention of county schoolmasters and schoolmistresses. She found what she described as an assembly of nearly two hundred intelligent, conceited, clever, eager-looking beings with sallow cheeks, large heads, and narrow chests and shoulders. They displayed all combinations of the physical characteristics which distinguished this restless, ambitious, pretentious, and ignorant people whose real desire for improvement seemed to be equalled only by the shallow empiricism of their cultivation. There was something ludicrous in the desire of the people of the New World for the "fine blossoms and jewels of civilization" while they neglected the roots and foundation of learning and civilization. These schoolmasters and mistresses desired to hear the celebrated actress read in order to catch something of her style. Then they would elocutionize from Shakespeare and Milton although in their daily conversation they employed *dog* English which neither Shakespeare nor Milton could have recognized as his native tongue.

Fanny's reading progressed in this fashion: "I will read you Hamlet's soliloquy and speech to the players." Having finished,

"The air of this room is pestiferous. You have here no ventila-
tion, and two rusty sheet-iron stoves all but red hot. I will
now read you the lament of her brothers over the supposed
dead body of Imogen." At the conclusion, "You have now
thrown open windows at the top and bottom, on opposite sides
of the hall, producing violent draughts of cold air. Such of
you as are exposed to them will get colds or the rheumatism.
I will now read to you Mercutio's speech about dreams."
Having finished it, "There is a strong escape of gas going on
in this room; the screws in the gas-burners are none of them
turned square; you are inhaling poison, and I am being
choked. I will now read you Othello's defense before the
Senate of Venice."

When she finished this selection, the reader determinedly
shut her book. What was the use, she questioned, of her
auditors' learning poetical declamation while they violated
every principle of health and neglected the most elementary
knowledge which concerned the well-being of themselves and
their pupils? So ended her first and only public lecture on
education.[81]

A summer at Lenox with Sarah and Fan passed quietly,
happily, and swiftly. Winter again brought with it the call of
the theater. In January, 1859, Fanny returned to New York
and repeated the successes of the previous year. An English
reviewer added to the *Albion* staff found many words of praise
for the work of his fellow countrywoman. To him she resembled
less a single reader than a whole stock company of actors.
She revived by her fancy and utterance memories of a whole
generation of dead English players. When listening to her, he
said, one approached as near as he could hope to the good, old-
fashioned legitimate drama which former generations knew
and loved in the great days of Drury Lane.[82] During this
season the reader first intimated her intention of taking a final
leave of the public. She hinted that she planned to read in
Philadelphia during the season of 1859, in New York during
1860, and in Boston in 1861, where she meant to give her

farewell interpretation.[83] Unforeseen happenings caused her to abandon this plan.

In the spring of 1859 she departed for England accompanied by her younger daughter. Up to that time Fan had expressed little desire to see Europe, and any thought of her going had been vigorously opposed. Now for some reason, either Fan asserted her own authority—she had celebrated her twenty-first birthday in May—or Mr. Butler relented in his opposition. Perhaps he was too busily occupied with other matters, and welcomed the chance to lessen his responsibilities.

On March 2 and 3, 1859, his half of the slaves from the plantations, 429 in number, were sold at public auction in Savannah to pay their owner's debts of one hundred thousand pounds incurred by dabbling with Wall Street friends and their ways.[84] Whether this circumstance counted for anything in bringing about Fan's trip to Europe is conjectural. The important consideration was that she went. Together she and her mother toured Scotland, crossed the Channel for a short stay in Paris, and visited English friends.

When the voyagers returned to Boston in the autumn, Sarah and her husband, Dr. Owen Wister, met them. Several days later they took Fan back to Philadelphia while her mother decided to spend the winter at Revere House in Boston, and at Lenox. The first news which greeted the travellers upon their arrival in the United States told of a slave insurrection, a duel between two senators, and the murder of a Boston business man by an associate. Fanny could have guessed where she was even if she had not known.[85]

CHAPTER X

LAST DAYS IN AMERICA

A QUIET year followed this return from England. In August, 1860, came a journey to Philadelphia to visit Sarah and her month-old son, Owen, for whom Fanny felt a most grandmotherly yearning. She anticipated a trip to Boston to honor her future sovereign, the Prince of Wales, during his visit there, but the arrival at Lenox of an invalid friend prevented her going. Fan danced with the royal visitor at the New York ball, and her mother consoled herself with that honor. Fan seemed less sensible of the distinction. When asked whether she had laid away in lavender the satin shoes in which she danced with such an illustrious partner, she shrugged her shoulders and laughed. He was a nice little fellow and danced very well, she said. Her mother was quite shocked to hear of her future king's being clapped on the shoulder in that fashion by a monkey of a democratic damsel. Did Americans consider marriage with foreigners a degradation, she wondered.[1]

In 1861 the peaceful quiet of the towns among the Berkshires where Fanny was staying came to an end. For years rumblings of a serious nature had been audible. The schism between the states now had become a yawning cleft. Manliness, patriotism, loyalty, and honor appeared to be stifled by material progress and by a total abdication to mere material prosperity. Slavery, it seemed to her, had made insane egotists of the Southerners, and the pursuit of gain, intolerable egotists of Northerners. She sometimes thought that a grievous civil war, shattering their financial and commercial idols and compelling them to find the connection between public safety and private virtue, might prove a salvation to the country.[2]

It came in 1861. "Fights and flights, weapons and wounds" became the daily topics of conversation among the Berkshires. The stars and stripes flaunting their red, white, and blue from every farm roof gave a sort of gala appearance to the New England landscape. All this would have been pretty enough had it not announced the interruption of national prosperity, impending danger and insecurity, and a disruption of national ties. The effects of the war already had penetrated into this remote region,[3] and the women hastened to express their sympathies. Their talk concerned hospital gowns, comfortable socks, and mittens. By summer the whole community from Mrs. Kemble to some of the Irish servants spent their leisure time in knitting.[4]

Although the state of the country seemed very sad, Fanny felt not a shadow of doubt in the ultimate success of the Federal cause. In 1838 she had hoped to alleviate the condition of the slaves. Prescience told her that they must soon be free and that it would then be preferable to count them as friends. The war meant the destruction of slavery. Years before, she had prophesied that the United States would become a monarchy before she was a skeleton, but a deeper knowledge of its people had dispelled that thought. She had learned their true temper, and she placed infinite confidence in their manhood and courage. This was their heroic war, without which the German scholar Waelcker said that no people could be truly great. "Admonished by its terrible experiences," she said, "I believe the nation will reunite itself under one Government, remodel its Constitution, and again address itself to fulfil its glorious destiny. I believe that the country sprung from ours—of all our just subjects of national pride the greatest—will resume its career of prosperity and power, and become the noblest as well as the mightiest that has existed among the nations of the world."[5]

Fanny anticipated a return to England in 1861, but circumstances delayed her. Fan spent four months of the summer at Lenox with her mother, and Sarah, one. Their contentment was interrupted by Mr. Butler's arrest and incarceration in Fort LaFayette on the charge of treason. Authorities claimed that he acted as an agent for the South during a visit to Georgia and that he received money for the purchase and transmission of arms.[6] After more than a month's imprisonment, he was released upon his pledge to do no act hostile to the Federal Government during the war and not to visit South Carolina without a passport from the Secretary of State.[7] When in the following year he attempted to sue former Secretary of War Simon Cameron for trespass, assault and battery, and false imprisonment, President Lincoln avowed Mr. Cameron's action as necessary for the prompt suppression of the existing insurrection.[8] This ended a matter which doubtless increased Mr. Butler's hostility towards the President and his subordinates.

Although her father was released in September, 1861, Fan again accompanied her mother to England in the following spring. After a summer in Germany and Switzerland, through the Rhone Valley and among the Alps, the travellers settled for the winter in Hampshire, where Adelaide had taken a cottage for them at her own gate.

In England the American civil war was the topic of absorbing interest. The people among whom Fanny lived, like most well-educated members of the upper classes of English society, were southern sympathizers. At every gathering she listened to ignorant and mischievous nonsense upon the subject of slavery. What did they know of the true conditions, she questioned. What could they know? False sentimentality for aristocratic slave owners who fought to protect their property and society against unlettered Yankees sprang from an ignorance of true conditions. She had seen slavery in its true setting. She determined that her apologetically inclined friends should see what she had observed thirty years ago.

She now felt free to publish the diary of her year on the

12

Altamaha plantations. She was no longer a slave-owner's wife; neither was she the mother of future slave-owners. Mr. Butler's adventure in Wall Street had settled that. She dragged the journal from among her papers and copied out those scenes and descriptions which pictured slavery as she had seen it. It was her payment of a debt due to the country which was and, as she thought, must continue to be her home.[9]

She did not present it as a record of the interior management of southern plantations in general. She published it only as an exhibition of the workings of the system on estates where she had resided and where the slaves believed themselves especially fortunate.[10] Southern sympathizers hastened to deny its authenticity; they charged that it was invented for the occasion. Friends who had heard the author read the accounts years before repudiated this false criticism.[11]

Some readers thought this diary the most powerful anti-slavery book yet written. They immediately missed the idealized and romanticized Negroes of the abolitionist publications. The author pictured no Uncle Toms. Instead she sketched beings which one might expect to find in such surroundings. During the tremendous debate of thirty years, this decisive voice had remained silent, but when it spoke it uttered no general statement, no sickening incident. Instead, it presented a summary of the ordinary life of a plantation owned by educated, intelligent, and most respectable people. It laid bare the spirit, the character, and the purpose of the Rebellion. Mrs. Kemble had spoken after years of silence, but her words, said reviewers, never before could have carried an equal power.[12]

Fanny's pictorial style and ability to describe in detail presented a vivid record of the happenings on the plantations. Her personality and her likes and dislikes colored every page. From the details of the requests addressed to her by slave women, she could turn to a colorful description of a southern sunset and present both with equal vividness. The reader followed her during her explorations of Saint Simon's or on an afternoon call upon a neighbor. He saw through her eyes the squalor of the dirty huts or the rich blue of the first spring violets. No incident suggested writing for effect. She penned no sensational passages. Although she violated grammatical mandates occasionally, the reader never failed to understand her meaning or to see a clearly drawn picture. Since the time of its publication, this record has remained 'a valuable contribution to American history.' From the American Freedman's Inquiry Commission of 1864[13] to the present student of slavery, all turn to this diary as a record of life on the plantation.

When Fanny returned to America in 1866, the fate of slavery had been settled forever. Although the government did not present a very edifying spectacle, that part of the country which she confined herself to seemed thriving and prosperous. The war only accelerated its vigorous action when once the people's energies returned to their usual channels.

Fan departed with her father for the plantations in March in the hope of salvaging something from the destruction there. Although Federal troops occupied Saint Simon's during part of the war,[14] the owners found some indications of their proprietorship. Many Negroes remained on the plantations, not only those who lived there when the war began but some of those sold in 1859 had wandered back. With these the owners made an agreement to work for half the crop. Although the former slaves talked a great deal about their desire and intention to labor, the idea unaided by stern law soon became vague. Some worked half the day, and others less. The success of the experiment soon depended upon Fan's ability to coax and to scold the erstwhile slaves.[15]

In August, 1867, Mr. Butler died in Philadelphia, and in the autumn Fan returned to the plantations with her brother-in-law. Her mother remained with Sarah until March when she no longer could resist the lure of the stage. She needed a great deal of money, she said, for the expenses of living in the simple, republican country of the United States. After presenting a series of readings in New York and one in Philadelphia,[16] she returned to Washington for the first time as an artist since 1833-1834.[17] Baltimore followed on her schedule just as in the days when she and her father won applause on the American boards.[18] Her three months' spring labor proved remunerative. A profit of £4,400, after she had paid all expenses, had given away £300, and had "read away" £1,100 for charities, was an acceptable return.[19]

Fan came from the plantations in May. She immediately went to the old farmhouse at Butler Place and began repairing it as a summer residence. Although her mother despaired of its being made habitable—it has been leased from the time of Mr. Butler's disastrous speculations—Fan patched and propped it until the "old barn of a building" looked charming. Fanny came from Lenox in August. Once again she frequented *her room.* Memories of happy days and sad days filled her thoughts. Twenty-six years had passed since she had inhabited it; thirty-four years, since she first entered there. The old place still seemed small and ridiculously inconvenient. The Frenchman who built it nearly one hundred years before was no architect, but with Fan's furnishings it looked cheery. Fanny was glad for the pleasant days in her "former purgatory."[20]

She regretted leaving it when on August 31 she started on a three months' tour of the West for her last series of public appearances as an interpreter of Shakespeare. Perhaps she did not intend this tour to conclude her career. She apparently never planned a farewell interpretation. One happened to be her last but not because she meant that it should be. She had seen many farewells to the stage. She knew that usually they were merely magnificent gestures and that unless death intervened the actor succumbed to the lure of the theater at stated intervals and returned for just one more night. She would not be guilty of this folly, not now after her partial succumbing to it in 1859.

With all her dislike for the life of the theater, something continually drew her to some profession associated with the drama. Money may have explained the attraction; the desire to prove her ability against younger competitors may have been added to the call of gold. A more plausible explanation was the inheritance from John Ward, Roger Kemble, and Therese Decamp. The irresistible lure of the stage repeatedly drew her back to the boards just as she believed that a Swiss grandmother called her to the Alps and to the Berkshires.

On September 2, Fanny commenced her tour with a reading in New Haven. Then Providence listened to *The Tempest* and *King Lear*. From Roger Williams's city she started to the West: Niagara, the Great Lakes, and the Mississippi. In spite of intensely disagreeable weather, an appreciative audience gathered at Young Men's Hall in Detroit. Those who had listened to the reader twenty years before claimed that her dramatic powers developed with the passing of time. Many believed that this tour would be her last to the West. Not to see and to hear her was to neglect the opportunity of seeing and hearing one of the great women of the age, reviewers said.[21]

In Chicago her popularity increased with each presentation. Many sensitive admirers of Shakespeare preferred her readings to stage portrayals. No unappreciative, incompetent makeshift of actors, and no stage clap-trap perpetually reminded the listener that the action before him was only a play. He saw a low crimson-covered table with a volume of Shakespeare lying open upon it, a tall candelabrum of thirteen burners on either side, and the figure of a woman with sable silvered hair sitting at the table before a plain red screen.[22]

Neither her friends nor her critics—they may have been slightly sentimental and gullible—were able to analyze or explain Fanny Kemble's peculiar powers as a reader. Of all dramatic artists, by their accounts, she remained the most difficult to study or to imitate. A subtle, intangible something always escaped definition. Her interpretations possessed a perfection which the observer saw and acknowledged, but he found it impossible to follow the successive steps by which she achieved her effects:[23]

> Her warbling voice, a lyre of widest range
> Struck by all passion, did fall down and glance
> From tone to tone, and glided thro' all change
> Of liveliest utterance.

Persons from the various walks of life and of all ages felt the power of her presentations. A little girl of nine turned away and hid her face in her hands when Shylock sharpened his knife: "O, I do not wish to see it! I do not wish to see him cut Antonio's flesh," she sobbed.[24] "What an abundance there is of her!" Emerson exclaimed when he first attended her readings. "She is Miranda, Queen Catherine, and many more at the same time!"[25]

The supreme test of her powers came when she accepted an invitation to read during one of the New York State Agricultural Fairs at Syracuse. On a hot September afternoon she mounted the rostrum of a church used as a lecture hall to read *Winter's Tale* to an audience composed for the most part of farmers. The heat was oppressive. She expected to see an empty auditorium before she half finished the presentation, but the men remained and listened with breathless interest. At the close a friend congratulated her: "Mrs. Kemble, you have never read better." "I know it, I know it, most certainly I know it," she replied. "I never did read better! I never read so well! It is the triumph of my life."[26]

When she first became a dramatic reader, she resolved to give her best efforts to every interpretation. She strove to make it as nearly worthy of Shakespeare as her strength and talents would permit. She continually asked herself what he would have preferred could he have sat in her audience. Although she never departed from the simple stage setting, the crimson-covered table and crimson screens, her artistic sense told her that her choice of costumes would add something to the effectiveness of her portrayals. A black velvet gown was beautiful and becoming, but it seemed incongruous in the fairy land of *Midsummer Night's Dream*.

With as much thought as she devoted to the interpretations of the dramas, she selected gowns appropriate to each story: moonlight gleam and the shadow of white satin for *Romeo and Juliet;* mossy-green velvet or white silk and lace for *Midsummer Night's Dream;* black silk relieved by a narrow lace collar fastened by a plain gold pin for *Coriolanus;* cream-colored silk trimmed with black lace upon the skirt, at the throat, and at the wrists for *Merry Wives of Windsor;* the somber richness of black velvet in *King Lear;* black velvet with a broad blue ribbon crossed on her breast in *Richard III;* dark blue or purple velvet with her Saint George badge for the other historical plays.[27] To a masculine, intellectual mastery of the plays, she added a feminine appreciation of the fitness of objective details.

In June, 1869, Fanny crossed the Atlantic for a four years stay in England, a visit interrupted by summer vacations among the Alps and by winter journeys to Italy. Sarah and Fan came during the next year, and together they visited Switzerland and Germany. Fan tired of trying to manage a planatation alone. The personal attachment which survived among the Negroes for a short time after their emancipation rapidly diminished. They asserted their natural and divine right to cultivate happiness—idleness—instead of cotton and rice. The ambitious girl overestimated the strength of their old superstitions and devotion. She was glad to escape from her lonely and disheartening surroundings and perhaps doubly pleased to return to England.

Although she expressed no enthusiasm for a trip abroad before the journey with her mother in 1859, England proffered inducements for future visits. Englishmen were more attractive than she had anticipated. At least one Englishman considered the democratic young lady who nonchalantly referred to his future sovereign as a "nice little man" charming enough to inspire a trip from England to Georgia. Fanny felt an unusual satisfaction in her son-in-law's being a native of her own country when on June 29, 1871, Little Fan became the wife of the Honorable and Reverend James Wentworth Leigh.[28]

In 1873 Mr. and Mrs. Leigh came to America, and Fanny accompanied them to Philadelphia. Although friends assured her that she could not remain away from England, she believed that she should never return. The four years there had been filled with priceless experiences. She had renewed friendships of other days with Lord Tennyson, Lord Houghton, Edward Fitzgerald, William and Mowbray Donne, and Arthur and Mary Anne Malkin. She crossed to Ireland to see again Harriet Saint Leger, that most constant friend of her life, who was now blind. Sadness mingled with the joys of these renewed acquaintanceships. When she looked at her companions, she saw the lines of age seaming their faces. They were growing old, and that meant that she, too, approached the "remembering time" of life. If she should live until the Leighs' return to England, she might accompany them back to see once more those of her circle who remained. But why should she speculate on the future? What could anyone anticipate when she had reached the age of sixty-four?[29]

In the autumn of 1873 Fanny took an apartment at 1812 Rittenhouse Square, Philadelphia. Fan and Mr. Leigh went South to the plantations soon after their arrival in America, but the winter brought Fanny other companions. Horace Furness and his wife came occasionally to pass an evening and to discuss the task of his *Variorum* Shakespeare. Of course Sarah's home was near by. On evenings when no callers came, Fanny divided the time until ten o'clock between Patience and knitting. Then she read until eleven. Occasionally she attended the theater either alone or in company with Sarah and Dr. Wister.[30]

Christmas was a merry time for Fanny. Presents were heaped on her desk, among others a pair of French candlesticks, one with a figure of Doré's Don Quixote, and the other, with Retch's Mephistopheles. There, too, were Furness's *Variorum* editions of *Romeo and Juliet* and *Macbeth*. At one side of the heap sat a large Catalonia jasmine in a delicate green china jardinière decorated with flowers, birds, and butterfles, a gift which seemed a strange blossoming of memories. The flower was Mr. Butler's first present. When her theatrical wanderings prevented her caring for the plant, she gave it to a friend who now returned it covered with fragrant blossoms.

In May, 1874, the Leighs returned from Georgia for the summer residence at York Farm. As soon as Fan could set the place in order, her mother came from Philadelphia on May 28, the birthday of both Fan and Sarah. In June Dr. Wister's family moved to Butler Place. Only a highway separated it from the yard of York Farm. There within sight of the old farmhouse which had been her only home in America, Fanny spent the remainder of her years in the United States. Remembrances of the long ago mingled with her present happiness. The sight of Sarah superintending the arrangement of furniture seemed to her mother an apparition of her own youth. She accompanied Fan to the little village church at Branchtown for the christening of little Alice Dudley Leigh although memories of other christenings blinded her. Recollections of past days combined with heartfelt thanks for the present blessings of being near her children.

Fanny was glad to leave Philadelphia for this country residence. She was tired of listening to the continuous wrangling over political and financial conditions which were the chief topics of conversation. She felt no sympathy for the Woman's Rights cause. Many laws were unjust to woman, but they would never be righted by women's platform speeches. Fredrika Bremer frequently became vehement on the subject. When she exclaimed in a frenzy of assertion that women had the right to be soldiers and to fight if they pleased, Fanny grasped the speaker's small fist which was clasped in warlike ardor: "If fisticuffs are to decide the matter, the weakest man's fist is stronger than the strongest woman's," replied her hearer. Fanny remembered that with all Margaret Fuller's claims to absolute equality with men, she remained extremely exacting in regard to the small courtesies which men never showed to each other. She expected her fallen glove or handkerchief to be presented or the door to be opened. Fanny always saw the inconsistencies in matters which did not concern herself too intimately.

The attempted adjustments of the Negroes' status also occasioned much discussion in Philadelphia. Mulattoes descended from slave parents or born in slavery were rapidly superseding the Irish as maids, waiters in hotels, and coachmen. Although they lied and pilfered, they were less insolent than the Irish and less insubordinate than poor whites. The Philadelphians' attitude toward Negroes, to Fanny, seemed self-contradictory. They welcomed these former slaves as laborers in their homes, but no theater in the city permitted a colored person to attend a performance. Negroes were citizens. They were elected as members of the public school boards, but their children were not admitted to the white schools. Custom and prejudice, which were stronger than law, determined these practices.[31]

Fanny welcomed escape from the discussions and observations of these conditions to the quiet of York Farm. The old place seemed less lonely now. Perhaps she demanded less excitement than she had craved forty years before. She had reached the age which preferred peaceful and happy monotony. Through her open windows on summer mornings came the sounds of the piano when her grandson practised his music. How she wished that his vacations might last indefinitely! She was proud of this tall, broad fellow in his teens. He was amiable, clever, and unusually well endowed with ability. He wrote good verses, and possessed an extraordinary talent for music. If he worked—she feared that he might not—he would become a remarkable person, not a book man, but a student of the natural laws of force and motion and of their results as applied to machinery.[32]

Her residence in the country also offered leisure for preparing and copying her memoirs. Harriet Saint Leger had preserved every letter which she had received from Fanny during forty

years. These she returned to their writer during her last visit
to Ireland. This collection of several thousand letters was a
ready written autobiography. Fanny knew that the passion
for universal history, anybody's and everybody's story, seemed
to render any personal recollections good enough to be printed
and read. Why should she not capitalize upon this insatiable
public appetite for gossip? Some day, doubtless, this craving
would be gratified at her expense. After her death some in-
genious person might publish some record of her similar to
those of the more celebrated members of her family. She
already had received notices and sketches more or less "men-
dacious and veracious." A *post mortem* examination seemed a
not improbable event. Why should her own gossip about
herself not be as acceptable as gossip about her written by
another? She had come to the garrulous time of life, to the
"remembering days" which preceded only a little the "forgetting days." She had leisure, and the writing of reminiscences
would amuse her. Reading them might entertain others no
busier than she.[33]

She set to work on the letters, copying out those portions
which she desired to retain and destroying all which revived
any distressing associations.[34] Throughout the year in Philadelphia she worked on the project. In the spring of 1875 the
editor of the *Atlantic Monthly* requested any article which she
might have available. She mentioned the memoirs and received
a liberal offer for them.[35] In the August issue the first installment of her *Old Woman's Gossip* appeared. She prefaced the
letters with an autobiographical sketch of the first sixteen
years of her life. At that age she made the acquaintance of
her friend, and from that time extracts from letters with
occasional explanations continued the record.

After she settled herself at York Farm, she worked tirelessly.
She feared to trust her only manuscript in the hands of the
publisher. That necessitated the re-copying of everything
which she had already written. In addition she continued the
original version, for she had completed the record only to

1841 at the time of the publication of her first installment. Although she did not plan to extend the account being published beyond 1832, she wanted to finish the copying from the series of letters. Upon Mr. Leigh's recommendation she bought a printing machine operated by striking the keys as though one played a piano. It was an admirable invention, a great relief from the fatigue of constant writing. Soon Fanny used it for all her copying.[36]

Throughout the spring and summer she worked diligently every day and into the night on her manuscript. Since she could not go to Lenox for the sultry months, she determined to make herself as comfortable as possible at York Farm. When in June the heat became intolerable, she decided to rid herself of her abundant mass of hair. After many protests her maid, Ellen, cut it to finger's length. Fanny knew that she looked "dreadfully frightful," but the relief was immense. Her only regret was that she could not shave her head and go about with only the skin for a skull cap, an idea suggested by Sydney Smith who wished that he could throw off his flesh and sit in his bones in hot weather.[37]

In October, 1875, came a request from the committee in charge of the Centennial Exposition in Philadelphia for one of her readings to be given in the Academy of Music. At last she felt compelled to resist the lure of the drama. She was quite incapable of such an exertion, she replied. Her strength was unequal to the effort, her voice which had lost its power could not be heard in a large auditorium, and the loss of her teeth impaired the distinctness of her speech.[38]

It must have cost her a pang to admit that never again could she respond to that urge which had dominated so large a part of her life. Although her theatrical days were over, she still remained dramatic. As long as she lived, associates saw expressions of that power which brought her popularity on the stages of two continents. Once as the guest of Mr. Curtis she suffered from a smoking chimney until her patience was exhausted. She summoned her host and questioned in her deepest, tragic tones, "William, do you think I am a herring?"[39] Years could not destroy the heritage from generations of histrionic artists.

When Fanny left England in 1873, she hoped that she might live until the Leighs completed their experiment with the Georgia plantations and were ready to return to Britain. Three years later, in 1876, Mr. Leigh decided that he could leave the care of these estates to the management of agents. His efforts had developed the plantations into valuable agricultural property of their kind. In addition he had labored incessantly among the colored people. He established Sunday schools and other religious services, night schools for adults, and day schools for the children. He enjoyed his work there, but he realized that the time had come for his return to England and to the profession which previously occupied his interests. He accepted a living in Staffordshire—Fanny wished he had accepted the one offered at Stratford-on-Avon—and prepared to return to this new field of duty.[40] At last Fanny was to have one child permanently located in England. She could pass her remaining years in the only country which would ever be home to her, for all her life she remained *la plus anglaise des anglaises.*

But she could not bring herself to leave the country where she had spent the happiest as well as the saddest days of her life without seeing her Berkshires once more. Only a few of her former friends remained there, but the Bowl had not changed, and the mountains retained their ruggedness. On June 27 she arrived at Lenox and took rooms for the summer at Curtis's Hotel, now the property of the man who as a boy had managed her boat on fishing excursions. The village seemed to have added to its attractiveness since her residence there. The trees along the streets had grown tall and thick, and the sidewalks were wider and paved or smoothed.

Early one morning she walked down Kemble Street to The Perch. She ventured inside the gate and up the carriage road until she glimpsed the house screened by oaks, maples, and chestnuts which were young trees when she lived there. Memories of the years when she called it home crowded upon one another. Often she had welcomed Catherine or Elizabeth Sedgwick at that front door. On summer evenings she and Sarah or Fan had walked over the lawn among the flowers. Many times she had galloped her black horse down the carriage road, off for a trip to Greylock.

Every spot about Lenox seemed to recall some unforgettable reminiscence. Here stood Mrs. Sedgwick's academy where Fanny had often read Shakespearean dramas to the girls. There was the hitching post where she had left the enviously admiring Judge Bishop aghast after having set him right about her superior riding ability: "The great difference between you and me is that when you are on a horse's back he knows you are afraid of him; when I am on his back he knows he is afraid of me."

From the distance through the trees peeped the lake where she had sometimes entertained the élite of Lenox at picnics. On one occasion when the hostess wished to provide unusual delicacies she had ordered them from New York. All went well until she neglected to add the water necessary for punch to the undiluted liquors. She smiled yet whenever she recalled that staggering group of gentlemen and ladies each trying to maintain his poise but none succeeding very well.

But an expression of sadness followed the moments of recollected merriment. Where were they, those former associates who welcomed her annual returns to Lenox? She looked towards the old church with the clock which she had donated and at the rows of white marble stones behind it. Most of her friends slept there now. If she returned to England she could never rest among them. Long ago she had agreed to lie on that hill if she might pop her head above the sod occasionally to catch a view of the surrounding valley.

But another object dispelled these melancholy reflections. She reached the steps of the hotel. Here she had often mounted into the carriage when William Curtis drove her about the country side. She smiled again as she recalled the day on which she interrupted his explanations of the landscape: "I hired you to drive, not to talk." When she dismounted on those same steps he claimed five dollars and a half instead of the customary amount and then silenced her objections by adding that the five dollars paid for the drive and the fifty cents, for the "sarce."

Fanny always enjoyed a joke, and she knew how to laugh at herself. She never failed to recollect and to repeat those told at her own expense. If any person outwitted her, he won her lifelong favor. Once, in the village shop she informed a tradesman in her best tragedy manner, "Gentlemen always take off their hats in my presence." "But I'm not a gentleman, I'm a butcher," replied the Yankee shopkeeper. His ready wit cemented an abiding friendship.[41]

During the last week of August she bade her last farewell to her American mountains, forever sacred to the friends she had loved there. She might return, but a woman aged sixty-seven could not anticipate many more summers. The goodbye would have been more bitter had it not been for her mountains in Switzerland.

After visits to several friends, Fanny returned to Branchtown to spend her last weeks in America with Fan and Sarah. Many times she looked from her windows at the trees of Butler Place, glorious in their autumn gold, and mused on her former years there, not evil years now for the gloom was far away. In her present calm it was easier to remember only the happiness. She felt an impulse to prostrate herself in thanksgiving for the quiet close to her tempestous life.

During these last days, Fanny turned again to literary work. Owen used his powers of persuasion to induce Grandmother to collaborate with him in the composition of an opera. If she would write the libretto, he pleaded, he would add the music. He chose the subject, a pretty fairy story, and outlined his proposed version. Under his directions she set to work, an instance of her amiable desire to please, she said, even when her faculties had grown stiff with almost seventy years of wear and tear.

Sarah spilled her mother from a sleigh and then fortunately for herself fell on top. Dr. Wister attempted to aid his mother-in-law over ice-covered steps. They both slipped down four steps and then landed opposite each other on the icy gravel walk. Fanny felt considerably shaken up after each accident but not in the least daunted. She climbed back into the same sleigh and drove with Sarah to Branchtown for her last church service in America. Nothing should mar the contentment of her last days in her adopted country.

Leavetaking brought a pang of sadness. Old country neighbors came to say goodbye and to wish her well. Sarah, Dr. Wister, and her grandson remained at Butler Place. But they could cross the Atlantic to visit her, and it was best that she should go. It would be easier to recall the beauty and to forget the monotony of other years at Butler Place when thousands of miles separated her from it. In the "remembering years" she wanted to recall the flower garden instead of the vegetable plat, the chivalrous young lover instead of the obstinate slave owner.

When the steamship *Britannica* drifted slowly from a New York pier on January 20, 1877, Fanny waved a last farewell to America. She was going home to Adelaide, to Harriet Saint Leger, to England.[42]

CHAPTER XI

MAUVE ANEMONES

IT WAS Christmas Eve. A fir tree stood in a corner of the nursery of Alverston Manor House at Stratford-on-Avon. Laurel and holly hung in the windows and festooned the walls of the quaint old thirteenth-century monastic house once the property of Worcester Abbey. Fire blazing in the huge chimney and the glow from a brass chandelier suspended from an oak rafter lighted the apartment. Servants stood on steps, mounted on ladders, and knelt about the tree while Fan and Mr. Leigh handed toys and decorations to them. While he hung more evergreens about the room, a Negro man-servant watched with a broad grin the decking of the tree. Fanny sat near the heavy oak table filling small bags, boxes, and baskets with bon-bons. Henry James, "a handsome, dark-bearded American," who had come to Stratford for a holiday visit with his friends, the Leighs, decided upon the most artistic placements for gifts and decorations. When the last sprig of holly hung about the room, and every gift found a place on the tree, the conspirators, who had transformed the nursery into a Christmas wonderland, extinguished the gas light, closed the door, and tip-toed past little Alice Dudley Leigh's room.[1]

When Fanny had returned from America in January, 1877, she temporarily took rooms at 23 Portman Street, Portman Square, London. Here she remained until April when she re-moved to 15 Connaught Square, where she rented a house for a year. The visits of former friends and preparations for house-keeping filled busy days. Mr. Leighton came to invite her to

13

see privately his collection of pictures before their exhibition at the Academy. Fanny Cobbe sought her assistance in a crusade against vivisection. Her niece, May Gordon, and Mr. Gordon rushed in for dinner when they came to London to practise for the Bach concert directed by Otto and Jenny Lind Goldschmidt. Harry Kemble came often to dine and to converse with his aunt. His visits always were welcome events. His Kemble face and voice, which were much like his father's and grandfather's, were pleasant to Fanny.

Because of ill-health she refused almost all social invitations. Even slight exertions appeared formidable. She never cared for purely social functions, and now her disinclinations and unfitness for them were insuperable. Morning visiting had become for the most part nothing except an exchange of bits of pasteboard, for everybody went abroad at the same hour of the day. When her friends the Donnes seemed annoyed at her reluctance to attend Valentia's wedding, she decided upon the extraction of her last shaky front tooth and the replacement of all four by false ones. If she were to go, she must look presentable.

The task of procuring acceptable servants caused immeasurable annoyance. Things and people had changed since the days when Fanny kept house in England. The absence of respectability in the attire and of respect in the demeanor of applicants took her breath away. America had come across the Atlantic with a vengeance. Kitchen maids, with their hands thrust into their jacket pockets, stood close to their prospective mistress. Before she could ask a single question, they demanded if the house was large or small, and how many servants she employed. She found it difficult to understand who did the work in an English house. If one hired a cook, she demanded a kitchen-maid. When one sought a kitchen-maid, she requested a scullery girl. Fanny's refusal to furnish the young women in her employ with either beer or beer-money increased her difficulties. When no other agreement seemed possible, she hired servants on board wages. If they chose to purchase beer out of their allowance, she could not interfere. This procedure at least prevented her countenancing the practice.[2]

In June Fanny departed for her mountains in Switzerland. Several weeks later Harry Kemble left his theatrical work to join her at Thusis. Together they travelled through the famous passes of the Alps into northern Italy and then back by Maloya Pass into the Engadine. Although Fanny thought that the Swiss people were the most disagreeable persons on either continent, their country was her Arcadia. Her diary recorded the journey from Splügen to Chiavenna: "Lordly, lovely, wonderful mountain pass; Italy at the bottom, cypresses, vines, chestnuts; every quarter of a mile a perfect picture, wretched population, hideous human dwellings, fit only for cattle; at the hotel, lofty rooms, scaliola floors, marble mirrors, magnificence, bad smells and—bed-bugs."

She preferred the Swiss to the Italian side of the Alps; it was grander, more rugged, and more sublime. The bright verdure of high Alpine meadows to her was more lovely than the vines of the South. The wild flowers of Switzerland were incomparable. One found masses of rhododendron and sheaves of blue-bells of every shade from white to deep purple and of every size from clumps of tiny blossoms shivering in the spray of the waterfalls to the large deep bell vibrating on its hairlike stem in the keen mountain breeze. The rose veronica, the deep blue dwarf gentian, and the ermine edelweiss, never found except with the everlasting snow as their neighbor, were beauties with which all the glowing, untidy southern landscape could not compare.

Harry proved an agreeable comrade. He was amiable and well-disposed, quiet and well-bred, kind, courteous, and affectionate to his aunt. Although Fanny feared that he found her a rather dull companion, he was more than pleased with their associations. Her enthusiasm and capacity for excitement surprised and amused him. Like many others, he marvelled at the youth of this lady of sixty-eight.

In September the travellers went to Paris, where Fanny remained for several weeks to shop. By the first of October she, too, returned to England. After a few days' rest in London, she proceeded to Wales for a visit with Harriet Saint Leger. Then when the holiday season drew near she went to Stratford-on-Avon where her English family lived.

When, during the summer, the vicar of Leamington died, Mr. Leigh accepted the living there and installed his family at Stratford. There Fanny found them within a quarter of a mile of the famous little inn of the Red Horse. She approved of Mr. Leigh's removal to his new vicarage. He seemed particularly well fitted for the work there. His activities always took him among the lower classes, to the mill people of Staffordshire, to the Negroes of Georgia, and now to the less fortunate groups of Leamington.

Fanny was glad, too, for the days on the Avon. She attended services in the old church where Shakespeare lay. Although the chanting of the service and the repetition of the Athanasian Creed were trials to her, she hoped they were acceptable, beneficial, and comforting to her fellow-worshippers. The church with its yard dotted by noble old elms and almost surrounded by the river excited a feeling of reverence and of worship which the service failed to inspire.[3]

In the spring of 1878 Fanny returned to London. In April she gave up the house at Connaught Square. It had been her home for a year, and twelve months were too long for her to remain satisfied with any one place. Something of the wanderlust which drove John Ward and Roger Kemble to lead their players year after year around the English countryside tugged always at her heart. She was a stroller first and last, and the impulse refused to be repressed.

Before her return from Stratford, Mr. Bentley wrote to suggest the publication in book form of her *Gossip*. She readily agreed to the plan, and in the autumn the three volumes called *Records of a Girlhood* came from the press. She extended the *Old Woman's Gossip*, first published serially in the *Atlantic*

Monthly, to include an account of her first two years in America. With this exception there was no important change in her autobiographical account.[4] The record was an interesting self-revelation of the author. It depicted the growth of the passion-ate, wayward though generous disposition which often threw shadows over her life. It showed her aspirations; it also revealed her faults, mistakes, and contradictions. She made no attempt to extenuate her immaturity or to reconcile her inconsistencies.

Incidental notices of persons of social, literary, or political distinction, sketches of London and impressions of American life added to the interest of the personal narrative. Since she wrote the accounts at the time of her observations, they were fresh and bright in tone. Each person stood out clearly and vividly. Readers wished that when she wrote of a friend she would have called her Harriet instead of H———, or Emily instead of E———. Mr. Butler apparently deserved some more descriptive designation than a blank when she mentioned him. This referring to a person by the first letter of his name was a provoking characteristic of her writing.[5]

From her girlhood Fanny's friends included many notable persons, men and women, who already had achieved renown or who became prominent figures of the later nineteenth century. Through her brother John's association with the Cambridge Apostles, she made the acquaintance of that remarkable group. Her family associations with the stage intro-duced her to the famous actors and actresses of that age. As the young débutante member of the Kemble family she re-ceived a welcome into the drawing rooms of London. Her own success as the author of *Francis I* established her relation-ship with literary circles. Her letters were mirrors of these associations.

In April, 1878, soon after Fanny gave up the house at Connaught Square, she returned to Stratford, where she took rooms at the Red Horse Inn. In June she accompanied Fan and little Alice to the Malvern Hills. In October she again departed for Switzerland, where she passed a month among her mountains at Lago Maggiore.⁶ In 1879 she took a residence for two years at Queen Anne's Mansions. By this time the course of her activities settled into a routine from which they rarely varied during the remainder of her life. She reserved a house or several rooms in London. Their location changed frequently, for she remained an addict to the moving habit. Months at a hotel, a residence at Hertford Square, and more hotel days followed her removal from Queen Anne's Mansions. Although she always referred to London when she spoke of home, her stays there usually were brief. She frequently visited the Leighs. Every summer until 1890 found her in France or Switzerland.

In 1886 she went to Smith's Hotel at Aix-les-Bains to meet Mrs. Anne Thackeray Ritchie. Fanny was lunching alone, a sad expression on her face, when her friend first found her. Immediately she brightened up and seemed eighteen again. "*Qu' est-ce donc, mon ami?*" she questioned a waiter who served the dessert. "It is a puddinge english, Madame." "I detest English cookery," she retorted, "and pray why do you speak to me in English and bring me this detestable thing? Is not my French good enough to exempt me from nursery pudding?"⁷ When she was seventy years old her strength yet sufficed for a tramp of fifteen hundred feet down the dry bed of a mountain torrent near Brunnen. After she was unable to walk or ride up the steep slopes of her Swiss mountains, she hired carriers. When they reached the summit of the mountain pass from Roselani, the bearers always paused. In her clear, rich voice she began, "I will lift up mine eyes unto the hills," continuing verse after verse of this favorite Psalm.⁸ At last she no longer felt equal even to the exertion of being carried. Instead, she sat for hours on the balconies of the hotels and looked at the overhanging snow-capped peaks. Ten years later, in the autumn of 1889, she felt that she was leaving her mountains for the last time. Her sorrow and regret found expression in her poem, *In Switzerland:*

"Oh look on me once more!" I cried.
But thickest mist encompassed every head.[9]

The Alpine guides called her *la dame qui va chantant par les montagnes*. No visitor was more universally known or loved.[10]

Adelaide's death in August, 1879, hastened Fanny's return to London. This sudden and unexpected blow crushed her. Life again seemed unusually cruel and unjust. In the natural course of human existence Henry and Adelaide should have outlived her, but now of that family of four children, she alone survived.[11] The mutual understanding between these two sisters was deep and lasting. Adelaide exemplified the qualities which her sister admired but did not possess. "You think me clever?" Fanny questioned in reply to a compliment. "My dear child, I'm a perfect fool! You should have known my sister Adelaide. Ah! she was a genius and the sweetest creature that ever breathed, very like her Aunt Dall, and very unlike me." Although Adelaide was a devoted sister, she was not blind to Fanny's faults. When acquaintances became cross and disagreeable, she said they were for all the world like Fanny.[12]

After her sister's death, the world to Fanny seemed emptier than ever before. But since she must live on, she could not be idle. As long as life remained, it demanded activity. Her restive disposition prevented idleness, and she again turned to writing. Many authors fail to reach the age of seventy; usually those who do survive have ceased creative work. But Fanny, in addition to short articles, poems, and pamphlets, published twelve books. Three of these were written and four others prepared for the press after her seventieth year.

Records of a Girlhood received immediate recognition, and by April, 1879, it had reached a third edition in England. Its proceeds encouraged Mr. Bentley to solicit more of Mrs. Kemble's "rubbish," her designation for the letter-memoirs. In 1882 he issued a three-volume sequel with the title *Records of Later Life.* The narrative of these volumes began with a letter of October 26, 1834, six months after her marriage. She already feared she had made a mistake and that her life at Philadelphia would be a disappointment, for the affections of her nature were out of harmony with everything and and everybody about her. *Records of Later Life* told the story of her experiences from that time until her return to America in 1848 to contest Mr. Butler's suit for divorce.

This second series failed to present a complete account of her activities such as the earlier volumes contained. She suppressed all except indirect references to her marital difficulties, and to the general reader this reticence was perplexing and annoying. He knew that Mr. Butler did exist, although his name never appeared except in incidental references. Sydney Smith's thrust that "this pleasing young woman labored under the singular and distressingly insane idea that she had contracted a marriage with an American" seemed hardly far-fetched.

In plan, these volumes did not differ from the earlier records. Selections from letters connected by links of narration or of explanation told the story. But the narrative included more than a study of a remarkable character and career. It contained criticisms, eloquent bursts of feeling, comments, and reflections on life, manners, books, and events. Especially significant were the criticisms of dramatic productions and the delineations of actors and musicians. The sketches of London life, together with the estimates of noted persons, formed the most generally attractive part of the story. Although the writer was frank and outspoken in her comments, she was rarely unkind. Many amusing passages occurred, and a sense of humor pervaded these sketches, for Fanny Kemble always enjoyed a joke.[13]

Because of the source of the material, the work was intimate. Meaning held precedence over form; the language and expression approached the informality of conversation. Although sentences were long and complex, they were lucid in meaning.

She coined words, and threw in French or Italian phrases; sometimes, as in the earlier records, she was ungrammatical. But the reader readily forgave these liberties even if the charm of the narrative permitted his noticing them.

During the same year, 1882, Mr. Bentley published Mrs. Kemble's *Notes upon Some of Shakespeare's Plays*, a volume containing interpretations of *Macbeth*, *Henry VIII*, *The Tempest*, and *Romeo and Juliet*. In addition, the author included her essay "On the Stage" which first appeared in 1863 in the *Cornhill Magazine*. Considering its brevity, this study contained perhaps the most careful analysis in dramatic criticism of the actor in juxtaposition with his art.[14] English people, said the author, frequently confused the terms "dramatic" and "theatrical" and spoke of them as synonymous. She tried to correct this misconception.

The passionate, emotional, humorous element in human nature, she said, is the dramatic. Beyond its momentary excitement and gratification it claims no relation with its imitative theatrical reproduction. The dramatic is the *real* of which the theatrical is the *false*. The combination of the power to represent passion and emotion with that of imagining or conceiving it, the union of theatrical talent with dramatic temperament, is essential to the good actor. Their combination in the highest possible degree makes a great actor.

The theatrical, according to this critic's interpretation, differs from all other arts. It has neither fixed rules, specific principles, indispensable rudiments, nor fundamental laws. It has no basis in positive science such as music, painting, sculpture, or architecture has. The appearance of spontaneity is it chief merit. Although it creates nothing and perpetuates nothing, it requires of its practitioners the imagination of the poet, the ear of the musician, and the eye of the painter and sculptor. In addition, it demands a faculty peculiar to itself, for the actor personally fulfills and embodies his conception. With all its demands, it requires no study worthy of the name. Actors delight only the play-going public of their own day. They cannot justly claim the rapture of creation, the glory of patient and protracted toil, or the love and honor of grateful posterity. Money and applause fitly compensate these performers.

Her notes on the various Shakespearean plays were for the most part interpretative. She designated *Macbeth* as a drama of conscience in which Lady Macbeth embodied evil strength, and Macbeth, evil weakness. *Henry VIII* presented the conflict between two types of pride—pride of power, and pride of birth. Instead of an analysis, the notes on *Romeo and Juliet* included only a few hints for the acting. Romeo seemed to represent the sentiment, and Juliet, the passion of love. The pathos was his, the power, hers. The comprehension of these distinctions furnished the key for the impersonation of these characters.

In her study of *The Tempest*, her favorite Shakespearean drama, she attempted to explain the reasons for this preference. The remoteness of setting allowed to the imagination a range permitted in no other play. The action presented the supremacy of the human soul over all things which surrounded it. The characters portrayed every plane of human life. Prospero represented wise and virtuous manhood in its relation to the combined elements of existence, the middle link in a chain of beings of which Caliban stood at the lowest and densest, and Ariel, at the most ethereal extreme. Caliban personified the more ponderous and unwieldy natural elements which, through knowledge, the wise magician compelled to serve him. Ariel embodied the keen perceiving intellect apart from all moral consciousness and sense of responsibility. Because he was a spirit only of knowledge, he became subject to the spirit of love. This wild, subtle, keen, powerful creature served the human soul with mutinous waywardness and unwilling subjection.

In these criticisms Mrs. Kemble proved herself a ready writer and the master of an easy and idiomatic English which used words exactly.[15] Although devotees of the theatrical art severely flayed the author for her strictures upon the actor's labor and reward,[16] her notes on the plays received favorable comment. They revealed clearness of insight and thoroughness of comprehension.

In 1883, Mr. Bentley printed a revised edition of her volume of poems, first published in 1859. The three hundred and forty pages included a few selections from the 1844 publication and almost all of those in the later volume. To these the author added twenty-five original poems, five short poems and sayings translated from Hugo, Millevoye, and Musset, and a Sicilian song.

Three short lyrics on the Civil War and one on the fall of Richmond were notable additions. Two of these voiced the concern of those who feared for the future of liberty and democracy. Both played on a mutual refrain:

> She has gone down! Woe for the world, and all
> Its weary workers! gazing from afar
> At the clear rising of that hopeful Star;
> Star of redemption to each weeping thrall
> Of power decrepit and of rule outworn;
> Beautiful shining of that blessed morn,
> Which was to bring leave for the poor to live;
> To work and rest, to labor and to strive!
> She has gone down! Woe for the struggling world
> Back on its path of progress sternly hurled!
> Land of sufficient harvest for all dearth.
> Home for far-seeing Hope. Time's latest birth,—
> Woe for the promised land of the whole earth.

Another expressed firm confidence in the future of the country then torn by civil strife. The *Fall of Richmond* echoed the thanksgiving freed from all spirit of gloating which attended the surrender of Lee:

> For our own guilt have we been doomed to smite
> These our own kindred, Thy great law defying,—

These our own flesh and blood, who now unite
In one thing only with us—bravely dying.

With all of the author's belief in abolitionist principles, references to slavery occurred in only two poems and then with no elaboration. She wrote of places which she visited, "The Syren's Cave at Tivoli" or "A Vision of the Vatican." Other poems were narrative or philosophical. Echoes of the seventeenth-century cavaliers sounded in such lighter love poems as "What Is My Lady Like?" Others on the same general theme presented the passion but not the sentimentality of unrequited love. Nature in its various forms inspired many of the poems: changes attending the different seasons, mountain crags, rare flowers, and aspects of the sky in the evening or at dawn.

Time mellowed the author's despairing pessimism. A note of hopefulness absent from her earlier poetry sounded from many of these later compositions. She still felt the mutability of all earthly things. Life was a struggle doomed to final defeat, but it was not meaningless. As long as one lived his existence held some purpose.

Her refusal to correct and to revise left many halting lines and hackneyed epithets. Bathos resulted from the stage temptation to anti-climax.[17] Although she wrote in an age during which many preferred sentimental poetry, her better poems possessed a strength which the popular writers of that time would have hesitated to express. They rang with genuine human emotion. They were intense and sincere. The reader gladly extenuated their slipshod style and "worn beauties" just as he excused the cut of his grandmother's frock. The rigid requirements of the sonnet proved useful to her "untidy muse." Her best poems were in that form.

Although she published no other volume until 1889, she continued to write, for she believed that inaction hastened senility, and she refused to grow old. What if one passed his seventieth birthday? What if he were eighty? His spirit, his interests in life and not the number of birthdays determined his age. Acquaintances continually wondered at her mental and physical energy. Friends who came to call found her by the fireside with her sampler, or at her writing desk at work on a poem or a novel. She wore black silk now, and, to relieve its somberness, a white lace cap. Her beauty bade defiance to time: "How handsome she used to look with her great expressive black eyes," remarked an aged acquaintance. "Yes," replied Robert Browning, who had just returned from a call on the septuagenarian, "and how handsome she is still."[18]

She wrote poems, some of which appeared in magazines,[19] an article on Salvini,[20] and a farce entitled *The Adventures of Mr. John Timothy Homespun in Switzerland*, the story of English, American, and Russian tourists and their mountain climbing. When she submitted this manuscript for publication in pamphlet form, in fun she added under the title "stolen from the French of Tartarion de Tariascon." Fanny had always had a scornful opinion of printers, but when she received her copies of this production, she felt inclined to believe that even she had been too liberal in her estimate of them. Although the publisher entirely omitted her name, the line which she added in mischief appeared on the title-page. That most literal of men, a publisher, had taken her literally. She was disgusted: "Why wasn't my name put on my farce?" she questioned of a friend who worked for the firm. "Did or does Mr. Bentley think I am ashamed of my natural condition which is farcical? My name is *Frances Anne Kemble*, and ought to be affixed to everything Mr. Bentley publishes for me. I wrote 'stolen' on my farce for fun and had no idea that it would be printed, whereas I expected my name would be."[21]

She also mentioned the writing of a tiresome novel of fifty chapters. Upon another occasion she said she felt proud and vain over having written a story, the first she ever told, at the age of seventy-eight. She composed it, she said, in the midst of a domestic earthquake occasioned by her discovery of the lying, drunkenness, and thieving of her servants. Disgust and distress drove her to seek relief. *The Rose Lily* enabled her to extricate her thoughts from this mire.[22]

In 1889 she submitted to the printer her first and only novel. Henry Holt and Company published the American edition in the Leisure Hour Series, "a collection of works whose character is light and entertaining, though not trivial, handy for the pocket or the satchel," but neither "in contents or appearance, unworthy of a place on the library shelves." Across the top of the volume a black oak limb loaded with acorns ornamentated the dull copper-colored binding. The title and the author's name appeared between this bough and an intricately meshed web with a prosperous looking spider crouched in his nest. Editors thought Mrs. Kemble's *Far Away and Long Ago* worthy of a place beside Richardson's *Clarissa Harlowe*, or Harriet Spofford's *Amber Gods*, previously published in this series.

The introduction resorted to a time-worn literary device. Among the personal effects of Miss Selbourne—the name and setting suggested Catherine Sedgwick—her niece found a bulky package marked "*Far Away and Long Ago*, to be published after my death." The story was a sociological study of life in the Berkshire country during the time when Fanny knew its conditions and customs. Industrialism had just begun to touch the sequestered towns of Lenox, Stockbridge, and Pittsfield, easily identified under their pseudonyms in the story. Democratic simplicity still characterized life there. Into such unpretentious surroundings James Morrison, an iron worker of Lancashire, England, brought his family. Relieved in his new surroundings from the sternly oppressive hand of English industrialism, he freely expressed his pent-up social and religious antagonism. During this first year of exciting self-expression, a daughter, Mary, was born. Although her older sister, Susan, was gentle, cheerful, respectful, and religious—the type of her parents' reserved life and repressed feelings in England—Mary was rebellious against all restraint, morbidly irritable, sensitive, and violently self assertive.

Years passed. James Morrison died from exposure following an attempt to procure water lilies from the edge of a marsh for his daughters. A new spiritual guide, Caleb Killegrew, came to minister to the Greenville Christians and to live at the widow Morrison's. Beauty, when it appeared as a young woman, attracted this quintessence of rampant proselytism. He determined to marry the proud, defiant, unorthodox girl to save her soul.

Chance seemed to favor him. Although William Morris, a young theological student, preferred Susan, Mary also loved him. In a burst of passion she betrayed her feelings; then, humiliated by her action, she left home to secure employment in the cotton mills at Gordonton. When the death of William's grandfather brought her to Greenville, William started to drive her back to her work. Before they traversed half the distance a blinding snowstorm made further progress impossible. They passed the night alone in the cottage of Mumbett, an old Indian woman who had strayed back to her early home from her tribe in New York.

On the following morning Caleb happened to come by just when Mumbett entered her cottage. His efforts to arouse the sleepers from the stupor which followed exposure in the subzero temperature, convinced him of their insensibility to their situation. But he recognized the favorable possibilities for his scheme. From him Mary learned the circumstances of the night in Mumbett's cottage together with his own fabrication, that gossip aired the story. But one escape from disgrace remained, he assured her. If she married him, no one would dare to speak evil of the minister's wife. Angered and humiliated, she fled to her favorite retreat on Monument Mountain, where, by accident, William found her. As she attempted to tell him of their mutual disgrace, she lost her balance and fell striking her head against a rock. In a few moments she lay dead at his feet. About her neck she wore a cord holding a tiny crucifix which Mumbett had given her. William grasped this cord as he attempted to prevent her fall. He now believed he had

strangled the girl. In fear he hid her body in a charcoal heap.
Brain fever obliterated all memory of the meeting on the
mountain. Friends thought Mary had fallen into the river and
the water had carried her body to sea.

Four years later children on a picnic found a blackened
crucifix near the charcoal heap. The glimpse of it restored
William's memory, but his weakened heart failed to survive
the nervous shock. Back in Lancashire again, Susan and Mrs.
Morrison recalled the events of the years in Greenville as the
half-effaced images of indistinct dreams.

As a work of art, this book deserves meager consideration.
It is loosely constructed. Interest shifts from Mr. Morrison in
the first third of the story to the relationships of William,
Caleb, and Mary. The author devotes much space to descriptions and to background. *Far Away and Long Ago* is primarily a
study of character and of social conditions. Although Caleb
Killigrew is its most vivid creation, the author disliked him.
The proselyting minister disrupts the peace and happiness of
the whole village. The only benevolent, magnanimous persons
are those whom the Reverend Killigrew counts among the
lost souls.

Only Mary is of special interest. Significantly, the phrases
which distinguish her are those most frequently applied to
the author. Pride is the predominant element of Mary's disposition, a pride which sustains her through all misunderstandings. She resents all attempts of others to restrain her actions.
Her excitable, impulsive, irritable, highly strung nervous
temper is ill adapted to contend with difficulties. She is morbidly sensitive and willfully capricious. To her, life is essentially
tragic because of her own temperament. After the death of
her father she feels kinship only with the old Indian, Mumbett.
Her other source of consolation comes from the wildness and
loneliness of nature. A force which says that pride is sin,
and beauty a snare of the evil one attempts to crush her.
A religion which falsifies facts to achieve its purpose drives her

to her death, but it fails to touch the determination of this willful resistant.

In the character of Mary Morrison, perhaps, the author voiced her own final defiance of the traditionalism and orthodoxy which attempted to crush her. Both Mary and her creator found themselves in uncongenial surroundings. Their artistic, impulsive, rebellious temperaments continually clashed with the blind conventions of a staid society. Each refused to accept custom. Each was an independent being with impulses and ideas of her own. Although convention attempted to destroy their individuality, both defied its demands. The integrity of their individualism remained their most sacred possession. Both preserved it no matter what the cost; both scorned compromise. The strength and weaknesses of Mary's character were also those of her creator.

In 1891 came the last of Mrs. Kemble's publications, *Further Records*, a sequel to her earlier autobiographical accounts. Although it lacked the charm of the former series, it was an interesting continuation of the narrative of her life. Two independent sequences of letters, one addressed to Arthur Malkin and the other to Harriet Saint Leger, revealed in general the events of her life and her interests from 1848 to 1883. A deplorable lack of good editing resulted in much confusion and repetition. Her failure to arrange the two series in chronological order showed a growing indifference to artistic principles. In the middle of the story, the reader must turn from an account of the author's Alpine journeys during the late seventies to the middle of her brilliant theatrical career in 1848.

Undated letters jumbled into the narrative without respect for time sequence disconcert the reader. He misses the charm of the *Records of a Girlhood* and the vigor of *Records of Later Life*.[23] A comparison of the two series of letters presents interesting differences. Those to Mr. Malkin as a rule tell of more trivial matters. They are records of commonplace interests. Those to

14

Miss Saint Leger include discussions of religious matters and of philosophical questions. Fanny tried to understand and to sympathize with this life-long friend who always was seriously inclined, and whose blindness now increased her sober thoughtfulness. To her Fanny wrote of her deeper feelings as well as of the mountains which she climbed or the miserly innkeepers whom she encountered. These letters contained expressions of her most mature ideas and beliefs.

Throughout her life, Fanny felt a great aversion to correcting proofs of her published writings. This in part explained the errors to be found in them, for the publishers frequently failed to decipher her writing. The information that she was reading a proof brought terror to the printer's heart. She felt no patience with his blundering mistranslation of her illegible penmanship. He was sure to find some such expression as "Don't be stupid" in the margin by a word which had caused him much irritating speculation. *Records of a Girlhood* came from the press without her seeing a single proof sheet. Without doubt, *Further Records* was the victim of similar inattention.[24]

Fanny was in her eighty-second year when *Further Records* came from the press. Although she was old in years, her spirit was still undaunted. She felt the throb of life more intensely than many less than half her age. She remained stately, upright, and ruddy of complexion. She retained the power of making new friends and of loving them. No matter whether expressions of esteem came in the form of white azaleas, a favorite song, or a visit, the bestower always received proof of her appreciation.[25] She possessed to a rare degree the gift of ennobling anything to which she turned her mind. By a touch almost divine she made others aware of qualities within themselves greater than they formerly were conscious of.[26]

No more sincere person ever lived. To be able to count her as a friend was to be sure of one thing in life. She would sacrifice herself and all of her belongings for what she conceived to be the truth. Instead of the conventional, "I hope I am not making a mistake," she substituted the more characteristic expression, "I hope I am not telling a lie." She valued at the worth of a shilling nothing except friendship, honor, and truth.

She encountered publicity as she encountered bad weather. The public was much more aware of her than she of it. A friend complained to her of an acquaintance's remarks: "I do not care what anyone thinks of me or chooses to say of me," she replied. "Nay more than that, I do not care what anyone chooses to say of the people I love; it does not in any way affect the truth. People are at liberty to speak what they choose, and I am also at liberty not to care one farthing for what they say nor for any mistakes they make."[27]

She retained, too, the vivacity, humor, and interest in events which characterized her earlier years. People who read accounts of her successes of 1829 and then met her during her old age frequently were astonished to learn that she still lived: "No wonder they were surprised and bewildered," she remarked with a twinkle in her eyes. "Poor things, they supposed that I was dead long ago." She remained susceptible to the lure of the playhouse even during her latest years. A friend persuaded her to attend a revival of *The Hunchback*. The performance was wretched. Actors mouthed their lines and stormed about the stage in undignified violence. Thoughts of the past recalled other performances and other actors in those dramatic rôles, her father, Mr. Knowles, and her own original creation of Julia. She sat through two acts. With tears in her eyes she demanded, "How could you bring me to see this thing?" She had survived the order of things which had distinguished her age.[28]

Conversation sometimes led to reminiscences. She talked of her mother, the god-daughter of Maria Theresa of Austria, of Aunt Dall and her faithfulness to her betrothed, and of her father's devotion to the stage. When upon rare occasions she mentioned her unhappy married life, she spoke tenderly of Mr. Butler. She blamed him for none of their misunderstandings. The censure was hers, she said. If she had been less self-willed and more conciliatory all would have been well.[29]

Conversation opened the doors to all her mind. She talked as she wrote, "observing, assenting, complaining, confiding, and contradicting." Companions felt a free sincerity and the absence of diplomacy in her intercourse. Wisdom and wit, criticism and keen analysis of character, and outbursts of eloquence entertained all listeners. With all her predilections for the stage, no one could have savored less of the "shop." She remained dramatic long after she had ceased to be theatrical. Her incomparable voice and nobility of expression existed independently of ambition or of cultivation.

She spoke in agreeable, uncontemporary, self-respecting, idiomatic English. She hated Gallicisms in English just as she winced at Anglicisms in French. She remained intensely English, the model of the English Philistine, she said. She knew what she meant, and so did her friends, but she always worded in French the statement of her chauvinistic faithfulness: "*Ah vous savez je suis anglaise, moi, la plus anglaise des anglaises.*" She was willing to entertain with her whimsicalities. If they failed, her eccentricities remained.[30]

Although she ceased to be a public figure, she retained a firm hold upon her circle of friends. She gave a continuity to the far away past. She exemplified an age's appreciation of culture, art, and literature.[31] Fredrika Bremer excused herself for not receiving her friend when she called: "I could not see so many people as you are when I had a headache." Mrs. Kemble was what this friend said, many people: actress, musician, reader, philosopher, journalist, critic, and poet.[32] Her diversity of interests stamped her as a true representative of the age in which she lived.

A richly gifted woman of genius, with a warm heart and a noble mind, animated by life and spirit enough to ride a horse to death every day or to dominate any man or woman who might attempt to master her, said one intimate acquaintance. One moment she seemed proud as the proudest queen;

the next, as humble and amiable as an unassuming young girl. Loving splendor, she cultivated expensive habits of life; yet she could be as simple as a peasant maid. Her eyes seemed to comprehend the whole world, and her dilated nostrils, to inhale all its affluent life. "For my part—to use the words of one of her friends —," concluded this penetrating observer, "I am glad there is *one* Fanny Kemble in the world, but I do not wish that there should be two."[33]

Friends who called on November 27, 1892, to congratulate her on her eighty-third birthday recognized the approaching end in her failing strength. For years she had suffered a painful martyrdom from asthma. Other ailments came with advancing age. Her eyesight failed slightly, and she also became somewhat deaf. To aid her hearing, she procured a kind of trumpet with a mouthpiece and a long India rubber tube, but she scorned and ridiculed it. Looking up with one of her mischievous old flashes, she demanded of a friend, "Should you like to talk to me at the other end of such a thing as that?"[34]

At last Fanny had given up her independent residence and had gone to Gloucester Place, Portman Square, to reside with the Leighs. Soon after the beginning of the new year she became ill, but in spite of her advanced age she regained her strength. During her earlier years she often thought of death. Of what would one think while he awaited it? When she almost drowned, all her past life seemed like a blank. Did one forget the past when one knew of the near approach of death, she wondered?

She wanted the end to come without warning, like a flash of lightning. If she could choose the circumstances, she said, she would prefer a broken neck sustained from a backward fall from her horse while he raced at full gallop. Pain was unbearable; she shrank from the thought of bedridden suffering. In part, her desire was realized. Without warning, on Sunday, January 15, 1893, she died.[35]

At two o'clock on Friday, January 20, friends gathered in the Church of England chapel at Kensel Green. The Reverend

M. C. Richardson read a simple burial service. For London in that season of the year the day was unusually warm and bright. Sunlight streamed over the flower-hidden casket on its way to the grave near that of her father in Kensel Green Cemetery. Wreaths of camelias, white tulips, chrysanthemums, hyacinths, and lilies-of-the-valley surrounded the family piece, a cross of double daffodils with an inner cross of anemones in Fanny's favorite color, mauve.[36]

When that group to whom she represented rare things turned away from the flower-covered grave, the world seemed emptier and meaner. To one mourner came memories of a dark-haired young woman on horseback, a passionate voice interpreting *King Lear,* and a stately old lady filling small bags with bon-bons. "A prouder nature never fronted the long humiliation of life," he mused.[37] To others came her own words:

> Let me not die forever! When I'm gone
> To the cold earth; but let my memory
> Live like the gorgeous western light that shone
> Over the clouds where sank day's majesty.

NOTES TO CHAPTER I

[1] Frances Anne Kemble, *Records of a Girlhood*, pp. 7-8. The eldest child, Phillip, died in infancy. John Mitchell was the oldest surviving child. Henry and Adelaide were younger than Fanny. In the interest of uniformity I have adopted the spelling "Anne." Fanny herself used either "Anne" or "Ann."

[2] Percy Fitzgerald, *The Kembles*, I, 11-13. Henry Siddons thought the names Campbell and Kemble were virtually the same. Cf. *Life and Letters of Thomas Campbell*, ed. William Beattie, III, 89. Mr. Campbell believed that the two names were originally the same and that the original sojourn of the Kembles was in Wales. Cf. Frances Anne Kemble, *Journal*, II, 18. Gouverneur Kemble was a great meddler in names. He told Fanny that the Kembles were originally Italian pirates by the name of Campo Bello. They belonged to the same family as the Scottish Campbells and the Norman Beauchamps. Cf. *The Kemble Papers* (by) Stephen Kemble. *Collections of the New York Historical Society*, 1884. Account of Peter Kemble of Mount Kemble, New Jersey, written in 1769. "In the north part of Wiltshire, near the edge of the county, within a few miles of Tilbury, Malmesbury, and Cirencester, near the source of the Isis, is a village and church or as I have been told a church only called Kemble, an ecclesiastical benefice in Malmesbury Deanery. . . . It is said that William Camden, Clarencieux King-at-Arms in the reign of Queen Elizabeth, did give George Kemble, of Wydell, or Widhill, in the country of Wilts, the coat-of-arms now used in the family."

[3] André Maurois, *Mape, the World of Illusion*, p. 151.

[4] Fitzgerald, *op. cit.*, pp. 12-14.

[5] *Ibid.*, pp. 15-16. Roger and Sally Kemble were the parents of twelve children: Sarah, John Phillip, Stephen, Frances, Elizabeth, Mary, Anne, Catherine, Lucy, Henry, Charles, and Jane. Eight grew to maturity. All devoted a part or the whole of their lives to the stage.

[6] Maurois, *op. cit.*, pp. 154-68. Cf. *Dictionary of National Biography*, xxx, 376-78.

[7] H. B. Baker, *History of the London Stage and Its Famous Players,* 1576-1903, p. 84.

[8] J. E. Murdock, *The Stage,* p. 194. Quoted from the *London Monthly Mirror,* 1801.

[9] Kemble, *op. cit.,* pp. 2-6. Cf. Murdock, *op. cit.,* p. 194.

[10] Kemble, *op. cit.,* pp. 2-7. Cf. Murdock, *op. cit.,* pp. 197-99. Three more of the Decamp children distinguished themselves in theatrical work. Adelaide (Aunt Dall) gave many years to the stage. Another daughter forsook the theater to become Mrs. Frederick Brown. Vincent Decamp came to the United States and established a theater chain in Charleston, Columbia, Savannah, and Augusta. The remaining child, Victorie, became a governess in a school at Lea.

[11] Anne Thackeray Ritchie, *From Friend to Friend,* pp. 40-41.

[12] Una Birch Pope-Hennessy, *Three English Women in America,* pp. 112-14.

[13] Kemble, *op. cit.,* pp. 1-2.

[14] *Ibid.,* p. 9.

[15] *Ibid.,* pp. 9-10.

[16] *Ibid.,* pp. 10-12.

[17] *Ibid.,* p. 25.

[18] *Ibid.,* p. 17.

[19] *Ibid.,* pp. 26-31.

[20] *Ibid.,* pp. 31-40.

[21] *Ibid.,* pp. 42-44.

[22] *Ibid.,* pp. 56-57.

[23] Frances Anne Kemble, "Old Woman's Gossip," *Atlantic Monthly,* xxxvi (1875), 589.

[24] Kemble, *Records of a Girlhood,* pp. 44-74.

NOTES TO CHAPTER II

[1] Frances Anne Kemble, *Records of a Girlhood,* p. 75. This chapter for the most part is based on Miss Kemble's own account For that reason I have allowed the references to include rather large units.

[2] *Ibid.,* pp. 74-81.

[3] *Ibid.,* pp. 82-84.

[4] *Ibid.,* pp. 85-86.

[5] *Ibid.*, p. 104.

[6] *Ibid.*, pp. 90-107.

[7] *Ibid.*, pp. 115-18.

[8] "Francis the First," *Quarterly Review*, XLVII (1832), 243-61. Cf. *Athenæum*, CCXXIX (1832), 170-71.

[9] Kemble, *op. cit.*, p. 122.

[10] *Ibid.*, p. 135.

[11] *Ibid.*, pp. 122-23.

[12] *Ibid.*, p. 136.

[13] *Ibid.*, p. 131.

[14] *Ibid.*, pp. 141-42.

[15] *Ibid.*, p. 142.

[16] *Ibid.*, pp. 160-61.

[17] *Ibid.*, pp. 165-66.

[18] *Ibid.*, p. 167.

[19] *Ibid.*, pp. 179-84.

[20] *Ibid.*, pp. 74-184, *passim*.

[21] H. B. Baker, *History of the London Stage*, 1576-1903, pp. 124-36. Cf. *Dramatic Magazine*, I (1892), 215. Cf. *Dictionary of National Biography*, XXX, pp. 365-76.

[22] Kemble, *op. cit.*, pp. 186-87.

[23] *Ibid.*, pp. 169, 187.

[24] *Ibid.*, pp. 168-87, 223.

[25] Frances Anne Kemble, *Journal*, II, 16-17.

[26] Kemble, *Records of a Girlhood*, p. 188.

[27] *Ibid.*, pp. 178-88.

NOTES TO CHAPTER III

[1] Frances Anne Kemble, *Records of a Girlhood*, pp. 196-97.

[2] The description of the theater is based on the following: *Ibid.*, pp. 219-20; Percy Fitzgerald, *A New History of the London Stage*, II, 372-73; H. B. Baker, *History of the London Stage, 1576-1903*, pp. 128-29; Percy Fitzgerald, *The Kembles*, II, 119; *Encyclopædia Britannica*, VII, 340.

[3] *Athenæum*, CII (October 7, 1829), 633. Cf. *Dramatic Magazine*, I (1829), 267-68. Cf. Kemble, *op. cit.*, pp. 219-20.

[4] Edward Robins, *Twelve Great Actresses*, pp. 283-84.

[5] Kemble, *op. cit.*, p. 220.

[6] William C. Russell, *Representative Actors*, p. 400. Quoted from *New Monthly Magazine*, 1829.

[7] *Athenæum*, CIV (October 21, 1828), 666. Cf. *Ibid.*, CII (October 7, 1829), 633.

[8] Russell, *op. cit.*, p. 400. Cf. *Dramatic Magazine*, I (1829), 268.

[9] *Athenæum*, CII (October 7, 1829), 633.

[10] Kemble, *op. cit.*, p. 221.

[11] *Ibid.*, pp. 220-22.

[12] Robins, *op. cit.*, p. 284.

[13] Kemble, *op. cit.*, p. 225.

[14] *Dramatic Magazine*, I (1829), 268-331. Throughout the months of October and November she appeared every Monday, Wednesday, and Friday night in this same rôle.

[15] Baker, *op. cit.*, p. 82.

[16] Kemble, *op. cit.*, pp. 225-37.

[17] *Athenæum* CXII (December 16, 1829), 780.

[18] *Ibid.*, pp. 780-82. Cf. *Dramatic Magazine*, I (1829), 331.

[19] *Athenæum*, CXVII (January 23, 1830), 44-45. Cf. *Gentleman's Magazine and Historical Chronicle*, C, Part I (1830), 75. Cf. *Dramatic Magazine*, II (1830), 22-25, 54-57.

[20] Robins, *op. cit.*, p. 285.

[21] Russell, *op. cit.*, p. 401.

[22] Kemble, *op. cit.*, pp. 199, 243.

[23] *Athenæum*, CXXII (February 27, 1830), 126. Cf. *Dramatic Magazine*, II (1830), 83-86. Cf. *The Greville Diary*, ed. P. W. Wilson, II, 546.

[24] Kemble, *op. cit.*, pp. 246-247.

[25] *Ibid.*, p. 224.

[26] Henry Lee, "Frances Anne Kemble," *Atlantic Monthly*, LXXI (1893), 664.

[27] Kemble, *op. cit.*, pp. 209, 237.

[28] *Ibid.*, p. 249.

[29] *Athenæum*, CXXVI (March 27, 1830), 188. Cf. *Dramatic Magazine*, II (1830), 86.

[30] *Athenæum*, CXXXV (May 29, 1830), 333. Cf. *Dramatic Magazine*, II (1830), 152-56, 182-84.

[31] *Dramatic Magazine*, II (1830), 186-187. Cf. *Athenæum*, CXXXV (May 29, 1830), 333.

[32] *Dramatic Magazine*, II (1830), 186-87.

[33] Baker, *op. cit.*, p. 136.

[34] *Dramatic Magazine*, I (1829), 215. The receipts for the season of 1828-1829 amounted to only £41,777.

[35] *Dramatic Magazine*, II (1830), 192, 287-88.

[36] Kemble, *op. cit.*, pp. 260-61.

[37] John G. Lockhart, *Memoirs of the Life of Sir Walter Scott*, V, 258-60. Entry in Scott's "Diary" under date of June 26, 1830.

[38] *Ibid.*, p. 258, June 17, 1830. Cf. Kemble, *op. cit.*, pp. 261-63.

[39] Kemble, *op. cit.*, pp. 266-67. Cf. *Dramatic Magazine*, II (1830), 287-88.

[40] Kemble, *op. cit.*, pp. 288-89. Cf. *Dramatic Magazine*, II (1830), 287-88. Engagements at Cork, Liverpool, Manchester, and Birmingham completed the summer tour.

[41] Kemble, *op. cit.*, pp. 293-94.

[42] *Ibid.*, pp. 295-304.

[43] *Athenæum*, CLIV (October 9, 1830), 637. Cf. *Dramatic Magazine*, II (1830), 314 and 377.

[44] Kemble, *op. cit.*, pp. 306-7. Cf. *Dramatic Magazine*, II (1830), 338.

[45] *Athenæum*, CLXIII (December 11, 1830), 780-81.

[46] *Dramatic Essays by Leigh Hunt*, edited by William Archer and Robert W. Lowe, p. 148.

[47] *Ibid.*, pp. 169-70.

[48] Fitzgerald, *A New History of the London Stage*, II, 424-25.

[49] Kemble, *op. cit.*, p. 417.

[50] *Op. cit.*, p. 206.

[51] Kemble, *op. cit.*, p. 416. Cf. *Dramatic Magazine*, III (1831), 192. Cf. Shakespearean Playbills, 55, 56, and 57. Manuscript Division, Library of Congress.

[52] Fitzgerald, *A New History of the London Stage*, II, 426.

[53] W. W. Clapp, *Records of the Boston Stage*, pp. 61-68.

[54] *Ibid.*, pp. 118-31.

[55] *Ibid.*, pp. 167-79.

[56] *Ibid.*, pp. 239-40.

[57] Kemble, *op. cit.*, p. 511.

[58] Baker, *op. cit.*, p. 95.

[59] Kemble, *op. cit.*, p. 458.

[60] *Ibid.*, p. 459.

[61] *Athenæum*, CCXI (November 12, 1831), 741.

[62] *Ibid*, CCXIII (November 26, 1831), 773.

[63] Kemble, *op. cit.*, p. 489.

[64] *Ibid.*, pp. 503, 518-19. Cf. *Athenæum*, CCXXIX (March 17, 1832), 181.

[65] *Athenæum*, CCXXXII (April 7, 1832), 229-30. Cf. Robins, *op. cit.*, pp. 290-91.

[66] Kemble, *op. cit.*, pp. 520-32.

NOTES TO CHAPTER IV

[1] Frances Anne Kemble, *Journal*, I, 1-47. The *Pacific* sailed on August 1 and arrived in New York on September 4. The first steamship crossed the Atlantic in 1819.

[2] Henry Wansey, *Excursion to the United States in 1794*. Salisbury, 1798.

[3] John Melish, *Travels in the United States, 1806-1811*. Philadelphia (   ), 1812, pp. x, 37.

[4] John Bernard, *Retrospections of America, 1797-1811*. New York, 1887.

[5] Thomas Cooper, *Some Information Respecting America*. London, 1794.

[6] This summary of early travellers and their reports follows Allan Nevins, *American Social History as Recorded by British Travellers*, pp. 3-107.

[7] "Inchiquen the Jesuit's Letters during a Late Residence in the United States of America," *Quarterly Review*, x (1814), 497-539.

[8] "On the Means of Education and the State of Learning in the United States of America," *Blackwood's*, IV (1819), 546-53, 642-49.

[9] "Statistical Annals of the United States of America by Adam Seybert," *Edinburgh Review*, XXXIII (1820), 69-80.

[10] Captain Frederick Marryat, *A Diary in America*. London, 1839.

[11] Thomas Hamilton, *Men and Manners in America*. Philadelphia, 1833.

[12] Mrs. Frances M. Trollope, *Domestic Manners of the Americans*. London (   ), 1832, pp. 56, 87-88.

[13] Nevins, *op. cit.*, pp. 111-38, is the source of this survey.

[14] Frances Anne Kemble, *Records of a Girlhood*, pp. 532-33.

[15] Frances Anne Kemble, *Fanny Thimble Cutler's Journal*, p. 3. I assign this journal to Miss Kemble on the basis of internal evidence.

The Library of Congress, which possesses the only copies which I have found, assigns it to her.

[16] Kemble, *Records of a Girlhood*, pp. 536-47. Cf. Kemble, *Journal*, I, 96.

[17] *New York Mirror*, September 15, 1832.

[18] *Diary of Philip Hone*, edited by Allan Nevins, I, 75.

[19] Kemble, *Journal*, I, 89-90.

[20] Hone, *op. cit.*, pp. 75-76.

[21] Kemble, *Journal*, I, 52-53.

[22] *New York Mirror*, September 22, 1832. Cf. Kemble, *Records of a Girlhood*, pp. 541-42. Cf. *Journal*, I, 47-96. Charles Kemble made his first appearance as Hamlet on September 17. The management thought it expedient for the two stars to act singly and then, as Fanny said, to make a constellation. The procedure at her début illustrated the attempt of managers to offer something acceptable to all tastes. A farce, *Popping the Question*, preceded *Fazio*.

[23] Hone, *op. cit.*, p. 77.

[24] *New York Mirror*, September 22, 1832.

[25] Pp. 11-12.

[26] *New York Mirror*, September 29, 1832.

[27] *Ibid.*, October 6, 1832.

[28] J. T. Morse, *Life and Letters of Oliver Wendell Holmes*, I, 83.

[29] J. G. Wilson, *Life and Letters of Fitz-Greene Halleck*, p. 365.

[30] *Ibid.*, pp. 368-69.

[31] *New York Mirror*, October 13, 1832. This first engagement lasted from September 17 to October 7. Plays included *Hamlet, Fazio, Romeo and Juliet, School for Scandal, Venice Preserved, King John, The Hunchback, Much Ado About Nothing*, and *The Inconstant*. Here in accordance with the usual theatrical speculation of the time, the manager employed one or two stars for the principal rôles and "nine or ten sticks for the rest."

[32] Kemble, *Records of a Girlhood*, p. 544.

[33] *Ibid.*, p. 542.

[33a] Kemble, *Journal*, I, 106. The servant must have been a freedman. Slavery did not exist in New York at this time. See *Niles' Register*, XL (1831), 170, for the census report of 1830.

[34] Kemble, *Journal*, I, 83-85n.

[35] *Ibid.*, p. 103.

[36] *Ibid., passim.*

[37] *Ibid.*, pp. 131-32.

[38] *Ibid.*, pp. 139-40, 143, 190-91. According to the 1830 census the population of Philadelphia was 161,410. See E. Channing, *History of the United States*, v, 82. The slave population of the entire state of Pennsylvania numbered 381. See *Niles' Register*, XL (1831), 170. A note adds that this number is in error—too large.

[39] *American Sentinel and Mercantile Advertiser*, October 16, 1832.

[40] *National Gazette*, October 13, 1832. Cf. *American Sentinel and Mercantile Advertiser*, October 16, 1832.

[41] Kemble, *Journal*, I, 159, 166. Cf. Kemble, *Records of a Girlhood*, pp. 540-41. The American extravagance in the enormous sums spent for flowers astonished the English girl. She disapproved of the custom.

[42] *American Sentinel*, November 1, 1832.

[43] Kemble, *Journal*, I, 140-41.

[44] *American Sentinel*, November 1, 1832. Cf. *National Gazette*, October 26, 1832, and November 2, 1832.

[45] *American Sentinel and Mercantile Advertiser*, November 8, 1832. Accounts of the performances may be found in the *National Gazette* and the *American Sentinel and Mercantile Advertiser* from October 8 to November 10, 1832.

[46] *New York Mirror*, November 10 to December 3, 1832. The New York engagement lasted from November 6 to December 2. The following Philadelphia engagement began on December 3 and lasted to December 30, 1832. See the *National Gazette*, December 4 to December 31, 1832.

[47] *Baltimore Republican and Commercial Advertiser*, January 4, 1833.

[48] Kemble, *Records of a Girlhood*, p. 560.

[49] *Ibid.*, p. 563. An account of the Baltimore performances may be found in the *Baltimore Republican and Commercial Advertiser*, January 4 to 15, 1833. The population of Baltimore in 1830 numbered 80,625. See Channing, *op. cit.*, p. 82. The Negro population for the State of Maryland was 102,878 to 291,093 whites. See *Niles' Register*, XL (1831), 170.

[50] Kemble, *Fanny Thimble Cutler's Journal*, pp. 34-36.

[51] *Autobiography of David Crockett*, edited by Hamlin Garland, pp. 154-55.

[52] Claude G. Bowers, *Party Battles of the Jackson Period*, pp. 1-9. The population at this time was about 20,000.

[53] Kemble, *Journal*, II, 92, 95-96.

[54] *Ibid.*, p. 89.

[55] *Life and Letters of Washington Irving*, edited by Pierce M. Irving, II, 275-76.

[56] Bowers, *op. cit.*, pp. 16-17. The *Washington National Intelligencer* contains accounts of the performances.

[57] In the meantime they had acted in Baltimore, Philadelphia, New York, Philadelphia, Washington, Philadelphia, and New York in the order named. See the *National Gazette*, the *Baltimore Republican and Commercial Advertiser*, *New York Mirror*, and the *Washington National Intelligencer* for accounts of performances in the various cities.

[58] *Boston Daily Advertiser and Patriot*, April 17, 1833.

[59] Kemble, *Records of a Girlhood*, p. 574.

[60] *Boston Daily Advertiser and Patriot*, April 19, 1833.

[61] Kemble, *Journal*, II, 132n.

[62] Shattuck Papers, XI. Ellen Shattuck to George C. Shattuck, April 21, 1833, and George Shattuck to his son, May 8, 1833. Massachusetts Historical Society.

[63] Henry Lee, "Frances Anne Kemble," *Atlantic Monthly*, LXXI (1893), 664.

[64] *Memoirs and Letters of Charles Sumner*, edited by Edward Price, I, 102-4. Cf. *Ibid.*, pp. 662-75.

[65] Kemble, *Records of a Girlhood*, p. 575.

[66] Jefferson Williamson, *The American Hotel*, pp. 13-25.

[67] Kemble, *Journal*, II, 133.

[68] *Boston Daily Advertiser and Patriot*, April 23, 1833. The highest premium paid for any one box was $10. Orders for more than forty-two boxes were received after the sale.

[69] Kemble, *Journal*, I, 161-62 n., 196-97, and n.

[70] Joseph N. Ireland, *Records of the New York Stage from 1750-1860*, pp. 42-53. The aggregate receipts for the sixty nights on which the Kembles appeared amounted to more than $56,000. The whole amount received for the season ending July 4, 1833, totaled $150,000. The season as a whole was not successful. Charles Kean did not draw a single full house except for his benefit.

[71] H. P. Phelps, *Players of a Century*, pp. 48, 168.

[72] Una Birch Pope-Hennessy, *Three English Women in America,* p. 117.

[73] Kemble, *Records of a Girlhood,* p. 580.

[74] *Ibid.,* pp. 580-86.

[75] *National Gazette,* October 9, 1833. Note from *London Globe.* Cf. *Records of a Girlhood,* p. 586.

[76] *Marriage Notices in the South Carolina Gazette and Its Successors, 1732-1801,* compiled and edited by A. S. Salley, Jr., p. 45. Cf. "Records Kept by Col. Isaac Hayne," *South Carolina Historical and Genealogical Magazine,* XI (1910), 95. This second record gives Miss Middleton's name as Mary.

[77] Information supplied by Dr. Owen Wister. Cf. U. B. Phillips, *Life and Labor in the Old South,* pp. 259-60.

[78] *Germantown Telegraph,* November 27, 1833.

[79] The Kembles had appeared for several nights in Montreal previous to their return to New York. They appeared in Boston during September; during October, at Park Theater, New York; during November, at Chestnut Street Theater, Philadelphia; in December, again at Park Theater; in January, 1834, in Washington, Baltimore, and Philadelphia; in February, in Boston and New York; during March and April in Philadelphia, Baltimore, Washington, and Boston; during the latter part of April and the first weeks of May, in New York; May 26 to June 6 in Philadelphia; from June 9 to June 16, in New York. The *New York Mirror* furnishes accounts of the engagements in that city; the *Pennsylvanian* and *National Gazette,* of those in Philadelphia; the *Boston Daily Advertiser,* of those in Boston; the *Washington Globe,* of those in Washington; the *Baltimore Republican and Commercial Advertiser,* of those in Baltimore.

[80] *Pennsylvanian,* January 1, 1834. Cf. James Murdock, *The Stage,* p. 18.

[81] *New York Mirror,* April 19, 1834. Cf. Ireland, *op. cit.,* pp. 75-85. The Kembles played 45 nights in New York during the 1833-34 season with an average of $732. Their eight benefits averaged over $1,200. The gross receipts for the season were not quite $135,000. Mr. Powers averaged only $480, and his benefits, only $960. Although Mr. Woods's first engagement of eleven nights including benefits averaged $960, his total engagements of thirty-

nine nights averaged only $490. Cf. Mary C. Crawford, *Romantic Days in Old Boston*, p. 242. An engagement of eighteen nights in Boston totaled $11,671. This was considered as unusually large receipts for this time. Cf. Clapp, *op. cit.*, p. 315. He indicated this return as being that from the September engagement. Cf. F. C. Wemyss, *Chronology of the American Stage, from 1752 to 1852*, p. 85.

[82] *Boston Daily Advertiser and Patriot*, April 22, 1834.

[83] Kemble, *Records of a Girlhood*, pp. 18-24.

[84] *Ibid.*, pp. 588-89. Cf. Frances Anne Kemble, *Further Records*, p. 199.

[85] *Pennsylvanian*, June 6, 1834. The engagement began on May 26, 1834. They had previously appeared at the Park Theater, New York. See *New York Mirror*, April 19 to May 26, 1834.

[86] *Pennsylvanian*, June 9, 1834.

NOTES TO CHAPTER V

[1] Pierce Butler, *Statement*, p. 24. Cf. Frances Anne Kemble, *Records of Later Life*, pp. 1-15.

[2] Pierce Butler, *Statement*, p. 22.

[3] *Idem.* Mr. Butler read the manuscript and proof sheets. He struck out passages and incidents until she threatened to leave him rather than submit to further curtailment of a work already sold to publishers.

[4] Letter written to H. S. Legaré. Private collection of Legaré letters in the library of Mr. W. G. Chisolm.

[5] Kemble, *op. cit.*, pp. 27-28.

[6] *Ibid.*, pp. 4, 13. Miss Frances Butler, an aunt of Fanny's husband, held a life interest in the place. The English girl could not think of making changes which might distress an elderly person.

[7] *Ibid.*, pp. 4-5.

[8] *Ibid.*, p. 6.

[9] *Ibid.*, p. 7.

[10] *Athenæum*, CCCXCVI (May 30, 1835), 404-6.

[11] *Niles' Weekly Register*, XLVIII (1835), 395.

[12] *Atlantic Monthly*, L (1835), 421-24.

[13] *Southern Literary Messenger*, I (1834-35), 524-31.

[14] *Quarterly Review*, LIV (1835), 39-58.

15

[15] I attribute this journal to Mrs. Butler on the basis of internal evidence and on the authority of the Library of Congress catalogue. It lists the only copy which I have been able to locate.

[16] Kemble, *op. cit.*, pp. 15-16. Written in 1835.

[17] Frances Anne Kemble, *Journal of a Residence on a Georgian Plantation*, p. 104. Cf. *Ibid.*, p. 29.

[18] Kemble, *Records of Later Life*, pp. 21-22. See E. Channing, *History of the United States*, VI, 275-85. See also *Niles' Weekly Register*, XLVII-XLIX, *passim*.

[19] Kemble, *Records of Later Life*, pp. 29-30. It is interesting to compare her plan for a savings bank with the policy of Brigadier-General Rufus Saxton who supervised the thousands of Negro refugees on the Sea Islands during the Civil War. See *Official Records of the Union and Confederate Armies*, Series III: IV, 1022-31.

[20] Kemble, *Records of Later Life*, pp. 24, 28-29. Cf. Butler, *op. cit.*, p. 11.

[21] Frances Anne Kemble, *Journal*, I, 106; II, 24.

[22] Kemble, *Records of Later Life*, pp. 40-41.

[23] *Ibid.*, p. 66.

[24] *Ibid.*, p. 48.

[25] *Ibid.*, p. 49.

[26] *Ibid.*, pp. 56-57.

[27] A. H. Quinn: *A History of the American Drama from the Beginning to the Civil War*, p. 253.

[28] *Macready's Reminiscences and Selections from His Diaries and Letters*, edited by Sir Frederick Pollock, p. 465.

[29] Butler, *op. cit.*, p. 79.

[30] Kemble, *Records of Later Life*, p. 79.

[31] *Ibid.*, p. 71.

[32] *Ibid.*, p. 92.

[33] *Ibid.*, p. 25.

[34] *Ibid.*, pp. 25-26.

[35] Mary Appleton later married Robert, son of Sir James Macintosh, and Fanny became the wife of the poet, Longfellow.

[36] Kemble, *Records of Later Life*, pp. 93-103.

[37] *Ibid.*, p. 139.

[38] *Ibid.*, p. 103.

[39] *Ibid.*, pp. 114-15.

[40] *Ibid.*, pp. 122-26.

[41] *Ibid.*, p. 131.

[42] *Ibid.*, pp. 131-33.

NOTES TO CHAPTER VI

[1] Frances Anne Kemble, *Journal of a Residence on a Georgian Plantation*, pp. 79-80. Hereafter cited as *Georgian Plantation*. This study does not attempt to appraise the value or validity of Mrs. Kemble's account of conditions on the Georgia plantations. Its purpose is to show what the experiences there meant to her and their influence on her later life. A discussion of the *Journal* will find a place among the events recounted in a later chapter, which concerns events at the time of its publication.

[2] *Ibid.*, pp. 176-77.

[3] Thomas Clarkson, *The History of the Rise, Progress, and Accomplishment of the Abolition of the African Slave-Trade by the British Parliament*, pp. 64-65. In 1772 Lord Mansfield rendered a decision on the case of James Somerset, an African slave brought to England by his master, Charles Stewart. His decision was that as soon as any slave set foot on English territory, he became free.

[4] Kemble, *Georgian Plantation*, pp. 15-16. Cf. Kemble, *Records of Later Life*, p. 137.

[5] W. E. Dodd, *Cotton Kingdom*, pp. 70-72.

[6] Kemble, *Georgian Plantation*, pp. 25-27.

[7] Kemble, *Records of Later Life*, p. 135.

[8] Frances Anne Kemble, *Further Records*, p. 198. Written August 18, 1876.

[9] Kemble, *Records of Later Life*, p. 144.

[10] In 1859 when the slaves were sold, Pierce Butler's half numbered 436. This meant that at least 872 slaves lived in not more than 80 huts, at least 11 to the hut.

[11] Kemble, *Georgian Plantation*, pp. 17-18.

[12] *Ibid.*, pp. 30-31.

[13] *Ibid.*, pp. 33-34.

[14] *Ibid.*, p. 35.

[15] I am indebted to Mr. Arthur Y. Lloyd's "Southern Justification of Slavery," an unpublished thesis in the Vanderbilt library, for this summary of pro-slavery arguments.

[16] Kemble, *Records of Later Life*, p. 139.

[17] *Ibid.*, p. 70.

[17a] *Georgian Plantation*, p. 65.

[18] *Ibid.*, p. 35.

[19] *Ibid.*, p. 43. For a statement of the usual instructions of owners to overseers see H. M. Henry, *Police Control of the Slave in South Carolina*, pp. 22-24, and U. B. Phillips, *Plantation and Frontier*, I, 115-26.

[20] Kemble, *Georgian Plantation*, *passim*.

[21] *Ibid.*, pp. 43-44, 209.

[22] *Ibid.*, pp. 44, 140. Cf. Henry, *op. cit.*, pp. 26-27 and Phillips, *Plantation and Frontier*, pp. 117, 127, for statements of the head driver's duties as generally defined by owners and overseers.

[23] Kemble, *Georgian Plantation*, p. 75.

[24] *Ibid.*, p. 28. For statements of the amount of work regarded by planters as a day's labor, see Phillips, *Plantation and Frontier*, p. 118; U. B. Phillips, *American Negro Slavery*, pp. 247-48; F. L. Olmsted, *Journey in the Seaboard Slave States, 1853-1854*, II, 62.

[25] Kemble, *Georgian Plantation*, pp. 25-28. Cf. Phillips, *Plantation and Frontier*, II, 38.

[26] A. B. Hart, *Slavery and Abolition*, p. 100.

[27] Kemble, *Georgian Plantation*, pp. 52-53, 229.

[28] *Ibid.*, p. 52. Cf. Phillips, *American Negro Slavery*, p. 265. Apparently there was no uniformity in the clothing distributed by various planters.

[29] Kemble, *Georgian Plantation*, pp. 64-65.

[30] *Ibid.*, p. 44.

[31] *Ibid.*, p. 30.

[32] *Ibid.*, p. 36. Statements of the rations deemed ordinarily sufficient may be found in Phillips, *Plantation and Frontier*, I, 18-126; Olmsted, *op. cit.*, pp. 19, 68; Dodd, *op. cit.*, p. 74; V. A. Moody, *Slavery on Louisiana Sugar Plantations*, pp. 74-77. Various statements occur. Dr. Dodd says that a week's allowance included four pounds of meat, a peck of meal, and a quart of molasses with something over for the little ones. Cf. Hart, *op. cit.*, p. 100. Cornbread and bacon with sweet potatoes and some vegetable was the ordinary diet. A peck of meal, three pounds of bacon, with a little sugar and wheat flour made a suitable ration for each hand.

[33] Kemble, *Georgian Plantation*, pp. 96-97.
[34] *Ibid.*, p. 127.
[35] *Ibid.*, p. 91.
[36] *Ibid.*, pp. 56-57.
[37] *Ibid.*, pp. 220-21, 238, 267.
[38] *Ibid.*, p. 85.
[39] *Ibid.*, 42-43.
[40] *Ibid.*, pp. 142, 153, 205, 235, 272, 228.
[40a] *Ibid.*, p. 228.
[41] *Ibid.*, p. 167.
[42] *Ibid.*, p. 207.
[43] *Ibid.*, pp. 55, 134, 199, 209, 227-29, 232, 240.
[44] *Ibid.*, p. 54.
[45] *Ibid.*, pp. 67, 156
[46] Kemble, *Records of Later Life*, p. 155.
[47] *Ibid.*, p. 153; Kemble, *Georgian Plantation*, p. 127.
[48] Kemble, *Georgian Plantation*, pp. 128-29.
[49] *Ibid.*, pp. 115-50.
[50] *Ibid.*, p. 79.
[51] *Ibid.*, pp. 157-59.
[52] *Ibid.*, p. 166.
[53] *Ibid.*, pp. 170-71.
[54] *Ibid.*, p. 171.
[55] *Ibid.*, pp. 230-31.
[56] *Ibid.*, pp. 171-72.
[57] *Ibid.*, p. 193.
[58] *Ibid.*, p. 130-31.
[59] *Ibid.*, p. 89.
[60] *Ibid.*, p. 263.
[61] Kemble, *Records of Later Life*, p. 137.
[62] Kemble, *Georgian Plantation*, p. 146.
[63] *Ibid.*, p. 249.
[64] *Ibid.*, p. 162.
[65] *Ibid.*, pp. 14-15.
[66] Kemble, *Records of Later Life*, p. 205.
[67] *Ibid.*, p. 31.
[68] Kemble, *Georgian Plantation*, p. 135.

NOTES TO CHAPTER VII

[1] Frances Anne Kemble, *Records of Later Life*, p. 176.

[2] Pierce Butler, *Statement*, pp. 52-53.

[3] Kemble, *op. cit.*, p. 150.

[4] Butler, *op. cit.*, pp. 9-11.

[5] Anne Thackeray Ritchie, "Chapters from Some Unwritten Memories—Mrs. Kemble," *Macmillan's Magazine*, LXVIII (1893), 195.

[6] "Fanny Kemble's Suddenness," *Critic*, XXII (1893), 291-92.

[7] Butler, *op. cit.*, p. 39.

[8] *Ibid.*, p. 28.

[9] *Idem.* See *Pennsylvanian*, March 21, 1836. Miss Frances Butler, daughter of Hon. Pierce Butler, died March 18, 1836.

[10] Butler, *op. cit.*, pp. 33-35.

[11] *Ibid.*, pp. 40-44. Fanny has left no statement of her marital difficulties before 1842. All references in her letters are carefully expurgated. Mr. Butler's *Statement* is practically the only source. One may suspect that he included only those letters or parts of letters which seemed to justify his procedure.

[12] Kemble, *op. cit.*, pp. 172-73. Cf. Letters from Pierce Butler to Mr. Tuckerman, February 7, 1840, Boston Public Library.

[13] Butler, *op. cit.*, pp. 53-56.

[14] Kemble, *op. cit.*, p. 204.

[15] *Ibid.*, pp. 193-202.

[16] Una Birch Pope-Hennessy, *Three English Women in America*, p. 208.

[17] Kemble, *op. cit.*, pp. 205-6. Cf. Butler, *op. cit.*, pp. 57-59.

[18] Kemble, *op. cit.*, pp. 207, 244-46.

[19] *Ibid.*, p. 227.

[20] *Ibid.*, p. 210.

[21] *Ibid.*, pp. 248-51.

[22] *Ibid.*, pp. 227, 239.

[23] *Ibid.*, pp. 253-69.

[24] *Ibid.*, p. 281.

[25] *Ibid.*, pp. 302-4.

[26] *Ibid.*, pp. 319-46.

[27] Butler, *op. cit.*, p. 13.

[28] *Pittsfield Sun*, December 7, 1848.

[29] Butler, *op. cit.*, pp. 15-17. Cf. Kemble, *op. cit.*, p. 324.

[30] Kemble, *op. cit.*, pp. 344-45.

[31] Butler, *op. cit.*, pp. 60-61.

[32] Letter, December 15, 1842, quoted in *Answer of Frances Anne Butler to the Libel of Pierce Butler Praying a Divorce*, p. 32.

[33] Butler, *op. cit.*, p. 76.

[34] *Ibid.*, p. 69.

[35] *Ibid.*, pp. 70-71.

[36] *Ibid.*, pp. 71-72.

[37] *Answer of Frances Anne Butler*, pp. 35-37.

[38] Butler, *op. cit.*, p. 79.

[39] *Ibid.*, pp. 79-91.

[40] *Answer of Frances Anne Butler*, p. 7.

[41] *The Greville Diary*, edited by P. W. Wilson, II, 547. Written December 8, 1842. This statement represents the only available scrap of unbiased material on the subject of the Butlers' marital difficulties. All other references come from either Mr. Butler's *Statement* or Mrs. Butler's writings. Likely neither told any considerable part of the circumstances which led to their separation.

[42] Kemble, *Records of Later Life*, p. 371.

[43] Butler, *Statement*, p. 63.

[44] *Ibid.*, pp. 107-13.

[45] Kemble, *op. cit.*, pp. 372, 383-85.

[46] *Ibid.*, p. 404.

[47] *Ibid.*, pp. 171, 406, 417.

[48] *Quarterly Review*, LXXV (1845), 325-34.

[49] *Athenæum*, DCCCLXXIV (1844), 687.

[50] *Ibid.*, DCCCLXXV (1844), 712-13.

[51] *Quarterly Review*, LXXV (1845), 325-34.

[52] Kemble, *op. cit.*, p. 417.

[53] *Ibid.*, pp. 387-88, 399, 404.

[54] *Ibid.*, pp. 379-84.

[55] *Answer of Frances Anne Butler*, p. 7.

[56] Butler, *Statement*, pp. 114-15.

[57] *Answer of Frances Anne Butler*, p. 7.

[58] *Philadelphia Public Ledger and Daily Transcript*, November 30, 1848.

[59] Butler, *Statement*, p. 97.

[60] *Ibid.*, pp. 98-100

[61] *Spectator*, Washington, D. C., April 16, 1844. Cf. *London Pall Mall Gazette*, February 11, 1893.

[62] James Schott, Jr., *Statement by James Schott, Jr., July 29, 1844*, pp. 2-21.

[63] *Spectator*, April 16, 1844.

[64] Butler, *Statement*, pp. 118-20.

[65] *Ibid.*, p. 109.

[66] *Answer of Frances Anne Butler*, p. 8.

[67] Butler, *Statement*, pp. 124-26.

[68] *Answer of Frances Anne Butler*, p. 9.

[69] Butler, *Statement*, pp. 131-32.

[70] *Answer of Frances Anne Butler*, p. 11.

[71] Butler, *Statement*, p. 134.

[72] *Ibid.*, pp. 139-40.

[73] *Answer of Frances Anne Butler*, p. 16.

[74] *Ibid.*, pp. 17-19.

[75] *Ibid.*, pp. 22-24.

[76] Letter, Frances Anne Butler, May 20, 1845 (?), Boston Public Library.

[77] *Answer of Frances Anne Butler*, p. 29. This *Answer* records the date of her sailing as October 16. This is evidently an error, for she was in London by October 3. See Kemble, *Records of Later Life*, p. 418.

NOTES TO CHAPTER VIII

[1] Frances Anne Kemble, *Records of Later Life*, pp. 418-32.

[2] *Ibid.*, p. 428.

[3] Mrs. Butler (Late Fanny Kemble), *A Year of Consolation*, I, 22.

[4] *Ibid.*, pp. 18-25.

[5] *Ibid.*, pp. 6-50

[6] *Ibid.*, pp. 59-61.

[7] *Ibid.*, pp. 76-86.

[8] *Ibid.*, II, 144-45.

[9] *Ibid.*, pp. 150-51.

[10] *Ibid.*, I, 89-90.

[11] Kemble, *Records of Later Life*, p. 465.

[12] *A Year of Consolation*, II, 97-98, 119. Cf. "A Mother's Memories," *Pittsfield Sun*, February 8, 1849.

[13] *A Year of Consolation*, II, 29.

[14] *Ibid.*, pp. 26-29.

[15] *Ibid.*, I, 65.

[16] *Ibid.*, II, 115.

[17] *Ibid.*, pp. 165-66.

[18] *Ibid.*, I, 133.

[19] Kemble, *Records of Later Life*, p. 474.

[20] *Answer of Frances Anne Butler*, p. 30. The letters were published in the *New York Weekly Express*, December 7 to 14, 1848.

[21] *Answer of Frances Anne Butler*, pp. 30-31.

[22] Kemble, *Records of Later Life*, p. 473.

[23] *Ibid.*, pp. 477-78.

[24] "A Year of Consolation," *Edinburgh Review*, LXXXVI (1847), 176-187.

[25] *Athenæum*, MXVIII (May 1, 1847), 460-62; MXIX (May 8, 1847), 491-93.

[26] "Mrs. Butler's 'Year of Consolation,'" *Living Age*, XIII (1847), 470-76. Quoted from the *Spectator*.

[27] *Ibid.*, p. 474. Quoted from the *Examiner*.

[28] *Athenæum*, MX (March 1, 1847), 263.

[29] Kemble, *Records of Later Life*, pp. 474-75.

[30] *Athenæum*, MXI (March 6, 1847), 265.

[31] *Theatrical Times*, II (March 6, 1847), 70.

[32] Kemble, *Records of Later Life*, p. 488.

[33] *Ibid.*, p. 490.

[34] *Theatrical Times*, II (March 27, 1847), 94. Cf. Kemble, *Records of Later Life*, pp. 494-95.

[35] *Theatrical Times*, II (March 13, 1847), 79.

[36] John Coleman, "Fanny Kemble," *The Theatre*, XXXIII (March 1, 1893), 144.

[37] Kemble, *Records of Later Life*, pp. 502-3.

[38] *Ibid.*, pp. 493-95.

[39] *Theatrical Times*, II (April 17, 1847), 120.

[40] Kemble, *Records of Later Life*, p. 495.

[41] *Theatrical Times*, II (1847), 31-56.

[42] Knowles's *The Hunchback* had been used for the first presentation at each of her engagements. *The Honeymoon, Romeo and Juliet, Macbeth, Henry VIII, School for Scandal*, and *Much Ado about Nothing* were the other presentations of these first engagements.

[43] *Athenæum*, MXVIII (May 1, 1847), 474-75.

[44] *Theatrical Times*, II (May 1, 1847), 133-34.

[45] *Ibid.*, II (May 8, 1847), 142.

[46] *Ibid.*, II (May 15, 1847), 149-50. Cf. *Athenæum*, MXX (May 15, 1847), 531.

[47] *Theatrical Times*, II (May 22, 1847), 157-58.

[48] *Ibid.*, II (May 29, 1847), 163-64.

[49] *Ibid.*, II (June 5, 1847), 176.

[50] Kemble, *Records of Later Life*, pp. 521-29. See *Theatrical Times*, II (1847), 311-98 *passim*. During the remainder of the summer and autumn she fulfilled contracts at Bristol, Bath, Plymouth, Exeter, Glasgow, Dundee, Perth, Greenock, Norwich, Ipswich, Cambridge, York, Leeds, Sheffield, Newcastle, Edinburgh, and Hull.

[51] Kemble, *Records of Later Life*, pp. 619-24. Cf. Playbills of the Princess's Theatre in Shakespearean Playbills 53 and 55, February 21 to March 17, 1848, Manuscript Division, Library of Congress. They presented *Macbeth*, *Henry VIII*, *Othello*, *Hamlet*, and *King Lear*, each at least twice.

[52] Kemble, *Records of Later Life*, pp. 636-51, *passim*.

[53] *Ibid.*, pp. 630-31. Cf. *Athenæum*, MLXI (February 26, 1848), 226.

[54] *Theatrical Times*, II (March 4 and 11, 1848).

[55] *Ibid.*, II (April 1, 1848).

[56] *Athenæum*, MLXII (March 4, 1848), 254.

[57] *Theatrical Times*, II (March 11, 1848).

[58] *Athenæum*, MLXXI (May 6, 1848), 468.

[59] *Theatrical Times*, II (April 8, 1848).

[60] Kemble, *Records of Later Life*, pp. 657-58.

[61] *Ibid.*, p. 657.

[62] *Ibid.*, pp. 632-33. She included *King Lear*, *Macbeth*, *Cymbeline*, *King John*, *Richard II*, both parts of *Henry IV*, *Henry V*, *Richard III*, *Henry VIII*, *Coriolanus*, *Julius Cæsar*, *Anthony and Cleopatra*, *Hamlet*, *Othello*, *Romeo and Juliet*, *Merchant of Venice*, *Winter's Tale*, *Measure for Measure*, *Much Ado about Nothing*, *As You Like It*, *Midsummer Night's Dream*, *Merry Wives of Windsor*, and *The Tempest*.

[63] *Ibid.*, pp. 633-34.

[64] *Athenæum*, MLXVI (April 1, 1848), 344.

[65] *Ibid.*, MLXVII (April 8, 1848), 372-73.

[66] Pierce Butler, *Statement*, p. 3, and *Answer of Frances Anne Butler*, p. 3.

[67] *Answer of Frances Anne Butler,* pp. 5-7.

[68] *Ibid.,* pp. 31-32.

[69] *American Courier,* October 28, 1848.

[70] *Philadelphia Public Ledger and Daily Transcript,* November 28, 1848, to December 7, 1848.

[71] *Ibid.,* January 22, 1849, and *North American and United States Gazette,* January 23, 1849.

[72] *American Courier,* April 14, 1849.

[73] *Philadelphia Daily News,* September 4, 1849.

[74] *Ibid.,* September 25, 1849. Cf. *Philadelphia Public Ledger and Daily Transcript,* September 24, 1849.

[75] *Philadelphia Public Ledger and Daily Transcript,* November 28, 1848.

[76] *New York Evening Mirror,* September 12, 1849.

NOTES TO CHAPTER IX

[1] *Philadelphia Public Ledger and Daily Transcript,* February 16, 1849. Quoted from the *Springfield Republican.*

[2] *American Courier,* March 3, 1849.

[3] "To Shakespeare," Frances Anne Kemble, *Poems,* 1859 and 1883.

[4] Frances Anne Kemble, *Further Records,* p. 287.

[5] Frances Anne Kemble, *Journal,* I, 196n.

[6] *New York Evening Mirror,* March 29, 1849. From the *Richmond Republican.*

[7] *American Courier,* November 3, 1849.

[8] *Philadelphia Public Ledger and Daily Transcript,* January 29, 1849. Note from the Boston correspondent. Cf. *North American and United States Gazette,* January 25, 1849.

[9] *American Courier,* February 3, 1849. From a Boston correspondent.

[10] *Philadelphia Public Ledger and Daily Transcript,* February 8, 1849.

[11] *Albion,* New York, February 17, 1849.

[12] *American Courier,* February 24, 1849. Original correspondence.

[13] *Life of Henry Wadsworth Longfellow,* ed. Samuel Longfellow, II, 141-45.

[14] *Evening Transcript,* March 12, 1849. Also in *Complete Poetical Works of Henry Wadsworth Longfellow,* Cambridge Edition, p. 112.

[15] *Albion,* March 10, 1849. Cf. *American Courier,* February 24 and

March 10, 1849. She had previously read at New Bedford and Cambridge.

[16] *Albion*, March 10, 1849.

[17] *Philadelphia Public Ledger and Daily Transcript*, March 10, 1849.

[18] *Albion*, March 10, 1849.

[19] *Ibid*, March 17, 1849.

[20] *Ibid*.

[21] *Philadelphia Daily News*, March 21, 1849.

[22] *New York Evening Mirror*, April 6, 1849.

[23] *Albany Journal*, March 31 to April 4, 1849.

[24] *Philadelphia Daily News*, April 13, 1849.

[25] *New York Evening Mirror*, May 1, 1849.

[26] *Ibid.*, April 14, 1849.

[27] *Philadelphia Daily News*, April 19, 1849.

[28] *Ibid.*, April 18, 1849.

[29] *American Courier*, May 5, 1849.

[30] *New York Evening Mirror*, May 12, 1849, and *American Courier*, May 26, 1849.

[31] *Philadelphia Daily News*, May 16, 1849.

[32] *Ibid.*, June 19, 1849.

[33] *American Courier*, June 23-30, 1849.

[34] Kemble, *Records of Later Life*, p. 158.

[35] R. DeWitt Mallory, *Lenox and the Berkshire Highlands*, p. 32.

[36] Julian Hawthorne, *Nathaniel Hawthorne and His Wife, A Biography*, I, 362-63.

[37] *Ibid.*, p. 409. Cf. Mallory, *op. cit.*, p. 17.

[38] Lewis Mumford, *Herman Melville*, pp. 135-57.

[39] C. B. Todd: "Fanny Kemble at Lenox," *Lippincott's Monthly Magazine*, LII (1893), 66-70; "The Late Fanny Kemble," *New York Times*, January 18, 1893.

[40] "The Late Fanny Kemble," *New York Times*, January 18, 1893. Cf. *Memoir and Letters of Charles Sumner*, edited by Edward Price, II, 318-19. She gave private readings at least in 1844. On September 3, 1849, she read in Burbank's Hall at Pittsfield. See *Pittsfield Sun*, August 30, 1849.

[41] Mallory, *op. cit.*, pp. 29-30.

[42] *Ibid.*, p. 32. Cf. "The Late Fanny Kemble," *New York Times*, January 18, 1893.

[43] Mallory, *op. cit.*, pp. 31, 75.

[44] Todd, *op. cit.*, pp. 66-70. Cf. *Philadelphia Daily News*, August 27, 1849.

[45] Todd, *op. cit.*, pp. 66-70. The aged man who supplied the reminiscences for this article was William D. Curtis, who in his youth frequently attended her on her rides and fishing trips. See *New York Times*, January 18, 1893.

[46] Sumner, *op. cit.*, II, 317.

[47] Todd, *op. cit.*, p. 70.

[48] "The Late Fanny Kemble," *New York Times*, January 18, 1893.

[49] *Philadelphia Daily News*, September 29, 1849.

[50] *Ibid.*

[51] *Ibid.*, October 1 to November 8, 1849, and the *Philadelphia Public Ledger and Daily Transcript*, October 1 to November 8, 1849. It is interesting to compare the *American Courier*, which carried unfavorable reports. On October 6, 1849, it reported that she attracted little notice in Philadelphia, a definite contradiction of the other papers. When she returned to the city for a second series in April, 1850, this paper urged all not to miss the opportunity to hear her inimitable readings of the immortal Bard. See *American Courier*, April 20, 1850.

[52] *Philadelphia Daily News*, November 15, 1849. Those named were Miss Kimberley, Richard H. Dana, Mrs. Kemble, Mr. Fleming, Mr. Allen, Miss Reid, and Mr. Lowell. With the granting of the divorce, Mrs. Butler resumed her maiden name. She was known during the remainder of her life as Mrs. Kemble.

[53] John Coleman, "Fanny Kemble," *The Theatre*, XXXIII (1893), 144.

[54] *New York Evening Mirror*, November 21, 1849.

[55] *Philadelphia Daily News*, November 28, and December 7, 1849.

[56] *Ibid.*, November 30 to December 6, 1849.

[57] *Ibid.*, December 18, 1849.

[58] *Savannah Daily Morning News*, January 17, 1850.

[59] *Albion*, December 1 and 22, 1849.

[60] *Ibid.*, December 22, 1849.

[61] Kemble, *Further Records*, pp. 299-300.

[62] *Ibid.*, pp. 295-98.

[63] *Philadelphia Daily News*, December 31, 1849. Her appearances included series at Albany, New Haven, Philadelphia, and Reading.

See *Albany Evening Journal*, January 9-13, 1850; *Philadelphia Daily News*, January 14, and March 1-19, 1850; *New York Evening Mirror*, January 22-24, and March 1-7, 1850; *Albany Evening Journal*, April 3, 1850; *Philadelphia Daily News*, April 9 to May 4, 1850; *American Courier*, April 9 to May 4, 1850; *Philadelphia Public Ledger and Daily Transcript*, April 10, 1850. The last appearance to which I have reference was in Reading on June 28.

[64] *Philadelphia Daily News*, April 22, 1850.

[65] A. H. Quinn: *A History of the American Drama from the Beginning to the Civil War*, p. 253.

[66] *New York Evening Mirror*, May 2, 1850; *Philadelphia Public Ledger and Daily Transcript*, May 2, 1850; *Philadelphia Daily News*, May 2, 1850.

[67] Eugene Tompkins, *A History of the Boston Theatre, 1854-1901*, p. 71.

[68] Kemble, *Further Records*, p. 289. Cf. *Philadelphia Daily News*, October 11 and 26, 1850.

[69] Kemble, *Further Records*, pp. 290-98. Cf. *Letters of Elizabeth Barrett Browning*, edited by Frederic G. Kenyon, II, 13-16.

[70] *Athenæum*, MCCLXV (January 24, 1852), 122.

[71] *Ibid.*, MCCLXVII (February 7, 1852), 178, and MCCLXXV (April 3, 1852), 387.

[72] Kemble, *Further Records*, p. 303. Adelaide had married Edgar J. Sartoris in 1843.

[73] W. H. Griffin: *Life of Robert Browning*, p. 194.

[74] E. B. Browning, *op. cit.*, II, 154-67.

[75] *Athenæum*, MCDXII (November 18, 1854), 1399.

[76] *Philadelphia Daily News*, May 31, 1856.

[77] Letter, Mrs. S. Plitt to Harriet Lane, June 19, 1856. Buchanan-Johnston Papers, Library of Congress.

[78] Kemble, *Further Records*, pp. 315-17.

[79] *Philadelphia Daily News*, February 11, 1857. After her return from the West, appearances in eastern cities including a prolonged stay in Boston preceded her departure for her summer home among the Berkshires. See *New York Daily Times*, December 2-12, 1856, for notices of her trip west and appearances in St. Louis. For accounts of her readings in the East, see *Boston Atlas*, February 16 to April 8, 1857; *Boston Daily Traveller*, April 18-29, 1857. In addi-

tion to appearances in Boston, she read at Cambridge, Springfield, and New Bedford.

[80] Kemble, *Further Records*, pp. 317-21.

[81] *Ibid.*, pp. 321-24. A prolonged engagement in New York preceded her tour of the smaller towns of Massachusetts and New York. According to one report seven readings in New York City netted $6,000. See *Albion*, December 12, 1857, to January 30, 1858; *New York Evening Post*, January 2 to April 21, 1858; *Boston Daily Traveller*, January 9, 1858.

[82] *Albion*, January 8 and 15, 1859.

[83] *Ballou's Pictorial Drawing-Room Companion*, XVI (January 22, 1859), 62.

[84] Mortimer Thomson, *Great Auction Sale of Slaves at Savannah, Georgia, Mar. 2d & 3d., 1859;* U. B. Phillips, *American Negro Slavery*, pp. 251, 374; Kemble, *Further Records*, p. 366. Dr. Owen Wister has supplied added information to that contained in these sources.

[85] Kemble, *Further Records*, pp. 318-29.

NOTES TO CHAPTER X

[1] Frances Anne Kemble, *Further Records*, pp. 333-34.

[2] *Ibid.*, pp. 330-31.

[3] *Ibid.*, p. 335.

[4] Mary E. Dewey, *Life and Letters of Catherine M. Sedgwick*, pp. 391-92.

[5] *New York Times*, January 17, 1893.

[6] *Official Records of the Union and Confederate Armies*, Series II, Vol. II, 505. Hereafter referred to as *ORUCA*.

[7] *Ibid.*, pp. 505-7.

[8] *Ibid.*, pp. 507-9.

[9] Frances Anne Kemble, *Records of Later Life*, pp. 159-60.

[10] *Ibid.*, pp. 159, 203-5.

[11] *Ibid.*, p. 160. Mr. John Forbes of Boston had the book republished in the United States.

[12] *North American Review*, XCVII (1863), 582; *Harper's New Monthly Magazine*, XXVII (1863), 416-17; *Atlantic Monthly*, XII (1863), 260-63; *Athenæum*, MDCCCVIII (1863), 737-39. For the most recent discussion of the possible influence of the book see Mildred E. Lombard,

"Contemporary Opinions of Mrs. Kemble's Journal of a Residence on a Georgian Plantation," *Georgia Historical Quarterly*, xiv (1930), 335-43.

[13] *ORUCA*, Series iii, Vol. iv, 329. Cf. Phillips, *American Negro Slavery*, p. 251.

[14] *ORUCA*, Series i, vol. xxviii, pt. 2, p. 5.

[15] Frances Butler Leigh, *Ten Years on a Georgia Plantation Since the War*, pp. 5-25. Cf. Kemble, *Further Records*, p. 342.

[16] *Philadelphia Daily News*, March 9, 1868, and *New York Tribune*, March 3, 1868.

[17] *Washington National Intelligencer*, March 31 to April 4, 1868.

[18] *Baltimore American*, April 4-7, 1868.

[19] Kemble, *Further Records*, p. 348. During this period the *St. Louis Times*, March 1, 1868, and the *Chicago Republican*, May 2, 1868, carried notices and reports of her readings, a rather significant comment on her hold upon public attention even after her absence of eight years from the reading stage.

[20] *Ibid.*, pp. 344-46.

[21] *Detroit Free Press*, October 3-9, 1868. She had stopped for readings at Worcester, Massachusetts, and Troy, and Rochester, New York. See the *Chicago Republican*, September 18, 1868; *New York Times*, September 27 to October 4, 1868.

[22] *Chicago Republican*, October 13-18, 1868. After a series at St. Louis she started east again. By December she had returned for the winter and spring to Philadelphia with more than two thousand pounds added to her earnings. See Kemble, *Further Records*, pp. 347-49; *Detroit Free Press*, October 25 to November 22, 1868.

[23] "Mrs. Frances Anne Kemble," *Galaxy*, vi (1868), 797-803.

[24] Mme. Augustus Craven (Pauline La Ferronnays), *La Jeunesse de Fanny Kemble*, pp. 11-12.

[25] Fredrika Bremer, *Homes of the New World*, tr. Mary Howitt, i, 227.

[26] A. J. Upson, "Fanny Kemble in America," *Critic*, xxii (1893), 152-53.

[27] *Ibid.*, pp. 151-53. Cf. *Chicago Republican*, October 13-18, 1868.

[28] Kemble, *Further Records*, pp. 349-50. Cf. Leigh, *op. cit.*, p. 199.

[29] Kemble, *Further Records*, p. 351. Cf. Hallam Tennyson, *Tennyson, A Memoir*, ii, 351; *Letters of Edward Fitzgerald to Fanny Kemble*, edited by W. A. Wright, pp. 3-28.

[30] Kemble, *Further Records*, pp. 1-31.

[31] *Ibid.*, pp. 13-36.

[32] *Ibid.*, pp. 354-56.

[33] Frances Anne Kemble, "Old Woman's Gossip," *Atlantic Monthly*, xxxvi (1875), 152.

[34] Kemble, *Further Records*, p. 129.

[35] *Ibid.*, p. 95.

[36] *Ibid.*, p. 121.

[37] *Ibid.*, p. 101.

[38] Letter, Frances Anne Kemble to Mrs. Henry Cohen, October 16, 1875 (?). Historical Society of Pennsylvania.

[39] "Fanny Kemble at Lenox," *The Berkshire Hills*, ii (June 1, 1902), 10.

[40] Kemble, *Further Records*, pp. 156, 198, 219. Cf. Leigh, *op. cit.*, pp. 340-46.

[41] R. DeWitt Mallory, *Lenox and the Berkshire Highlands*, pp. 163-64; H. H. Ballard: Address delivered at the dedication of the Hawthorne and Kemble markers in Lenox on August 6, 1929, *Berkshire Evening Eagle*, August 10, 1929; Walter P. Eaton, "The Berkshires: Old Style," *American Mercury*, xxii (1931), 325-27.

[42] Kemble, *Further Records*, pp. 203-20.

NOTES TO CHAPTER XI

[1] Frances Anne Kemble, *Further Records*, pp. 233-34.

[2] *Ibid.*, pp. 200-38.

[3] *Ibid.*, pp. 231-72.

[4] *Ibid.*, pp. 236-41. Henry Holt and Company published a one-volume edition in 1879.

[5] *Living Age*, xxiv (1878), 628-33. Cf. *Theatre*, December 1, 1878, pp. 392-93.

[6] Kemble, *op. cit.*, pp. 244-58. Cf. *Letters of Edward Fitzgerald to Fanny Kemble*, edited by W. A. Wright, pp. 138-43.

[7] *Thackeray and His Daughter*, edited by Hester Thackeray Ritchie, pp. 211-12.

[8] Anne Thackeray Ritchie, "Chapters from Some Unwritten Memories—Mrs. Kemble," *Macmillan's Magazine*, lxviii (1893), 204.

[9] Frances Anne Kemble, "In Switzerland, 1889," *Temple Bar*, lxxxviii (1890).

[10] "Some Recollections of Yesterday," *Temple Bar*, cii (1894), 315-39. Cf. Henry James, *Essays in London and Elsewhere*, pp. 115-16.

[11] Kemble, *op. cit.*, p. 365. Cf. Fitzgerald, *op. cit.*, p. 154.

[12] "Some Recollections of Yesterday," *loc. cit.*, p. 334.

[13] *Athenæum* MMDCCCXLV (July 8, 1882), 39-40. Cf. *Quarterly Review*, CLIV (1882), 83-123. Henry Holt and Company also issued a one-volume edition of *Records of Later Life* in 1882.

[14] George Arliss, Introduction to *On the Stage*, published by the Dramatic Museum of Columbia University, p. 1.

[15] *Ibid.*, pp. 27-29; "Some Recollections of Yesterday," p. 331; *Athenæum*, MMDCCCLXXVII (December 16, 1882), 823; *Quarterly Review*, CLV (1883), 354-88.

[16] *The Theatre*, May 1, 1879, pp. 224-27, and February 1, 1893, p. 115.

[17] "Frances Anne Kemble's Poetry," *Critic*, IV (1884), 105-6.

[18] W. H. Griffin, *Life of Robert Browning with Notices of His Writings, His Family and His Friends*, edited by Harry C. Minchin, p. 194.

[19] *Temple Bar*, LXXXII-LXXXVIII (1888-1890), *passim*.

[20] Frances Anne Kemble, "Salvini," *Temple Bar*, LXXI (1884).

[21] "Some Recollections of Yesterday," *loc. cit.*, pp. 337-38.

[22] *Ibid.*, p. 332. I have been unable to identify this novel, but I am inclined to think that it became *Far Away and Long Ago*.

[23] "Mrs. Kemble's Letters," *Atlantic Monthly*, LXVII (1891), 688-94.

[24] "Some Recollections of Yesterday," *loc. cit.*, p. 333.

[25] Anne Thackeray Ritchie, *op. cit.*, p. 192.

[26] *Ibid.*, p. 205.

[27] "Some Recollections of Yesterday," *loc. cit.*, p. 327. Cf. Anne Thackeray Ritchie, *op. cit.*, p. 193; James, *op. cit.*, p. 83.

[28] James, *op. cit.*, pp. 81-97.

[29] "Some Recollections of Yesterday," *loc. cit.*, pp. 333-34.

[30] James, *op. cit.*, pp. 93-114. Cf. George Bentley, "A Note on Mrs. Kemble," *London Daily Mail*, January 20, 1893.

[31] James, *op. cit.*, pp. 81-84.

[32] Anne Thackeray Ritchie, *op. cit.*, p. 195.

[33] Fredrika Bremer, *Homes of the New World*, tr. Mary Howitt, I, 227-37, and Fredrika Bremer, *America of the Fifties*, edited by Adolph B. Benson, pp. 75-76.

[34] "Some Recollections of Yesterday," *loc. cit.*, pp. 338-39.

[35] *Pall Mall Gazette*, January 17, 1893.

[36] *Ibid.*, January 21, 1893. Cf. *Critic*, XXII (1893), 54.

[37] James, *op. cit.*, pp. 81-83.

BIBLIOGRAPHY

The following list is not presented as an exhaustive bibliography. With a few exceptions it consists of material cited in the footnotes of this study.

I. MANUSCRIPTS

Kemble, Frances Anne, *An English Tragedy.* Manuscript Division Library of Congress.

Letter, Frances Anne Kemble to Mrs. Henry Cohen, October 16, 1875. Historical Society of Pennsylvania.

Letter, Frances Anne Kemble, Mansion House, Tuesday 17 (1834?). Historical Society of Pennsylvania.

Letter, Mrs. Pierce Butler to Mrs. Wallace, Washington Square. Historical Society of Pennsylvania.

Letter, Fanny Kemble to Mr. Gerhard. Washington, Friday, 25. Historical Society of Pennsylvania.

Letter, Fanny Butler, Saturday, 9. Germantown Historical and Genealogical Society.

Letter, Fanny Kemble to Mr. Mason, 20 Dover Street, Monday. Germantown Historical and Genealogical Society.

Letter, Frances Ann Kemble to Elias Nason, Esq., Albany, Wednesday, 9. Germantown Historical and Genealogical Society.

Letter, Fanny Kemble to Mrs. Edwards, Saturday, 4. Boston Public Library.

Letter, Fanny Kemble, Philadelphia, May 20. Boston Public Library.

Letter, Fanny Kemble to Mr. Bellows, Clarendon, Tuesday, 8. *Washburn Papers*, XIX, 30. Massachusetts Historical Society.

Letter, Fanny Kemble to Rev. William Furness, Philadelphia, December, 1844. *Washburn Papers*, XIX, 30. Massachusetts Historical Society.

Letter, Pierce Butler to Mr. Tuckerman, February 7, 1840. Boston Public Library.

Letter to Hugh S. Legaré, Charleston, May 8 (1835?). Private collection of W. G. Chisolm.

Letter, Mrs. S. Plitt to Harriet Lane, June 19, 1856. Buchanan-Johnston Papers. Library of Congress.

Letter, Ellen Shattuck to George C. Shattuck, Brookline, April 21, 1833. Shattuck Papers, xi. Massachusetts Historical Society.

Letter, George Shattuck to his son, Boston, May 8, 1833. Shattuck Papers, xi. Massachusetts Historical Society.

Letter, George B. Shattuck. February, 1860. Shattuck Papers, xxiii. Massachusetts Historical Society.

II. PUBLISHED WRITINGS

Kemble, Frances Anne, *Adventures of Mr. John Timothy Homespun in Switzerland*. London. 1889.
Rare, One copy seen in the Widener Library at Harvard University.

Kemble, Frances Anne, "A Mother's Memories," *Pittsfield Sun*, February 8, 1849.

Kemble, Frances Anne, *Answer of Frances Anne Butler to the Libel of Pierce Butler Praying a Divorce*. October 9, 1848.
Rare. One copy seen in the Rare Book Room of the Library of Congress.

Kemble, Frances Anne (Mrs. Butler), *A Year of Consolation*. London. 1847.

Kemble, Frances Anne, *Fanny Kemble in America or Journal of an Actress with Remarks on the State of Society in America and England. By an English Lady Four Years Resident in the United States*. Boston. 1835.
Rare. One copy seen in the Library of Congress.

Kemble, Frances Anne, *Far Away and Long Ago*. New York. 1889.

Kemble, Frances Anne, *Francis I*. London. 1832.

Kemble, Frances Anne, *Further Records*. New York. 1891.

Kemble, Frances Anne, "In Switzerland," *Temple Bar*, lxxxviii (1890).

Kemble, Frances Anne (Frances Anne Butler), *Journal*. Philadelphia. 1835. Also published in Paris in 1835.

Kemble, Frances Anne, *Journal of a Residence on a Georgian Plantation*. New York and London. 1863.

Kemble, Frances Anne, "Lament for a Mocking-Bird," *Temple Bar*, LXXXII (1888).

Kemble, Frances Anne, "Lines," *Sedgwick Papers*, XX. Massachusetts Historical Society.

Kemble, Frances Anne, "Lines Addressed to Miss L. W.," *Temple Bar*, LXXXV (1889).

Kemble, Frances Anne, *My Conscience! Fanny Thimble Cutler's Journal of a Residence in America whilst Performing a Profitable Theatrical Engagement: Beating the Nonsensical Fanny Kemble Journal All Hollow*. Philadelphia. 1835.
Rare. Two copies seen in the Library of Congress.

Kemble, Frances Anne, *Notes upon Some of Shakespeare's Plays*. London. 1882.

Kemble, Frances Anne, "Old Woman's Gossip," *Atlantic Monthly*,
XXXVI (1875), 152-166; 282-296; 444-459; 583-597; 722-735.
XXXVII (1876), 76-90; 198-207; 316-328; 450-463; 591-606; 711-726.
XXXVIII (1876), 32-43; 185-202; 330-341; 431-443; 602-614; 705-717.
XXXIX (1877), 73-87; 209-223; 342-352; 432-445.

Kemble, Frances Anne, *On the Stage*. Republished from the *Cornhill Magazine*, 1863, with an introduction by George Arliss. New York. 1926.

Kemble, Frances Anne, *Outline Illustrative of the Journal of F—— A—— K——*. Boston, 1835.

Kemble, Frances Anne, *Plays*. London. 1863.

Kemble, Frances Anne, *Poems*. London. 1844.

Kemble, Frances Anne, *Poems*. Boston. 1859.

Kemble, Frances Anne, *Poems*. London. 1883.

Kemble, Frances Anne, *Records of a Girlhood*. New York. 1879.

Kemble, Frances Anne, *Records of Later Life*. New York. 1882.

Kemble, Frances Anne, "Salvini's Othello," *Temple Bar*, LXXI (1884).

Kemble, Frances Anne, *Star of Seville*. New York. 1837.

Kemble, Frances Anne, *The Essence of Slavery. Extracted from a Journal of a Residence on a Georgian Plantation* by Isa Craig. (Ladies' London Emancipation Society. Tract Number 2.) London. 1863.

III. SHAKESPEAREAN PLAYBILLS

Files of the Manuscript Division, Library of Congress.
Shakespearean Playbills, 55, 56, and 57.
Princess's Theatre, London, February 25 to March 17, 1848.
Shakespearean Playbills, 56 and 57.
Theatre Royal, Birmingham, September 6 to September 13, 1830.

IV. BOOKS AND PAMPHLETS

Adams, John Quincy. *Memoirs*, ed. Charles Francis Adams. VIII. Philadelphia. 1877.

Baker, H. B. *History of the London Stage, and Its Famous Players, 1576-1903*. N. Y. 1904.

Bassett, John Spencer. *The Southern Plantation Overseer As Revealed in His Letters*. Northampton. 1925.

Bernard, John. *Retrospections of America, 1797-1811*. N. Y. 1887.

Beveridge, A. J. *Abraham Lincoln, 1809-1858*. II. Boston. 1928.

Boston Theaters and Halls Past and Present with Diagrams. Boston, 1907.

Bowers, Claude G. *Party Battles of the Jackson Period*. N. Y. 1922.

Bremer, Fredrika. *America of the Fifties*, ed. Adolph B. Benson. N. Y. 1924.

———. *Homes of the New World*, tr. Mary Howitt. I-II. N. Y. 1854.

Brooks, John G. *As Others See Us*. N. Y. 1910.

Broughton, Lord. *Recollections of a Long Life by Lord Broughton* (John Cam Hobhouse), ed. his daughter, Lady Dorchester. IV. N. Y. 1910.

Brown, T. Allston. *A History of the New York Stage, 1832-1901*. N. Y. 1903.

Browning, Elizabeth Barrett. *Letters of Elizabeth Barrett Browning*, ed. Frederic G. Kenyon. I-II. N. Y. 1889.

Browning, Robert and Elizabeth Barrett. *Letters of Robert and Elizabeth Barrett Browning, 1845-1846*. N. Y. 1899.

Butler, Pierce. *Statement*. Philadelphia. 1850.

Campbell, Thomas. *Life and Letters of Thomas Campbell*, ed. William Beattie. III. London. 1850.

Carlyle, Jane Welsh. *Letters and Memorials of Jane Welsh Carlyle*. Prepared for publication by Thomas Carlyle; ed. J. A. Froude. N. Y. 1883.

Channing, E. *History of the United States*. V. N. Y. 1921; VI. N. Y. 1925.

Clapp, W. W. *Records of the Boston Stage*. Boston. 1853.

Clarkson, Thomas. *The History of the Rise, Progress, and Accomplishment of the Abolition of the African Slave Trade by the British Parliament.* I-II. Philadelphia. 1808.

Coad, O. S. *William Dunlap.* N. Y. 1917.

Conway, Moncure Daniel. *Autobiography and Experiences of Moncure Daniel Conway.* I. Boston. 1905.

Cooper, Thomas. *Some Information Respecting America.* London. 1794.

Craven, Mme. Augustus (Pauline La Ferronnays). *La Jeunesse de Fanny Kemble.* Paris. 1888.

Crawford, Mary C. *Romantic Days in Old Boston.* Boston. 1922.

———. *The Romance of the American Theater.* Boston. 1925.

Crockett, David. *Autobiography of David Crockett,* ed. Hamlin Garland. N. Y. 1923.

Dewey, Mary E. *Life and Letters of Catherine M. Sedgwick.* N. Y. 1871.

Dodd, W. E. *Cotton Kingdom.* New Haven. 1919.

Drew, Elizabeth. *Jane Welsh and Jane Carlyle.* N. Y. 1928.

Drew, Mrs. John. *Autobiographical Sketch of Mrs. John Drew.* N. Y. 1899.

Firkins, O. W. *Ralph Waldo Emerson.* N. Y. 1915.

Letters of Edward Fitzgerald to Fanny Kemble, 1871-1883. ed. William Aldis Wright. N. Y. 1895.

Fitzgerald, Percy. *The Kembles.* I-II. London. 1871.

———. *A New History of the London Stage.* II. London. 1882.

Florida Plantation Records. From the papers of George Noble Jones. ed. U. B. Phillips and J. D. Glunt. St. Louis. 1927.

Furness, H. H. *The Letters of Horace Howard Furness,* ed. H. H. F. Jayne. I-II. N. Y. 1922.

Greville Diary, The, ed. P. W. Wilson. II. N. Y. 1927.

Griffin, W. H. *Life of Robert Browning with Notices of His Writings, His Family and His Friends,* ed. Harry C. Minchin. N. Y. 1912.

Hamilton, Thomas. *Men and Manners in America.* 3 vols. Philadelphia. 1833.

Hart, A. B. *Slavery and Abolition.* N. Y. 1906.

Hawthorne, Julian. *Hawthorne and His Circle.* N. Y. 1903.

———. *Nathaniel Hawthorne and His Wife, A Biography.* Boston. 1885.

Hawthorne, Nathaniel. *Passages from American Notebooks,* ed. G. P. Lathrop. N. Y. 1896.

———. *Wonder Book,* ed. George Parsons Lathrop. IV. Boston and N. Y. 1898.

Henry, H. M. *Police Control of the Slave in South Carolina*. Emory, Va. 1914.

Higginson, Thomas W. *Henry Wadsworth Longfellow*. N. Y. 1902.

Hone, Philip. *Diary of Philip Hone, 1828-1852*. 2 vols. ed. Allan Nevins. N. Y. 1927.

Hornblow, Arthur. *A History of the Theater in America*. 2 vols. Philadelphia. 1919.

Howe, P. P. *Life of William Hazlitt*. N. Y. 1922.

Hunt, Galliard. *Life in America One Hundred Years Ago*. N. Y. 1914.

Hunt, Leigh. *Autobiography of Leigh Hunt*. London. 1860.

————. *Dramatic Essays by Leigh Hunt*, ed. William Archer and Robert Lowe. London. 1894.

Ireland, Joseph N. *Records of the New York Stage from 1750-1860*. N. Y. 1860.

Irving, Washington. *Life and Letters of Washington Irving*. II. ed. Pierce M. Irving. Philadelphia. 1872.

James, Henry. *Essays in London and Elsewhere*. N. Y. 1893.

Kemble Papers, The (by) Stephen Kemble. Collections of the New York Historical Society for 1884. N. Y. 1885.

Kennedy, Lucy. *Visit to Washington, 1835*.

Leigh, Francis Butler. *Ten Years on a Georgia Plantation Since the War*. London. 1883.

Lockhart, John G. *Memoirs of the Life of Sir Walter Scott*. v. Boston. 1902.

Lloyd, Arthur Y. "Southern Justification of Slavery." (1929). Unpublished thesis in the Vanderbilt University Library.

Henry Wadsworth Longfellow, Life of, ed. Samuel Longfellow. II. N. Y. 1886.

Longfellow, Henry Wadsworth. *Complete Poetical Works*. Cambridge Edition. N. Y. 1893.

Lyell, Charles. *Travels in North America in the Years 1841-1842*. 2 vols. N. Y. 1845.

Macready's Reminiscences and Selections from his Diaries and Letters, ed. Sir Frederick Pollock. N. Y. 1875.

Mallory, R. DeWitt. *Lenox and the Berkshire Highlands*, N. Y. 1902.

Marryat, Capt. Frederick. *A Diary in America*. 3 vols. London. 1839.

Martin, E. S. *The Life of Joseph Hodges Choate*. I. London. 1920.

Martineau, Harriet. *Retrospect of Western Travels.* 3 vols. N. Y. 1838.
———. *Society in America.* 3 vols. N. Y. 1837.
Maurois, André. *Mape, the World of Illusion.* N. Y. 1926.
Melish, John. *Travels in the United States, 1806-1811.* 2 vols. Philadelphia. 1812.
Melville, Lewis. *William Makepeace Thackeray.* N. Y. 1928.
———. *The Life of William Makepeace Thackeray.* 2 vols. N. Y. 1899.
Merwin, Henry C. *The Life of Bret Harte.* N. Y. 1911.
Mesick, Jane L. *The English Traveller in America.* N. Y. 1922.
Moody, V. A. *Slavery on Louisiana Sugar Plantations.* New Orleans. 1924.
Morse, John T. *Memoir of Colonel Henry Lee.* Boston. 1905.
Morse, J. T. *Life and Letters of Oliver Wendell Holmes.* I. N. Y. 1896.
Moses, Montrose J. *The Fabulous Forrest.* Boston. 1929.
Mumford, Lewis. *Herman Melville.* N. Y. 1929.
Murdock, James. *The Stage.* Philadelphia. 1880.
Nevins, Allan. *American Social History as Recorded by British Travellers.* N. Y. 1923.
Odell, George C. D. *Annals of the New York Stage.* III. N. Y. 1928.
Official Records of the Union and Confederate Armies. Series I, Vol. 28, Part 2. Washington. 1890.
Series II, Vol. 2. Washington. 1897.
Series III, Vol. 4. Washington. 1900.
Olmsted, F. L. *Journey in the Seaboard Slave States, 1853-1854.* I-II. N. Y. 1904. Originally issued in 1856.
Perry, Bliss. *Life and Letters of Henry Lee Higginson.* Boston. 1921.
Phelps, H. P. *Players of a Century.* (Record of the Albany Stage.) Albany. 1880.
Phillips, U. B. *Documentary History of American Industrial Society. Plantation and Frontier.* I-II. Cleveland. 1910.
———. *American Negro Slavery.* N. Y. 1918.
———. *Life and Labor in the Old South.* Boston. 1929.
Poore, B. Perley. *Perley's Reminiscences of Sixty Years in the National Metropolis.* I. Philadelphia. 1886.
Pope-Hennessy, Una Birch. *Three English Women in America.* London. 1929.
Quinn, A. H. *A History of the American Drama from the Beginning to the Civil War.* N. Y. 1923.

Reid, T. Wemyss. *Life, Letters and Friendships of Richard Monckton Milnes, First Lord Houghton.* I-II. N. Y. 1891.

Ritchie, Anne Thackeray. *Chapters from Some Unwritten Memories.* N. Y. 1895.

———. *From Friend to Friend.* N. Y. 1920.

Robins, Edward. *Twelve Great Actresses.* N. Y. 1900.

Russell, William C. *Representative Actors.* London. 1875.

Salley, A. S., Jr., comp. and ed. *Marriage Notices in the South Carolina Gazette and Its Successors,* (1732-1801). Albany. 1902.

Schott, James, Jr. *Statement by James Schott, Jr., July 29, 1844.* Philadelphia. 1844.

S. D. L., "Memoir of the Dramatic Life of Miss Fanny Kemble," in Kemble, Frances Anne, *Francis the First,* N. Y. 1833 (Sixth American edition).

Sedgwick, Catharine M. *Letters from Abroad to Kindred At Home.* N. Y. 1841.

Sedgwick, Mrs. Charles. *A Talk with My Pupils.* N. Y. 1863.

Sumner, Charles, Memoirs and Letters of. ed. Edward Price. 4 vols. Boston. 1877.

Taylor, John. *Records of My Life.* N. Y. 1833.

Tennyson, Hallam. *Tennyson, A Memoir.* I-II. London. 1897.

Thackeray, W. M. *Thackeray and His Daughter,* ed. Hester Thackeray Ritchie. N. Y. 1924.

Thomson, Mortimer. *Great Auction Sale of Slaves at Savannah, Georgia, Mar. 2d and 3d, 1859.* Reported for the *Tribune.* N. Y. American Anti-Slavery Society. 1859.

Tompkins, Eugene. *A History of the Boston Theater, 1854-1901.* Boston. 1908.

Trent, William P. *William Gilmore Simms.* N. Y. 1892.

Trollope, Mrs. Frances M. *Domestic Manners of the Americans, in America, 1832.* 2 vols. London. 1832.

Vigne, G. F. *Six Months in America.* 2 vols. London. 1832.

Walker, Hugh. *The Literature of the Victorian Era.* Cambridge. 1913.

Wansey, Henry. *Excursion to the United States in 1794.* Salisbury. 1798.

Wemyss, Francis C. *Twenty-Six Years of the Life of the Actor and Manager.* N. Y. 1847.

———. *Chronology of the American Stage from 1752 to 1852.* N.Y. 1852.

Williamson, Jefferson. *The American Hotel.* N. Y. 1930.

Wilson, J. G. *Life and Letters of Fitz-Greene Halleck.* N. Y. 1869.

Wyman, Mary Alice. *Two American Pioneers: Seba Smith and Elizabeth Oakes Smith.* N. Y. 1927.

V. NEWSPAPERS

Albany Evening Journal, 1849-1850.
American Courier (Philadelphia), 1848-1850.
American Sentinel and Mercantile Advertiser (Philadelphia), 1832-1834.
Baltimore American, 1868.
Baltimore Republican and Commerical Advertiser, 1833-1834.
Berkshire Evening Eagle (Pittsfield, Mass.), 1929.
Boston Atlas, 1857.
Boston Daily Advertiser and Patriot, 1833-1834.
Boston Daily Traveller, 1857-1858.
Boston Herald, 1893.
Chicago Republican, 1868.
Detroit Free Press, 1868.
Evening Transcript (Boston), 1849.
Germantown Independent Gazette (Pennsylvania), 1922.
Germantown Telegraph (Pennsylvania), 1833.
London Daily Mail, 1893.
London Times, 1893.
Nashville Daily American, 1850.
National Gazette (Philadelphia), 1832-1834.
New York Daily Times, 1856.
New York Evening Mirror, 1849-1850.
New York Evening Post, 1858.
New York Mirror, 1832-1834.
New York Times, 1868-1870; 1893.
New York Tribune, 1868.
New York Weekly Express, 1848.
North American and United States Gazette (Philadelphia), 1849.
Pennsylvania Inquirer (Philadelphia), 1832-1834.
Pennsylvanian (Philadelphia), 1834-1836.
Philadelphia Daily News, 1849-1850; 1856-1857; 1868.
Philadelphia Public Ledger and Daily Transcript, 1848-1850.
Pittsfield Sun (Massachusetts), 1848-1849.
Providence Journal, 1868.
Republican Banner and Nashville Whig, 1850.
Saint Louis Times, 1868.

Savannah Daily Morning News, 1850.
Spectator (Washington), 1844.
Washington Globe, 1834.
Washington National Intelligencer, 1833; 1868.

VI. MAGAZINES

1. Miscellaneous Articles

Adams, Ephraim D. "The Point of View of the British Traveller in America," *Political Science Quarterly*, XXIX (1914), 244-64.

Aide, Hamilton. "A New Stage Doctrine," *Nineteenth Century*, XXXIV (1893), 452-57.

Address of Mr. H. H. Ballard at the dedication of the Hawthorne and Kemble markers at Lenox, Massachusetts, August 6, 1929. *Berkshire Evening Eagle*, August 10, 1929.

"A Lady Who Remembers Her in Her Youth," *New York Times*, January 18, 1893.

Bentley, George. "A Note on Mrs. Kemble," *London Daily Mail*, January 20, 1893.

Coleman, John. "Fanny Kemble," *The Theatre*, XXXIII (1893), 139-45.

"Death of Fanny Kemble," *Critic*, XXII (1893), 37.

"Death of Fanny Kemble," *New York Times*, January 17, 1893.

Eaton, Walter P. "The Berkshires: Old Style," *The American Mercury*, XXII (1931), 323-39.

"Fanny Kemble," *Saturday Review*, LXXV (1893), 67-68.

"Fanny Kemble at Lenox," *The Berkshire Hills*, II (1902), 10.

"Fanny Kemble's Death," *Philadelphia Times*, January 17, 1893.

"Fanny Kemble's Suddenness," *Critic*, XXII (1893), 291-92.

Fleming, Walter L. "The Freedmen's Savings Bank," *Yale Review*, XV (1906), 40-67; 134-46.

"Inchiquen the Jesuit's Letters during a Late Residence in the United States of America," *Quarterly Review*, X (1814), 497-539.

"Law of Divorce—The Butler Case," *Living Age*, XX (1849), 350-51.

Lee, Henry. "Frances Anne Kemble," *Atlantic Monthly*, LXXI (1893), 662-75.

Lombard, Mildred E. "Contemporary Opinions of Mrs. Kemble's Journal of a Residence on a Georgian Plantation," *Georgia Historical Quarterly*, XIV (1930), 335-43.

MacMahon, Ella. "Fanny Kemble," *Living Age*, CXCVII (1893), 692-97.

"Mrs. Frances Anne Kemble," *Galaxy*, VI (1868), 797-803.

"Mrs. Fanny Kemble and the Stage," *The Theatre* (1879), 224-27.

"Obituary of Frances Anne Kemble," *New York Sun*, January 17, 1893.

"On the Means of Education and the State of Learning in the United States of America," *Blackwood's*, IV (1819), 546-53; 642-49.

"Records Kept by Colonel Isaac Hayne," *South Carolina Historical and Genealogical Magazine*, XI (1910), 95.

Ritchie, Anne Thackeray. "Chapters from Some Unwritten Memories—Mrs. Kemble," *Macmillan's Magazine*, LXVIII (1893), 190-96.

"Some Recollections of Yesterday," *Temple Bar*, CII (1894), 315-39.

"Statistical Annals of the United States of America by Adam Seybert," *Edinburgh Review*, XXXIII (1820), 69-80.

"The Late Fanny Kemble," *New York Times*, January 18, 1893.

Todd, C. B. "Fanny Kemble at Lenox," *Lippincott's Monthly Magazine*, LII (1893), 66-70.

Upson, Anson J. "Fanny Kemble in America," *Critic*, XXII (1893), 152-53.

Walford, L. B. "A London Letter," *Critic*, XXII (1893), 79-80.

Woolson, Constance F. "Henry Middleton, President of the First Continental Congress," *Pennsylvania Magazine of History and Biography*, III (1879), 179-82.

2. Reviews

"A Year of Consolation," *Athenæum*, MXVIII (1847), 460-62; MXIX (1847), 491-93.

"A Year of Consolation," *Edinburgh Review*, LXXXVI (1847), 176-87.

"A Year of Consolation," *Quarterly Review*, LXXXI (1847), 440-68.

"A Year of Consolation," *Living Age*, XV (1847), 481-94.

"Fanny Kemble's Journal," *Niles' Weekly Register*, XLVIII (1835), 379.

"Far Away and Long Ago," *Athenæum*, MMMCCXV (1889), 725-26.

"Far Away and Long Ago," *Nation*, XLIX (1889), 120.

"Frances Anne Kemble's Poetry," *Critic*, IV (1884), 105-6.

"Francis the First: an Historical Drama," *Athenæum*, CCXXIX (1832), 170-71.

"Francis the First," *Quarterly Review*, XLVII (1832), 243-61.
"Journal of Frances Anne Butler," *Athenæum*, CCCXCVI (1835), 404-6.
"Journal of Frances Anne Butler," *Edinburgh Review*, LXI (1835), 379--406.
"Journal of Frances Anne Butler," *Southern Literary Messenger*, I (1834-35), 524-31.
"Journal of a Residence on a Georgia Plantation," *Athenæum*, MDCCCLVIII (1863), 737-39.
"Journal of a Residence on a Georgian Plantation," *Atlantic Monthly*, XII (1863), 260-63.
"Journal of a Residence on a Georgian Plantation," *Harper's New Monthly Magazine*, XXVII (1863), 416-17.
"Journal of a Residence on a Georgian Plantation in 1838-1839," *North American Review*, XCVII (1863), 582.
"Miss Fanny Kemble's Reminiscences," *Theatre* (1878), 392-93.
"Mrs. Butler's Year of Consolation," *Living Age*, XIII (1847), 470-76.
"Mrs. Butler's Journal," *Quarterly Review*, LIV (1835), 39-58.
"Mrs. Kemble's Letters," *Atlantic Monthly*, LXVII (1891), 688-94.
"Mrs. Kemble's Memoirs," *Atlantic Monthly*, L (1882), 421-24.
"Mrs. Kemble's Records of Her Life," *Living Age*, CLIV (1882), 707-29.
"Mrs. Kemble's Reminiscences," *Temple Bar*, LXVI (1882), 172-91.
"Notes upon Some of Shakespeare's Plays," *Athenæum*, MMDCCCLXXVII (1882), 823.
"Poems by Frances Anne Butler," *Athenæum*, DCCCLXXV (1844), 712-13.
"Poems by Frances Anne Butler," *Quarterly Review*, LXXV (1845), 325-34.
"Records of Later Life," *Athenæum*, MMDCCCLIV (1882), 39-40.
"Records of a Girlhood," *Quarterly Review*, CLIV (1882), 83-123.
"The English Stage," *Quarterly Review*, CLV (1883), 354-88.
"The Star of Seville: a Drama in Five Acts," *Athenæum*, CCCCXCIV (1837), 258-59.

3. Notes and Criticisms

Albion, 1849; 1857-1859.
Athenæum, 1829-1832; 1835-1837; 1847-1849; 1852-1854.
Ballou's Pictorial Drawing-Room Companion, 1859.

Critic, 1893.

Dramatic Magazine (London), 1829-1830.

Gentleman's Magazine and Historical Chronicle, 1830-1831.

Illustrated London News, 1893.

Pall Mall Gazette, 1893.

Niles' Weekly Register, 1831-1835.

South Carolina Historical and Genealogical Magazine, 1908, 1910.

Theatre, 1893.

Theatrical Times (London), 1846-1848.

INDEX

Beverley, Mrs., Fanny as, 40; at Princess's Theatre, 148.

Bianca, Fanny as, 47; characterization of admired by Halleck, 59; at Chestnut Street Theater, 62; at Tremont Theater, 66.

Birmingham, England, Roger Kemble at, 2; Fanny visits factories at, 45; summer tour to, 47; workers of contrasted with those in America, 60; Baltimore like, 64; theater at, 147.

Bishop, Judge, 190.

Blackwood's, denounced America, 53.

Bladensburg, Md., duel at, 133.

Blithedale Romance, The, 163.

Bluebeard, staged by puppets, 11.

Border Minstrelsy, Scott's, Fanny read, 28; region of, 149.

Boston, Kembles go to, 66; Charles Sumner in, 67; like English cities, 67; social status in, 68; Kembles return to, 71; Butlers in, 129, 131; Fanny read in, 156, 157, 158-60; Julia Dean Hayne in, 169; Fanny planned farewell appearance in, 173-74; Fanny and Fan in, 174.

Branchtown, Penna., Butler Place near, 75; village school in, 75; no poor at 76; Alice Dudley Leigh christened in 185; Fanny returns to, 191; church in, 192.

Bremer, Fredrika, 185, 212.

Bristol, summer tour to, 47; Fanny on stage in, 147.

Britain, all the world in, 52; America more prosperous than, 53; institutions of defended, 54.

British periodicals, condemnation of America in, 53.

Brookline, Mass., inhabitants of attended Tremont Theater, 67

Brooklyn, N. Y., Fanny read in, 161.

Brougham, H. P., with *Edinburgh Review*, 27.

Browning, Elizabeth B., 170.

Browning, Robert, 170, 205.

Bryant, William C., 68, 163, 164.

Buffalo, N. Y., Fanny read in, 162.

Burns, Robert, 28, 149.

Butler, A., *Lives of the Saints*, read by J. P. Kemble, 3.

Butler, Frances Anne (later Mrs Leigh), birth of, 86; admired by Negroes on plantation, 108; with mother at Butler Place, 114; at Newport, 134; taken to country, 135; with mother at Lenox, 173; accom-

panied mother to England, 174; returned to Philadelphia, 174; danced with Prince of Wales, 175; visited mother, 177; went to Europe, 177; on the Butler plantation, 179; repaired Butler Place, 180; mother visited, 180; travelled in Europe, 183; married, 183-84; returned to the United States, 184; went to plantations, 184; returned to York Farm, 185; Fanny at home of, 185; daughter born to, 185; mother at home of, 193, 197-98, 213.

Butler, John Mease, brother of Pierce, 70; Pierce and Fanny at home of, 74, 118; went to plantations, 82; would not allow Fanny's return to plantations, 112.

Butler, Major Pierce, 70, 107.

Butler, Pierce Mease, sketch of, 70; married Fanny Kemble, 72; ideas of concerning marriage, 72; at Butler Place, 74; objected to publication of Fanny's journal, 74; went to plantations, 82; visited England, 83; objected to publication of *An English Tragedy*, 84-85; took family to Georgia, 87; on Butler's Island, 91-107; attitude of toward slavery, 91-107; on St. Simon's Island, 107-13; trouble between wife and, 115-20; with family abroad, 120-27; Greville's estimate of, 128; returned to Philadelphia, 129; sold wife's riding horse, 129; accused of unfaithfulness, 131-32; duel of with James Schott, Jr., 133; conduct of toward Fanny, 133-44; filed suit for divorce, 153, 157; wife's answer to suit of, 153; admitted wife's conduct pure, 154; offered annual allowance, 155; divorce granted to, 155; newspaper gossip about, 158; opposed his daughter's going abroad, 174; slaves of sold, 174; charged with treason, 177; released from prison, 177; went to plantations, 179; death of, 179.

Butler, Sarah (later Mrs. Wister), birth of, 79; accompanied mother to England, 82; birthday celebrated, 86; admired by Negroes, 108; with mother at Butler Place, 114; at Newport, 134; taken to country, 135; with mother at Lenox, 170-71, 173; returned to Philadelphia, 172; married, 174; Fanny visited, 175; visited mother, 179; in Europe, 183; Fanny